ARRANGER
REVOLUTION

D1276844

*© 2021 Arranger Revolution
www.arrangerrevolution.com
www.alfonsogirardo.com
info@arrangerrevolution.com
ISBN 979-12-210-0579-0*

ALFONSO GIRARDO

THE COMPLETE
MODERN
INSTRUMENTATION

ALL THE MUSICAL INSTRUMENTS
FROM BAROQUE TO THE SYNTHESIZER

To Daniela, Giorgia and Ginevra

CONTENTS

This book was born from my curiosity and the incurable desire to understand what surrounds the musical world.

Having been a musician for almost forty years, I have had the opportunity to touch many aspects of the musical experience. As is typical of my character, I never stopped, thirsty for knowledge.

By now, my primary job is the arranger, and I can assure you, dear reader, that it is a profession so full of concepts that you never stop learning.

Musical instruments have always been my passion.

I remember when I was studying History of Musical Instruments at the University: I was fascinated by the lessons of my professor, and I looked at X-rays every single musical instrument that presented itself in front of me, from ancient times to the present day.

I discovered countless fascinating musical instruments there that have positively shaken my every desire for knowledge.

Beyond this, the book you will study is a Manual, a text you will constantly consult that will be beneficial for the composition and arrangement work you will have to do.

For this reason, I wanted to write this book in a conversational tone; I find it useful and simple to make you understand every concept.

Many audio examples accompany this book that you can consult for free to enter better the fantastic world of each musical instrument that I explain. You will find a link at the end of this introduction to download all the musical examples. They will be beneficial to accompany your reading and your study.

The treatises on instrumentation and orchestration of the past are undoubtedly useful (Berlioz, Rimskij-Korsakov...), but you cannot take the fact that musical instruments evolve continuously into consideration; all the more so now, a period in which technology travels at the speed of light.

If you think that until the middle of the 19th century, the violin did not yet have a chin rest, the saxophones in practice did not exist, the serpent still represented the tuba. The synthesizers were a science fiction dream, and one realizes that the road traveled so far is really long.

One aspect that I like to emphasize is linked to the fact that the evolution of musical instruments goes hand in hand with the music itself.

The bigger extension of many musical instruments, the use of keys in wood, pistons and valves in brass, and many other mechanical changes occurred just because music required it.

Today, everything has changed a bit. Everything has obviously evolved. The advent of the synthesizer gave the moment of splitting as a commonly used musical instrument and computer music.

The idea of transforming a simple electrical signal into a sound to one's liking has undoubtedly influenced the unlimited creativity of composers of both so-called 'serious' and 'popular' music.

The digitization of everything, the advent of MIDI (therefore of communication between machines), DAWs (Digital Audio Workstations), Plug-ins, and Virtual Instruments have completely upset the way of treating musical instruments themselves and their integration within an arrangement.

Today, VST instruments are so well made that you can easily confuse the authentic sound from the sampled one if you don't have a trained ear.

The instrumentation is a fundamental aspect of the creative process.

Comparing it to the work of a painter, it somewhat represents the large palette of colors available; it is, therefore, the necessary preamble for orchestration (you cannot orchestrate if you do not know musical instruments).

Instrumentation is not orchestration; they are completely different, even if complementary, aspects ... orchestration always comes after and represents, always using the same metaphor, the ability to best mix the colors on the palette.

This book does not presume to be a treatise on orchestration; it is an instrumentation book. Still, it can certainly be a means of getting to know it better later and making each composition or arrangement worthy of one's taste and the taste of those who listen to it.

Copy this link to download all the audio files that accompany the book

https://drive.google.com/drive/folders/1_zwOTk4n510Ye8iJHfHS3ZVHobw8GtwE?usp=sharing

Acknowledgment

I don't think it's possible not to start a page of thanks thinking about the loves of your life: my wife and my two daughters.

Without them, everything I compose, arrange, play, would not have much sense, and obviously, who allowed me to enjoy the pleasure of being a musician: my parents, my brother, and my sister.

Since I was just three years old, I thank music, my life partner, which, between happy moments, disappointments, quarrels, and love, has always been close to me a bit as if it were my shadow even during a day without sun.

I thank all the people I have collaborated with as composer, violinist, arranger, and conductor, all my musician friends - classics, jazz musicians, metalheads, 'funketters', artistic and orchestra directors - all the orchestras and big bands that I have conducted in Italy and abroad.

I wholeheartedly thank Paolo Fresu: guru, friend, father, brother, teacher of all of us Italian and non-Italian musicians ... it would take thousands of people and musicians like him!

I thank my students because I always learn a lot from them, whether they are beginners or are forward with the study ... they are my strength and always give me the energy to deepen my knowledge.

I want to thank all my professors, from all the musical fields that I have dealt with: from violin to composition, from arrangement to jazz and, in this regard, I cannot fail to mention my Professor of Film Music Composition Luis Bacalov: what there is in here is also thanks to his valuable advice.

Finally, I thank life, the only element that allows music to be what it is, making a world rich that is often not so rich.

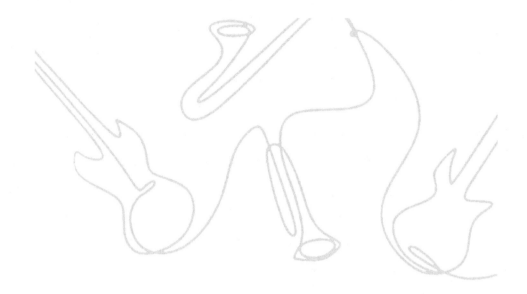

CHAPTER 1

**EVOLUTION
AND
CLASSIFICATION**

EVOLUTION OF INSTRUMENTS (THE BAROQUE)

The history of music has always been the child of man somehow.

Musical instruments even more.

The orchestra (and the musical instruments inside it) in the Baroque period is the daughter, in this context, of a very evolutionary musical period, namely the Renaissance.

The Baroque period I want to tell you about is the one that starts from around 1600 until 1750, the year of the death of J.S. Bach.

During the Renaissance, we witnessed real emancipation of instrumental music from vocal music, even if we must specify that still in the 17th century, many compositions had as subtitles "per sonar e cantar", so they could be both played in some way and sung.

From this point of view, there is no stability of the specific instruments in the score, as will be done later, but the concept of Orchestration began to be born a few years earlier.

In the beginning, it was at the performer's discretion: it was the performers who decided the musical instruments to use, then it became so important that the composer himself necessarily indicated it.

Now, we can obtain specific information on the orchestras of the Baroque period not only from the musical iconography but also from very important theoretical treatises that have come down to our days.

One of all, the 'Syntagma Musicum' by Praetorius, a fundamental work for organology published in 1618 in which there were the intonation and quality of all the instruments of the period and which has left us tables like these (below):

There is still no mention of the violin, for example, but there is a lot of stuff on the wind, plucked, and keyboard instruments of those decades. The Baroque period is characterized by the use of music and musical instruments to create emotions. Somehow, they wanted to touch the listener's hearts, so much so that this is precisely the period in which Melodrama was born.

This desire to excite inevitably led to wanting to imitate the voice somehow as much as possible, so much so that musical instruments underwent a real selective process since they wanted them to "sing" like a human voice.

Many wind instruments, for example, were abandoned, starting with those with encapsulated reeds, leaving space, for instance, for flutes, bassoons, and oboes.

In the Baroque orchestra, however, the string instrument dominates, first of all, the viola.

But precisely in this period, those that are now part of the strings family take their final form.

This family of musical instruments has an uncertain origin. Still, they certainly had as their reference the medieval ribeca, the vielle, the 'violas da braccio', and 'violas da gamba', which have undergone a process of reducing the strings up to today's four violin, viola, or cello strings tuned in fifths.

Ribeca *Viella* *Viola da Gamba* *Viola da Braccio*

Let's say that the violin somehow already existed at the end of the 16th century and had only three strings; then, they added the treble one a few years later.

The bowed instruments of the Baroque orchestra are not precisely those of today: this is primarily due to the music written at that time, to the fact that they were not kept with the chin as they were absent from the chin rest, but only resting on the clavicle.

The bridge was lower. The strings were strictly gut and thicker than those of today.

Even the bows were completely different and underwent a radical transformation both in shape and length until the arrival of Tourte, who invented today's screw mechanism to stretch the bow's hair.

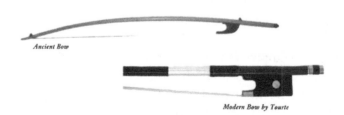

Ancient Bow

Modern Bow by Tourte

There were different sizes of string instruments in the orchestras of that period: from the violin (which acted as a soprano) to the alto viola, from the tenor violin (not very common) to the cello, born as a low 'viola da braccio'.

At the time, there was also a 5-string cello ... Bach himself indicated it around 1720 in the sixth of his suites for solo cello.

Often you could meet the so-called 'viola d'amore', very particular because, under the usual gut strings, it had metal strings that had a sympathy vibration without being touched by the bow, creating a sort of echo.

There was also the double bass at the time. Praetorius had already indicated it in his Syntagma Musicum. One could distinguish the different shapes given by the German luthiers, similar to a viola da gamba, and Italians, similar to a violin.

It usually counted five strings, and when the fifth was omitted, the tuning was, as today, for fourths.

On the other hand, 5-string double basses are still used in orchestras today.

Also, the lutes, archlutes (for example, the Chitarrone, the Tiorba, the Pandora, and the guitar), organs, and keyboard instruments (first of all, the harpsichord ... think to Bach's Well-Tempered Clavier ... monumental work!) dominated this whole century and a half.

However, the Baroque is the period of the string orchestra.

Viola d'Amore

Chitarrone

Tiorba

Pandora

Harpsichord

Let's say that this concept is not absolute ... in fact, there were not only strings orchestras.

The winds were used a lot in this period.

The flutes, oboes, and bassoons were the first to be readmitted into the orchestra with some modifications to make them compete with violins.

Precisely for this reason, they began to build wind instruments in several interlocking pieces (like today) rather than in a single piece. This allowed the performer to lengthen or tighten the pipe and, therefore, tune the instrument.

The ancestor of the transverse flute was used, although Bach, when writing Flute, indicated the recorder, that is, the one with the mouthpiece on the top instead of the side.

Even the oboe changes somehow: the performer also had three keys that increased its range. Not to mention the other oboes (the oboe d'amore, for example, very popular in the first twenty years of the 1700s, or the alto oboe, which should be the equivalent of today's english horn.

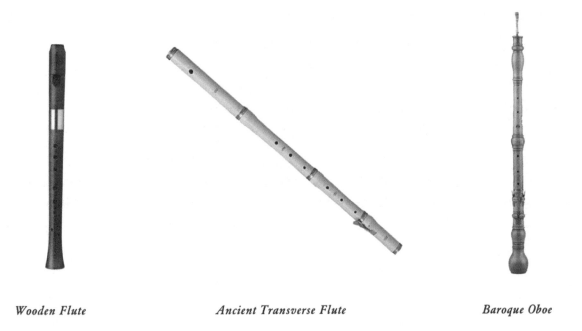

Wooden Flute   *Ancient Transverse Flute*   *Baroque Oboe*

The Baroque is also the emancipation of the French Horn, which from a hunting instrument becomes an instrument of art even if it is not very present in the scores or most it was found with the words 'horn trumpet' because it was still in evolution.

The trumpet also begins its ascent in this period.

In this period, the brass did not have pistons, and everything was at the discretion of the bore and the performer's lips.

Coulisse trumpets already existed, a bit like our trombones today, and Bach indicated them as 'Trumpet to be pulled' and has used them a lot in some of his Cantatas.

The success of these instruments will come later precisely because of their difficulty in playing them.

Just think of the serpent, an instrument that I know very well because I wrote a concert for it.

Today's Tubas then supplanted it in the orchestra due to the too low sound volume and the difficulty of intoning given the absence of keys in the beginning.

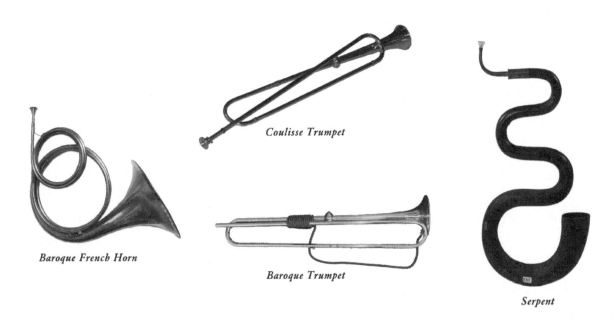

Coulisse Trumpet

Baroque French Horn

Baroque Trumpet

Serpent

The interesting thing that cannot be missing in this context is undoubtedly the orchestra's tuning.

Now we all tune with A at 440Hz as a reference, and today's Baroque music is played at 432Hz, about a semitone below.

There was no predetermined diapason at the time: organs of the period have a tuning even at 337Hz, corresponding to our F sharp on the first space in the treble clef.

The concept of the orchestra as we know it now is still a long way off.

Obviously, everything is based on the evolution of the music itself, the compositions, and technological development.

But the Baroque orchestra has left us priceless treasures as it has been handed down to us.

Think of the enormous work of Vivaldi, Bach, Handel, and many other less known composers who made this period unique and unrepeatable, not only from the point of view of organology.

EVOLUTION OF INSTRUMENTS (ROMANTICISM)

A crucial aspect that characterized the history of music in romanticism is the incredible timbral growth.
In this period, musical instruments are born and developed that today are the backbone of music.

Strings Family

This organological exponential growth has in some way elevated the desire to express emotions, preserving the trend that had been manifesting itself for a century before.
Thanks to this timbral variety, the feeling can now be highlighted in all its nuances.
A large number of new musical instruments made orchestration become, in this period, a separate subject of musical composition.
The existing musical instruments had to undergo improvements, thus trying to reach the highest peak of their technical possibilities to get this enormous timbral variety.

A pivotal element of romanticism is the need for a louder sound volume. This is undoubtedly due to the transition to a democratic rather than aristocratic culture, in which large concert halls replaced small living rooms.

Musical instruments had to be somehow within everyone's reach. Often, they were transportable or even hidden (I am thinking of pianos hidden inside desks, for example).
This is because emotion had to be the priority.
The instrument had to pass from forte to sudden piano and vice versa, to perform a colorful crescendo and decrescendo or perform
any musical articulation efficiently.
For this reason, many instruments that had already reigned were replaced with significantly modified instruments.

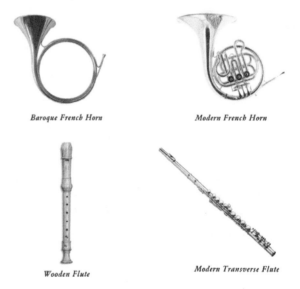

Baroque French Horn   *Modern French Horn*

Wooden Flute   *Modern Transverse Flute*

Think of the recorder, which was replaced by the modern transverse flute; to the hunting horn, replaced by the modern French horn; to the new stability of the string family (now divided into violins, violas, cellos, and double basses); up to the invention of perhaps the best-known instrument today: the piano.

The piano was born precisely for the need to color the music, which the harpsichord could not possibly do. In the early 700s, Bartolomeo Cristofori, a Florentine harpsichord maker, invented the mechanism that gave life to the modern piano. The so-called 'escapement' mechanism triggered the hammer against the string, leaving it to vibrate. So, the string is now no longer plucked but struck by a little hammer. Although the invention of this instrument can be attributed to the Italians, it was the Germans who improved it.

Acoustic Piano

The piano is the best-known example of innovation in this period.

But romanticism gave birth to the improvement of clarinets, which from lower-ranking Chalumeaux became clarinets taking the shape of the oboe, giving rise to an entire family; to the new pedal mechanisms of the harp; to the birth of Adolph Sax's saxophone, which was also later incorporated into an entire family;

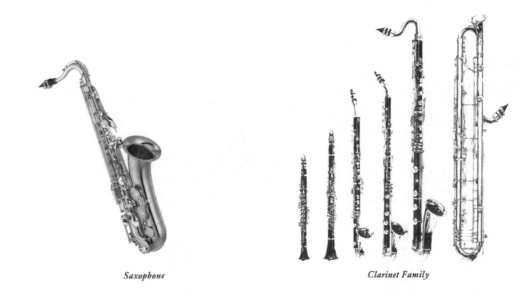

Saxophone   *Clarinet Family*

to the incredible improvement of the brass, trumpets, trombones with the use of pistons, up to the entry on the scene of the Tuba, the extremely low brass instrument.

The brass family increased a lot: think of the various Flugelhorns or the Euphoniums. In short, instruments of all sizes and registers useful to cover the whole range in some audible ways are born.

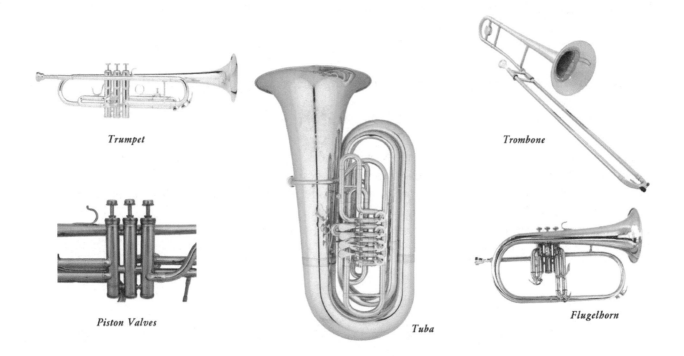

Trumpet   *Trombone*

Piston Valves   *Flugelhorn*

Tuba

This desire for sonority inevitably increased the technique and number of percussions.

Think of the timpani, which in this period take on a very important role in the orchestra and are no longer used as a simple filling of the trumpets, but are also able to emit a scale.

Think also of all the small instruments, super used in the orchestra.

Timpani

Hector Berlioz and Rimski-Korsakov write treatises on instrumentation and orchestration and are still texts of fundamental importance for an orchestrator.

Even the tuning of the instruments begins to approach that of today.

In 1834 the 440Hz diapason was already proposed (like today), but they did not accept it.

In a conference of physicists and musicians, which Berlioz was also part of, they decided to set the height at 435Hz.

We recall that they set today's 440Hz diapason during the London conference in 1953.

Romanticism brought the instruments and the orchestra to enormous improvements in timbre and dynamics.

Today's acoustic music is the daughter of that period, so it will be the reference point for us to understand and study musical instruments and their possibilities.

This period is, in practice, the opening of the modern period, also opening to electromagnetic experiments that will come shortly after.

The music of the twentieth century was certainly upset by the invention of electricity.

EVOLUTION OF INSTRUMENTS (THE 20TH CENTURY)

We will always remember the twentieth century as the period of electricity.

It was one of the centuries in which technological and social innovations were most evident and numerous.

In this period, everything changes: communication, the dissemination of information, in short, life in general.

From the point of view of musical instruments, at first glance, it would seem that the twentieth century was a century of continuity of the romantic line.

The orchestras have certainly expanded a lot.

If we think of baroque orchestras, formed only by strings and then the gradual addition of wind instruments, we must think of 20th-century orchestras such as those in which percussion has taken a lot of space.

The last century was the century of the "continuous rhythm," comparing it to the "basso continuo" of the Baroque.

We think of Schönberg's big scores, Stravinsky's 'the Rite of Spring' or 'Histoire du Soldat or Gershwin's orchestral compositions.

So.... Percussions.... Percussions.... Percussions.

This preference for rhythm was undoubtedly helped by the advent of jazz and swing in particular.

Even stringed instruments, such as the piano or the guitar, are used in orchestral ensembles.

For example, let's think of the banjo, which dominated the first swing orchestras.

We think of the essential role of the drums and the detachment of the double bass from the orchestra.

Banjo   *Drum Set*

However, as I pointed out earlier, the twentieth century is the century of electronic music and the advent of music recording.

Surely Edison played a pivotal role with the phonograph and Berliner for the microphone in 1876.

Phonograph

Microphone

Tube Amplifier

Pickup

1897 TELHARMONIUM

Theremin

RCA Synthesizer Mark I

The desire for sound volume was the basis of everything.

1915 was the advent of tube amplifiers, and the radio certainly contributed to the development of microphones, first with condenser ones and then with ribbon ones.

Not to mention the advent of the pickup to amplify some musical instruments, born from Rickenbacker and also called Horseshoe for its horse "shoe" shape.

The first electromechanical instruments are born:

the Telharmonium in 1897, ancestor of our Hammond organ with a part dedicated to controls and one, that of circuits, made up of more than 2000 switches and over 150 dynamo alternators.

The theremin or Termèn, an electronic monophonic instrument in which the performer does not have physical contact with the musical instrument for the first time, is born from modifying an alarm system designed by Termen himself.

These instruments, for example, are also used for the first significant movie soundtracks.

The evolution of electronic instruments alone is very long and very specific, so in this context, I will limit myself to introducing you to the most important ones.

We can divide electric instruments into two large families:

1. _Electromechanical instruments_, i.e., those produced by the usual mechanical way, such as an electric piano, a Rhodes Piano, for example.

2. And finally, _Electronic instruments_, that is, based on circuits or valves.

The synthesizer, which has totally revolutionized the musical timbre and the way of making music, was born in this century.
We started with the first synthesizers, so large that they occupy an entire room (think of the RCA Synthesizer Mark I), and everything stems from the studies on oscillators made as early as the 1920s.
After the end of the Second World War, however, electronics take up more and more space from the point of view of organology.
One of the first was the Electronic Sackbut, the electronic Sack, a synthesizer that already allowed you to vary the volume, pitch, and timbre of a sound.
The RCA Synth also had a Mark II version, a precursor of the first Moog or the VCS3, one of the first portable subtractive synthesizers.
The synth became increasingly portable until Robert Moog's revolution with the Mini-Moog in the early 1970s.

Electronic Sackbut

Moog

VCS3

Minimoog

Now synthesizers are completely digital, and, in 1981, after the advent of MIDI (Musical Instrument Digital Interface), computer music has practically taken most of the mainstream market, especially in the popular sector.

The very famous Fairlight had already been released in 1979, in practice one of the first samplers on the market.

At the turn of the 80s and 90s, the first Waveform-based synthesizers were born (Yamaha's DX7, Korg's M1, Roland's D50 ...)

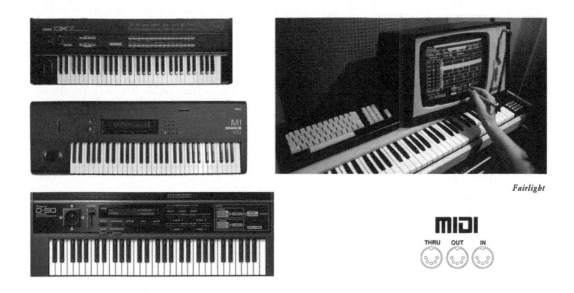

Fairlight

At the end of the 90s then the physical instruments will be increased by the virtual ones, the so-called Virtual Instruments. Today they are widely used through the DAW (Digital Audio Workstation). In practice, they are the so-called Plug-ins that we find in our software or the different Players that the musicians acquire and that practically reproduce the real sound of a physical instrument, pre-recorded and reproduced from a workstation.

As you have seen, the instruments have evolved, and I believe that there will never be an end in their evolution. This is because the musical instrument changes, improves, and progresses based on many aspects, not only musical but also social, so not necessarily related to music. It comes naturally to me to ask myself: "Where will we arrive?". This is a question that only time can give a satisfactory answer to.

CLASSIFICATION

The classification of musical instruments has always been a heated problem: many musicologists have reasoned and expressed their point of view.

Today for simplicity, we classify the instruments into four essential groups:

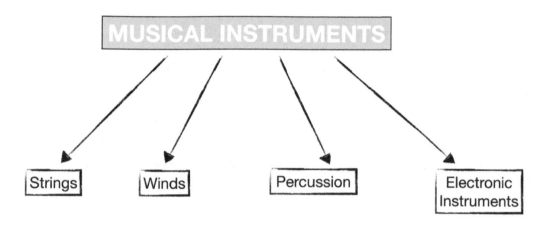

This classification is very abstract, and it is right to go to the bottom since we based it only on the way to play the instrument. There are already two types of wind instruments in an orchestra:

1. Woods
2. Brass

So, we have to go further, and in any case, we are also very superficial here because this classification is theoretically based on the construction material of the instruments.

An example of all is the Sax: The sax is a brass instrument, yet it is part of the wood family. Let's say that these classifications are very simplified and serve just to indicate something, but they are not precise. A classification that is constantly used also in Instrumentation and orchestration texts is that composed of 5 main groups:

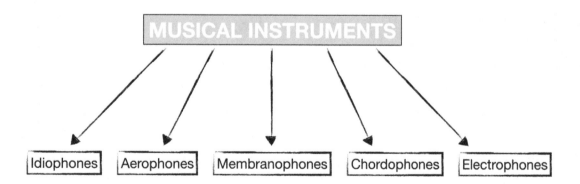

However, these are macro-categories with sub-categories that go further into the organological classification.

Idiophones

By Idiophones, we mean that circle of instruments that do not need extra tension, for example, strings or skins; the musician gives the tension to make the instrument vibrate with his action.

Percussion is part of this group:

There are idiophones with reciprocal percussion (for example, orchestral cymbals or castanets....); The struck idiophones (cymbals, all percussion keyboards, i.e., xylophone, marimba, vibraphone, glockenspiel, or tubular bells), which need to be hit by a hand to vibrate.

Then there are other idiophones, such as shaking ones (rattles, shakers, maracas, cabasa, and many others similar), scraping (one of all and very important for Latin American music: the guiro), or even plucking, like the harp.

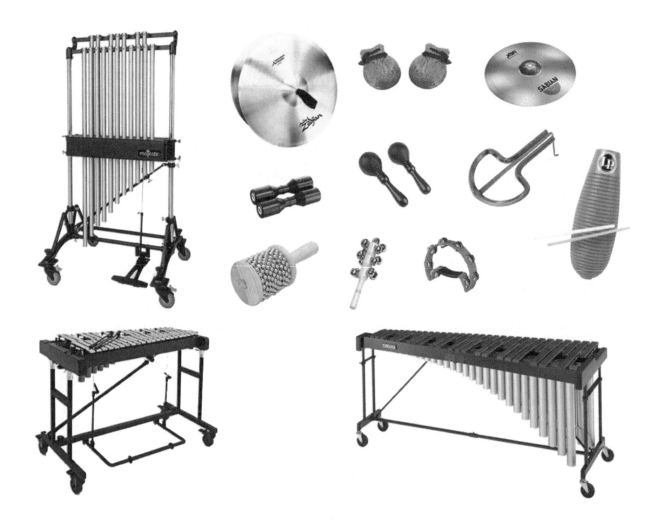

Aerophones

As the term itself implies, Aerophones are instruments that presuppose the use of air, so all wind instruments belong to them.

They all have a tube inside which the air circulates and is blown in by the performer precisely to set it in motion.

Woods usually use a reed that generates the motion of the air by vibrating. It can be simple (for example, in clarinets, saxes) or double (for example, in oboes, bassoons).

Brass instruments (horns, trumpets, trombones, tuba ....) Use a mouthpiece that varies in size depending on the size of the instrument.

There are also free aerophones, such as accordion, harmonica, bandoneon, and some organ pipes, especially in ancient organs.

Woodwinds   *Brass*

SIMPLE   DOUBLE

Membranophones

In this case, as the name may imply, we speak of the vibration of a membrane, obviously of a different type.

All drums belong to this category, whether they are played using a mallet or bare hands.

Obviously, the dimensions of these instruments vary a lot: you can start from the size of the timpani or the bass drum up to the smallest tambourines.

The membrane used by these instruments is usually defined as 'Skin' since they used animal skin in ancient times (but also today).

The tension and fixing of the skin can occur in different ways: either by using gut laces or frames, metal circles, they can be glued or nailed ... ... it depends in short on the specific instrument.

Chordophones

There are so many chordophones! Yes... because, as the name makes explicit, these instruments have strings. The way of vibrating the string changes according to the instrument. They can be hit with sticks (many Middle Eastern instruments are like that), plucked with bare hands or with a plectrum like in a guitar, rubbed with a bow like in violins or cellos. Regardless of their way of playing, all chordophones, except in form, are composed of the same parts:

1. The soundboard or resonance box (in which the air somehow moves).
2. The bands, which are the lateral parts of the soundboard.
3. The soundholes from which the sound comes out: in the classical guitar, for example, it is in the shape of a circle; in the stringed instruments, it is in the shape of an F ... in short, the shape of the hole also changes.
4. A neck, where there is the fingerboard on which the performer lengthens or shortens the length of the string with the use of his fingers.
5. The Pegs, i.e., the pins used to change the tension of the strings and then tune them.

The chordophones are thousands from all cultures and are essential for all musical sub-genres.
I will elaborate on this concept in the course of the book.

Electrophones

Electrophones are the youngest category.
They are those instruments that require electricity, therefore, in a certain sense, the most recent from a chronological point of view.
They can be summarily divided into:

1. Electromechanical, that is played mechanically and then see their vibrations electronically transformed (think of the Rhodes Piano)
2. Electronic, based on oscillators that emit sounds of different frequencies (first of all, the synthesizer).

As you noticed from this chapter, classification is a real problem.
In our work as composers, arrangers, and orchestrators, it will be undoubtedly difficult to call or indicate an instrument such as "Chordophone" or "membranophone" because, in the workplace, we always go to the specific. But the classification also serves to incorporate the instruments into different categories to understand their generic functioning, the invoice, and the possibilities.
There have been many classifications and some, that of Mahillòn, for example, had flaws since it was created to classify the instruments present in the museum of musical instruments in Brussels.
Please do not underestimate the classification; it will help you better understand the fantastic world of musical instruments.

CHAPTER 2

THE STRINGS FAMILY

As I said in the paragraph on classification, the string family is part of the so-called chordophones. Today the standard orchestral bowed instruments are divided into four different sizes but are very similar in construction.

Contrabass

Cello

Viola

Violin

The composers have used and still use this family a lot......practically always in the orchestra...for various reasons that make this family almost the most popular.

Why are they so used?

- They can perform practically any type of dynamics effortlessly, from pianissimo to fortissimo.

- The tonal possibilities are many (from the use of the bow to pizzicato to the wood of the bow, up to the chop... a technique widely used by Fiddler Violinists)

- All four instruments are tonally homogeneous, and this gives the composer the possibility of using them often as if it were a real piano.

- Last but not least: the enormous range they cover, in practice from the lowest sound of double bass and the highest of violins, they cover seven octaves ... so a vast range.

The string family is undoubtedly the largest in the orchestra......more than half of the entire orchestra is occupied by this family.
Violins are usually divided into two groups (Violins I and II). Together with Violas, Celli and Contrabasses, they form the classic orchestral string quintet.
The number of musicians can change according to the composition, but it can also reach 16 first violins, 14 seconds, 12 violas, 10 cellos and 8 double basses.
Obviously, here we are talking about a score where the need for timbre requires that number of musicians.
But, of course, there are the smaller groups down to the small chamber group.
The numbers often change simply to balance the forces well with the other instruments.
Since there are so many, they are divided into "rows" in the orchestra, but even these rows can break up...... I'll explain it shortly.

From a construction point of view, they are all very similar......but I'll get to the bottom of that when I talk to you about every instrument in the family.

As for the tuning, which I will discuss in more detail later, I just tell you that all the strings are tuned for fifths, except the double bass, which is tuned for fifths.

Furthermore, it must be specified that the Double Bass is the only transposing instrument of the family and the effect obtained by reading a part of this instrument is an octave below.

THE VIOLIN

As I have already explained to you in the previous module, the violin was an instrument that took hold in the 17th century.
Since then, the technical changes it has had have been many.
This does not only concern the instrument itself but also the bow.
Today, the violin we see in orchestras results from countless transformations that have led it to be what you see today.
Now I will give you some historical hints to make you understand the instrument well. I will try more to focus on the technical aspects and how it is used in the arrangements and the orchestras without touching elements of orchestration, even if it is inevitable.

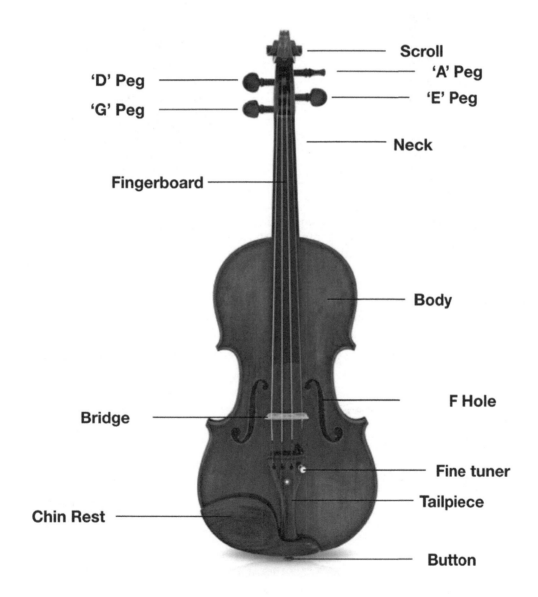

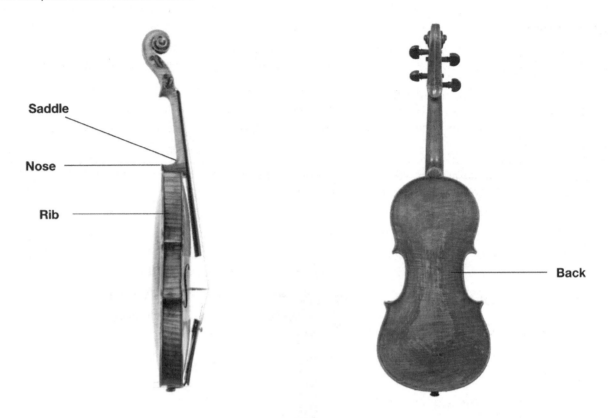

It is interesting to understand how the instrument actually works.
(Obviously, I will not go specifically from the point of view of acoustic physics, even if there is really a lot to say... ..and not just about the strings).
But I would like to show you how the instrument is made inside.

Here is a section of the violin and the bow.
All string instruments are like this, obviously changing their size.

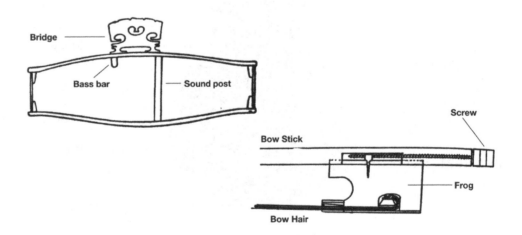

The parts that have substantially changed in the end are not so many.
The top, the back, the sides and the hedgehog have not changed.
It was the need to increase the sound volume that caused some parts of the instrument to change:
For example, the height of the bridge;

the length of the internal chain ... since the strings are no longer made of gut and the tension of which needs to be supported as it is more significant;
The sound post has been strengthened;
the length of the fingerboard and strings has been increased;
the shape of the neck and fingerboard has been changed, now tilted slightly back

As I showed you before, the bow has also changed a lot, up to the Francois Tourte screw mechanism of 1780.

All these changes occurred, as for all musical instruments, due to the evolution of the composition itself.
The short bows of the seventeenth century made it possible to play the dance music of the time at its best.
With the advent of the Opera and the Sonata, the violin triumphed somehow.
But the instrument had its organological growth in the 18th century, thanks to the great virtuoso composers of the period (Tartini, Viotti, and Paganini, for example). They pushed the instrument to extreme technical levels.

These compositional changes introduced new parts to the violin and a different way of playing it.

Look at these two images, for example:

Gerard Dou, Violin Player, 1653

David Oistrakh

In the painting on the left, you can see a 17th-century violinist holding the violin on his clavicle: that was the way at the time.
On the right, we see an image of David Oistrakh, a great violinist of the last century, who holds the violin practically to the left of his neck, on his shoulder.

The position on the clavicle, as Leopold Mozart, the father of the more famous Amadeus already said, "is pleasant but not firm"; in fact, the music of the time allowed changes of position using the thumb of the left hand and not very high notes ... the keyboards were shorter.
In 1820 Spohr, a great virtuoso violinist, introduced the chin rest, which is still present on the instrument today.
It allows for a firmer hold and provides agility to the performer, who was only a dream in the Baroque period.

Now beyond the historical aspect, let's go to the technical and start with the instrument's tuning. The violin is an instrument tuned by fifths and is not a transposer.

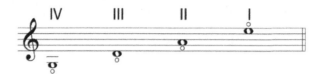

The violin parts are written in the G clef, also commonly called the treble clef.

Like all string family instruments, it is a versatile musical instrument with a vast range.

In fact, it covers a range that starts from G2 to E6 and beyond, in the solo steps (up to B6) and allows all the sounds of the chromatic scale.

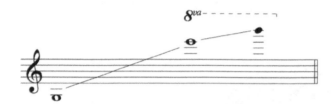

As in all the instruments of this family, the more you go up in the register, the more the difficulty increases as the spaces available between the fingers become smaller
.

It was used to reach a maximum of A5 in the classical period, which is the seventh position.
Then, of course, the composers went further and made some steps complicated to perform.

Let's go deeper and see how the execution mechanism works.

The primary technique that allows you to reach all the available sounds is called positions.

We have seen the four open strings of the instrument.
Obviously, you have to feel on the string to shorten its length and obtain a sharper sound.

What are the positions?

Positions represent the practice of placing a specific finger at a certain height of a string.
From the theoretical (but truly theoretical) point of view, a position should occupy an interval of fourth; this is because this distance represents in some way the ease of placing all four fingers of the left hand in sequence.

I'll give you an example of placing the fingers in the first position on the G string:

As you can see, with the 4th finger, you can take the following empty string in the first position, so you can continue playing on that one without moving up in position.

The most used positions on the violin are 7, even if we go far beyond with the music written today.
What arises from the use of different positions is the so-called fingering.
It is nothing more than the practice of choosing a specific finger to be placed on a particular string concerning another finger.

It is obvious to specify that the same note can be taken on different strings and with other fingers, depending on the performer's choice to justify the convenience of playing a sure step.

There are exceptions concerning those notes that are too low that can only be taken on the G string and those that are too high that can be taken only on E.

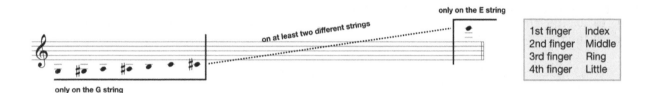

Usually, the fingering is an aspect borne by the performer; I can confirm this as a violinist.
Often composers who may not have studied the violin delight in fingering some points without knowledge.
It leads the performer to unnecessary difficulties.

I advise you to study the mechanism of fingering, and this table will be handy to you:

TABLE OF THE POSITIONS - VIOLIN

	1 pos.	2 pos.	3 pos.	4 pos.	5 pos.	6 pos.	7 pos.	8 pos.	9 pos.	10 pos.	11 pos.	12 pos.
I												
II												
III												
IV												

Fingering is real science, in my opinion.
The great violinist and teacher of the last century, Carl Flesh, has even written a treatise concerning only the fingering.
For this reason, the advice I can give you, if you compose or arrange, is to let the violinist do it.

If you want to use a particular fingering, it must be done possibly for timbral reasons, such as playing a whole step on a single string.

I will also explain the timbres of each string so that you can understand this aspect well.

The only constructive intervention that an arranger/composer can do about fingering is to indicate which string you want to play a particular passage (for example, everything on the fourth string).
This requires the performer not so much the fingering but the obligation not to go to the other strings.
This aspect is crucial for the timbre since the violin's four strings have a sonority that differs significantly in some cases.
The extreme strings (i.e., the first and fourth) have incredible personalities.

- The fourth string is very passionate, intense
- The II and III strings, on the other hand, are less characteristic
- On the other hand, the first string is bright and particularly resonant because it is the only one not covered but usually made of steel.

This aspect seems not very relevant, but it is essential.
Often, to exploit the passion of the fourth string, melodies are entrusted to it that could also be played on the third.

Example n. 1

Ravel writes a good part of the initial cadence of his Tzigane on the 4th string precisely to differentiate the timbre.

Same thing Tschaikowsky does in the second movement of his Fifth Symphony.
After a beautiful solo of the 1st horn, the theme is presented by the 1st violins and the composer specifies to play it on the G string.

(Empty page)

Example n. 2

P.I. Tschaikowsky, Symphony n. 5 – II mov.

Camille Saint-Saëns, in his famous III Concerto in B minor op. 61 for violin and orchestra, lets the soloist begin with the exposition of the whole theme on the fourth string.

 Example n. 3

Let's now proceed with the technical aspects of the violin:
What can a violin do or not do?
All bowed instruments are summarily very agile and consequently have few technical impediments related to the different possible articulations.

The violin, however, was born as a monodic and non-polyphonic instrument, even if the most incredible polyphonic work for violin is by Bach (the Sonatas and Partitas for solo violin).
Since there are also polyphonic parts in the violin repertoire, it is helpful to understand how double, triple and quadruple strings are managed.
Due to the arched shape of the bridge, theoretically, the violin cannot simultaneously perform more than two sounds made explicit by two adjacent strings.

A violin's intervals on a double string are very large if one of the two strings is empty.

Instead, they are limited from the second to the tenth if both strings are felt.
So, the violin can play the entire chromatic scale for second, third, fourth, fifth, sixth, seventh, octave, ninth, and tenth.

Let's now see the problems related to triple and quadruple strings.

I have already explained to you the morphology of the violin and the particular shape of the bridge, so inevitably, a violin will never be able to play 3 or 4 strings simultaneously with the simplicity of a guitar, for example.
To allow the execution of 3 or 4 notes together, the performer must somehow divide the chord by letting the upper notes resonate:

Beethoven, for example, begins his sonata for violin and piano "To Kreutzer" with a beautiful A major chord which, considering the speed of the piece and the type, will necessarily be divided:

 Example n. 4

An example in which the chords are 'torn' is given by Paganini in his Capriccio for solo violin no.14. Here the violinist uses unison, three and four sounds:

 Example n. 5

The empty strings have a particular timbre, especially in an orchestral context.

Open strings are defined as playing without being touched by the fingers, actually empty.

The sonority of the open strings is very bright as the string vibrates along its entire length.
The empty string cannot be vibrated with the left hand, except by using a vibrato for (say) "sympathy" by vibrating the neighboring string that is not played.

They are very sonorous when pizzicato is used with the left hand and are ideal for playing natural harmonic sounds (I will talk about these techniques shortly)
They are indicated with the number 0 above the note.

Apart from this, generally in the orchestra, they are used little because they substantially differ in sonority with the keyed notes.

But if used well, they have great expressive potential.
The example below shows how Copland uses all the string family instruments with empty strings.
The resulting sonority is very bright, brilliant and particular.
The composer could have easily written the parts in 'divided' without using double strings. Still, his choice was prudent and aimed only at the timbre purpose rather than at the execution of the notes themselves.

Aaron Copland, Saturday Night Waltz da "Rodeo III"

Example n. 6

The solo violin is a used instrument in the orchestral field, not just classical.
Think about the role of the violin in Argentine tangos and milongas.
Many and important composers use and have used the violin as a solo instrument in the orchestra.
You will see two very famous examples in orchestral literature in the examples below.
Here the violin comes out of the orchestral compartment and is accompanied or left alone.
The first example will be one of the famous first violin solos in Rimsky-Korsakov's Sheherazade, accompanied only by the harp, and an excerpt from the second movement of Symphony no. 1 by Johannes Brahms.

N. Rimskij-Korsakov, Sheherazade

 Example n. 7

J. Brahms, Symphony n.1 – II mov.

 Example n. 8

The violin has had such a solid musical and social impact that it has managed very well to expatriate from the frame of classical music.

There have been violinists such as Joe Venuti, Stephan Grappelli and Jean Luc Ponty. They have made the jazz violin a real cult, for example, from Grappelli's Jazz Manouche to Ponty's electric jazz.

Joe Venuti

Stephane Grappelli con Django Reinhardt

Jean Luc Ponty

With technology development, the violin has also become very popular in the electrical field.

The instruments of the electric arc family are now on the agenda.

Lately, the compositional needs have also led this instrument to become a hybrid between violin, viola and cello. Some composers have written pieces for 5-string and even 6-string violin.

The 5-string violin is practically a hybrid between violin and viola, the fifth string added is the low C, so it covers the empty strings of both the viola and the violin.

The 6-string violin, on the other hand, has the addition of a low sixth string, precisely the F, therefore very close to the cello in the low register.

In fact, in practice, the score can be read in a double key: bass clef for the low notes and violin for the high notes.

In the next page I'll bring you, for information, their tuning:

5 STRINGS VIOLIN

6 STRINGS VIOLIN

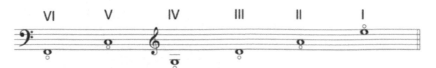

THE VIOLA

If we were to compare the family of strings to human voices, the viola would take the place of the altos.

The viola is a slightly larger instrument than the violin (about ten centimeters); its technique is practically the same as that of the violin.

But, being larger, it needs extra effort. For this reason, the dimensions of the instrument often vary depending on the size of the hand of the performer who plays it.

A lot of music has been written on the viola, from Stamitz to Mozart, but it has an essential role in the orchestra in the nineteenth century with Berlioz.

It is now an integral part of the string family in all orchestras and plays a significant role.

This is a modern Viola:

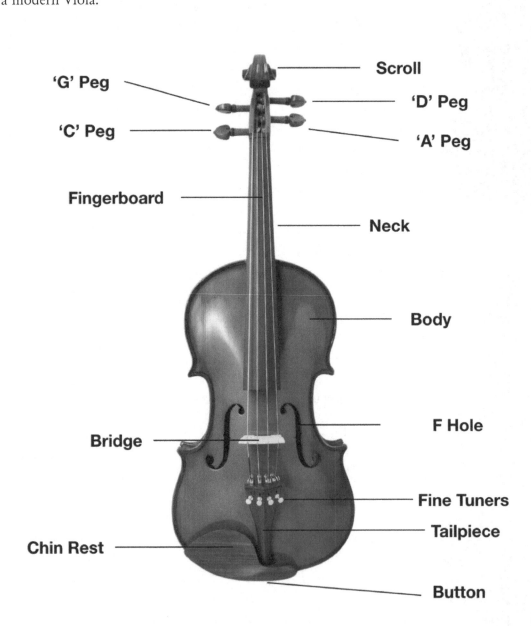

The viola, like the violin, is an instrument tuned by fifths and is not a transposing instrument. It has a range one fifth below the violin:

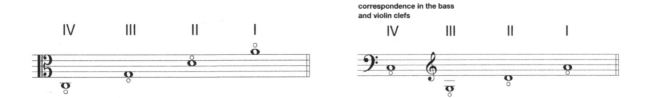

Viola's parts are written in the alto clef in the normal register and the treble clef in the acute. This is also a very versatile instrument with a considerable range.

This is its range:

Also in the viola, the more you go up in the register, the more the difficulty increases since the spaces available between the fingers become smaller and smaller, a fact also aggravated by the greater size of the instrument compared to the violin.

As I told you, it is very similar to the violin; looking at it from a distance, one hardly notices who is viola and who violin.

However, there are three small differences that can also help in writing.

-   The viola has the thickest strings, so it needs more strength to play

-   Violists use a heavier bow

-   And, given the greater thickness, it is easier to play harmonic sounds

Let's now look at the concepts based on positions and fingering.
Obviously, from now on, I will not give you a definition since I have already made it explicit in the chapter on the violin, but it is helpful to see how the viola behaves.

As in the violin, the most used positions on the viola are seven. The appearance of the fingering is practically the same as that of the violin, taking into account the fingers precisely as on the violin.

1st finger	Index
2nd finger	Middle
3rd finger	Ring
4th finger	Little

Also, in this case, I bring you a practical table:

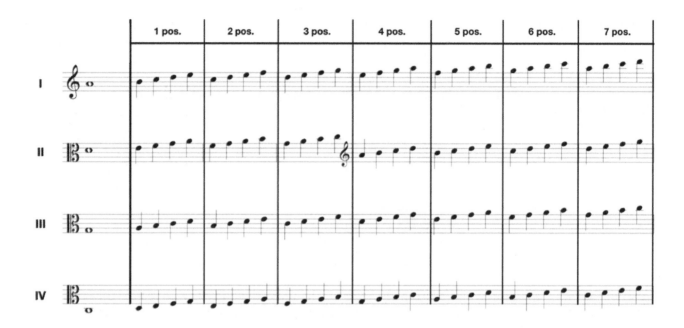

As for the timbre, we can note that the viola has a much more nasal sound than the violin; it is easily recognizable and distinguishable between the two instruments.
This is undoubtedly due to the greater thickness of the strings and the size of the soundboard.
The I string has a particularly shrill sound in the viola, but it is nasal.
The II and III, as in the violin, are less characteristic; in the orchestra, they are often used for accompaniment.
Instead, the fourth string has an intense sound and doubles some solo parts of the cellos to give a greater sound volume in orchestration.

The discourse on the Double, Triple and Quadruple Strings is the same for the violin.

The viola can practically play the entire chromatic scale starting from the second up to the tenth interval in double strings on two adjacent strings. The intervals that a viola can take on a double string are very large if one of the two strings is empty:

Instead, they are limited from the second to the tenth if both strings are felt.

The same rules apply to the viola for double, triple, and quadruple strings.

The open strings of the viola also have a particular brilliance.
Look at the example on the empty strings of the violin and look at the score that I brought back to you on the Copland Ballet.
Although the viola is less agile than the violin, the composers have dedicated a lot of literature to this instrument, even as a soloist (Mozart's Sinfonia Concertante for violin and Viola, Stamitz's Viola Concerto). The twentieth century was in practice the one that gave more space to the viola, making it equal to the other instruments of the family, see Walton's concert, The compositions of Hindemith.
Many concertos for solo viola have been written, and it has often been used for a solo in the orchestra.
In the following example (next page), I bring you a fantastic viola solo taken from "Le Jarden feerique" by Maurice Ravel.
Here the instrument is gently accompanied by the orchestra in a truly celestial texture by the composer:

 Example n. 9

M. Ravel, "Le jarden feerique" – 'Ma la mère l'oye'

Another example of great importance given to this instrument was transmitted to us by Igor Stravinsky in his "The Rite of Spring."
Even here, the composer uses 6 divided violas that play real parts, and the effect is truly fantastic:

I. Stravinsky, extract from "The Rite of Spring"

 Example n. 10

THE CELLO

The cello takes the place of tenors and basses in the string family.
Due to its size, it cannot be played by placing it between the shoulder and the chin like the violin and viola, but it can be played seated by placing it between the legs and resting the neck on the performer's left shoulder.
Another help is given by a removable endpin, placed under the instrument, fixed to the floor.

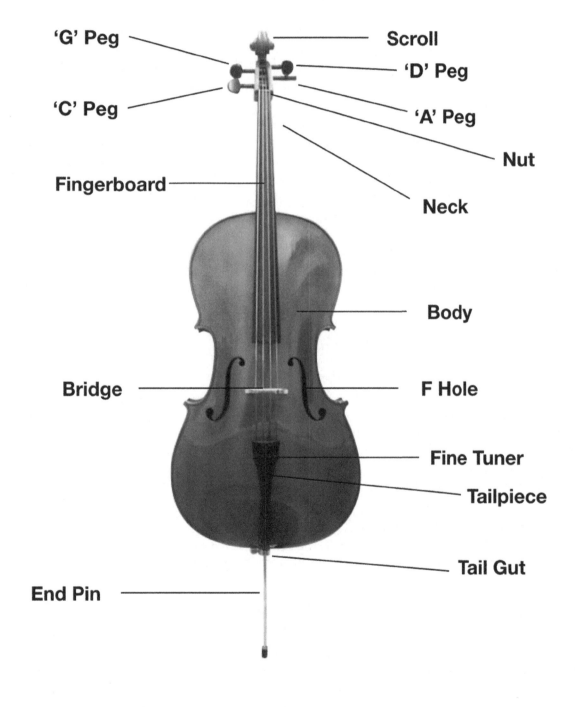

The cello, like all strings, except the double bass, is tuned by fifths and practically one octave below the viola.

The cello reads mainly in the bass clef, but moving towards the high pitch, it also uses the tenor and violin clef to avoid ledger lines.

Like all bows, the cello has a considerable range:

A separate discussion must be made for the fingering and positions on the cello, being a much larger musical instrument than the viola and the violin.
We know that the distance between the first and fourth fingers is a fourth interval in the first position on the violin and viola.
In the cello, on the other hand, the distance is a third due to the length of the strings.
In fact, the second finger is used in the first positions only for the chromatic passages. Then, as you go up in pitch, all four fingers are used under the handle as the distances get smaller.
The novelty in the cello is that to fingering, the thumb is also used.
Since the hand does not hold the instrument, the thumb is free to be used as it rests on the shoulder.
It is always used in the higher positions ... ... even from the seventh position, it leaves just the normal position to intervene in the fingering.

I'll show you an example of fingering on the cello of the C major scale in the first position:

It is always better, in any case, as I mentioned earlier, to leave the arrangement of the fingers to the performer.

A fundamental element in the fingering of the cello is undoubtedly the use of the so-called "nut."

The nut is a technique that involves using the thumb in fingering in high positions.

It is usually used starting from the seventh position.

With the thumb, using the shorter finger (the little finger) is usually excluded from the fingerings.

The use of the nut takes place precisely because the soundboard takes up space, and the thumb leaves its position behind the fingerboard.

Let's say that its use brings the hand to a decidedly unnatural position; in fact, it is used only in the conditions I have explained to you.

This does not mean that it is sometimes also used in the low positions, for example, to make chords.

The graphic sign that distinguishes the nut is this sign placed above the note:

Regarding the use of bichords or chords, a consideration must be made:

The cello has empty strings tuned for fifths, such as the viola and the violin, except that it is placed between the legs. In this case, the order of the strings will be reversed for the performer.

This is a big problem.

To fix this problem, the player usually strains on the lower strings (to the right of the instrument) with the heel of the bow and finally rotates towards the higher strings.

Indeed, it will never be able to be "rip" as a violin do.

Cellists often rip in reverse, starting from the up bow, even if it is a cellist technical expedient.

The cello can take different intervals within the sixth in a double string. Octaves are possible thanks to the use of the nut.

For triple strings, we must consider possible chords that contain two sixths, or a fifth and a sixth or two fifths.

The same goes for adding the fourth string to 4-note chords.

I close now with the timbral characteristics of the instrument:

- The first string (A) is obviously the brightest

- The second string (D) is the hottest and most intense

- The third-string (G) is the least sonorous one, but it holds up well the others

- The fourth string (C) is very rich in harmonics and sonorous

The literature for cello is vast.

Many pieces have been dedicated to this instrument for both solo, chamber and orchestral use; just think of Bach's 6 Suites for solo cello, a monumental work.

In this book, however, I will give more space to the use of instruments in the orchestra, at least for most of them.

Look at the example below: It is an excerpt from Brahms' second piano concerto.
Here the solo cello comes out of the orchestral team in an amazing lyricism:

J. Brahms, Piano Concerto n.2 III mov.

 Example n. 11

In the following example (next page), instead, I'll show you the very famous intro of Tschaikowsky's 1812 Overture.
Here are four solo cellos playing a fantastic choral:

 Example n. 12

R. H. 272a

THE DOUBLE BASS

The Contrabass is the low end of the strings, rather, I would say of the whole orchestra (together with the tuba, the contrabassoon).
It is a huge instrument that forces the performer to play it either standing or sitting on a high stool resting it on the knee.
This mammoth instrument was created to double the cello to the lower octave: all baroque and classical period music relied on this principle for the double bass.
It is the only instrument of the family to be a transposer; that is, the real sounds that you listen, have the effect of one octave below compared to the writing.
Although, as you have already seen, the bows have more or less the same construction types, the double bass differs in some little details.
Its shoulders are slightly inclined (especially in the German models), and the pegs have completely different mechanics like a toothed wheel because of the thickness of the strings; they are also often, but not always, positioned behind the curl (especially in the German models).
As you know, the double bass is used in the orchestra and is the backbone of the rhythm section, especially in jazz.

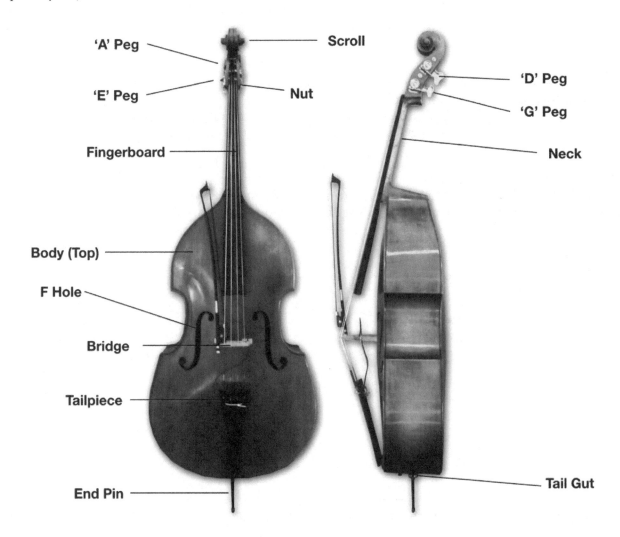

The Double Bass is the only strings to be tuned in fourths.

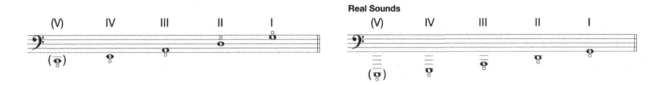

It is usually 4-stringed, but an additional fifth string (C) is often used.

Like the cello, to avoid ledger lines, the double bass reads mainly in the bass clef and the tenor and violin clef.
Its range is remarkable, like all the strings:

As the double bass is huge, left-hand positions are essential.
Obviously, the distances are more significant.
Double bass strings require a lot of pressure, and even small intervals need ample space.
For example, a major second interval is covered in the first position from the first to the fourth finger.
Often the third finger has the function of reinforcement of the fourth; in fact, it is not summarily used alone up to the fifth position.
The double bass also uses the thumb (nut) starting from the seventh position.
Given the size of the instrument, the so-called Half Position is often used, i.e., the one adjacent to the nut.
For example, look at this F major scale:

Look at this G major scale in the first position and notice how the pitch distance is also fingered with the 1st - 4th finger.

Also, in the double bass, as in the cello, the "nut" technique is fundamental, therefore using the thumb for fingerings under the neck or particular effects.
In addition to the use starting from the seventh position, the nut in the double bass is very important for playing, for example, artificial harmonics and multiple strings.
In fact, with the nut, an interval between two fingers can increase by even a third.
The graphic sign that distinguishes the nut is the same used for the cello

About using multiple strings, it is advisable not to use them in an orchestra unless an empty string is also used.

As a soloist, the double bass can produce bichords from the perfect fifth to the minor third up to the fourth position, from the fifth position, you can also reach the interval of the minor sixth and from the seventh position also the major sixth, up to the octave under the neck.

From a timbral point of view, the double bass is not very powerful despite being large.

Due to the thickness of the strings, the sound is slow in articulation. In many orchestral scores, even when the double basses double the celli, especially in speedy steps, some notes are omitted; in short, the writing is specially composed in a gaunter way.

For this reason, harmonic sounds are widely used by double bass players, especially in the solo field.

Although I will talk about bow strokes later, in the chapter on the technical specifications of the string family, I find it helpful to specify a few things for the double bass.

The double bass has a much shorter bow than all the other instruments in the family.

The agility of the instrument is poor compared to the others in the family, considering the thickness of the strings: you can do most of the bow strokes that a violin makes (martellato, balzato, spiccato ...) and, in any case, with reduced agility; for example, the picchettato, the ricochèt and many other bow strokes typical of the literature of the other instruments are almost unused.

Even the use of the bow, being shorter, can change.

In fact, two very different schools still coexist for holding the bow.

The German school, known as the "Dragonetti" (Domenico Dragonetti was a very important double bass player who lived at the turn of the eighteenth and nineteenth centuries) where the handle provides that in the frog there are the middle and ring fingers, instead of the thumb and the medium that distinguishes the Italian school.

German School ("Dragonetti")

Italian School

Here, some examples are taken from double bass literature both in the solo and orchestral fields. The first example I show you is from Camille Saint-Saëns' Carnival of the Animals:

🔊 Example n. 13

In the following example, note how Mahler uses the double bass only in one movement of his First Symphony "Titan":

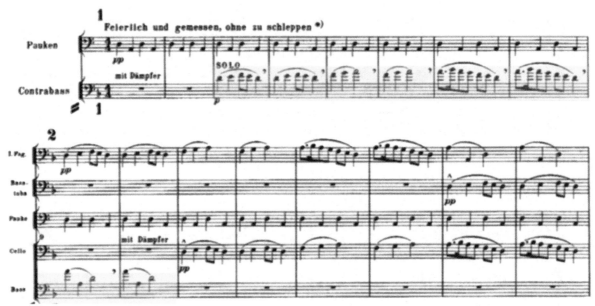

G. Mahler, Symphony n. 1 "Titan" – III mov.

 Example n. 14

Here is an example taken from the solo repertoire of the double bass (next page). I am showing you the score from Bottesini's Gran Duo Concertante for violin and double bass, the Paganini of the double bass. Note how the instrument becomes agile here thanks to the use of harmonic sounds:

(next page)

Example n. 15

G. Bottesini, Grand Duo Concertante for Violin, Double Bass and Orchestra

Today, the double bass is an essential instrument, not only in the orchestra.

As I already mentioned, any jazz rhythm section needs a double bass.

The classic jazz trio is composed of a polyphonic instrument (piano, guitar), the drums, and the bass articulation given by a double bass or electric bass.

I just wanted to clarify that the electric bass is born and develops from the double bass, so much so that it has the same tuning.

But be careful! A 5-string electric bass does not have a low C as the fifth string, as in the double bass used in an orchestra, but a low B, one semitone below.

In addition, the electric bass had further modifications, and a sixth acute string has also been added that does not exist in the acoustic double bass.

An arranger must know this musical instrument well, especially if he works in the jazz field.

Of course, today, the so-called slash notation is often used in the popular field, without therefore specifying the notes to be played but only indicating the chord on which to play with some indication.

On the other hand, I find it essential to be able to write well for double bass, since sometimes an arranger may decide to compose himself, for example, the walkin' of a jazz piece or the obstinate part of a pop song to follow the rhythm of the drums.

THE TECHNIQUE OF THE STRINGS (LEFT HAND)

Starting from this chapter, we go beyond the organological aspects and explore the technical aspects of the string family.

Something I already told you in the chapters about the individual instruments, but it is useful, for optimal writing, to know the possibilities, the timbres and the articulations that the instruments of this family can do.

Since the elements that allow the creation of the sound are two (the left hand and the right hand), I decided to subdivide them to investigate the question further because each has a different task in setting the string into vibration.

Let's start with the left hand.

First of all, it's helpful for you to understand how sound is produced on a string instrument.

When a string is put into vibration, it is impressed on the bridge, which vibrates.

Through the feet, the bridge transmits the vibrations to the soundboard.

These vibrations are expanded by the bass bar inside the soundboard, and the soundpost transmits them to the bottom.

So, it is a total and imperceptible vibration of the instrument.

The sound then comes out of the F-holes, creating that beautiful voice that distinguishes this family of musical instruments.

Now, I don't want to give you a lesson in acoustic physics, it would be a bit out of place since we are still talking about instrumentation, but at least these things, in my opinion, you must know.

The primary function of the left hand is to shorten the length of the string by touching it and thus obtaining distinct and sharper sounds than the string played open.

This is not the only function that this hand has.

The musician can only perform many bow strokes with the help of the left hand (first of all, the legate).

The articulation of the fingers of the left hand allows the performer to change the length of the string obviously: the smaller the remaining string, the sharper the intonation.

The keyboards of the instruments of the strings family do not have the frets (such as a guitar), which distinguish the exact position of the finger. So, the player, since he begins to practice the instrument, always has to do with solving the intonation problem.

The task of intoning becomes more difficult naturally by going up to the high positions, especially for the violin and the viola, where, under the neck, already the finger's movement by a millimeter or an exaggerated and poorly executed vibrato, totally changes the intonation of the note.

Therefore, it is up to the performer to carefully study the intonation and find reference points, not only auditory but also tactile, for example, the curve of the anklet or the contact with the soundboard or with the heel of the neck.

However, all stringed instruments use specific finger applications taking tone and semitone as a reference point.

This allows them to have excellent control over the keyboard and learn the distances of these intervals across the keyboard in their studies.

Let's see specifically the techniques that require the left hand and the right, of course.

Let's start with the *Vibrato*:

Vibrato is the expressive technique of the left hand most used by all string instruments.

It consists of the more or less rapid oscillation of the hand and finger, which must vibrate forward and backward to slightly change the note's pitch taken into consideration and thus create a vibrato effect (think, for example, of a singer when he vibrates).

By vibrating, we say that the note's frequency changes slightly, and the effect obtained does not disturb; it is more pleasant indeed.

Vibrating also slightly increases the intensity of the sound.

Theoretically, as I have already explained to you before, an open string, for example, cannot vibrate. It can only have a "sympathy" vibration. You can only make it vibrate by shaking at a certain height on the string adjacent to the empty one you are playing.

Usually, the vibrato is not marked in the score; it is at the performer's discretion in execution speed and amplitude. He has to consider the type of piece, its historical period, or any other aspects related to the kind of music he is playing.

All this unless the composer explicitly writes on the score "very vibrato" or "vibrato" or "without vibrato" for purely timbral purposes and his clear choice.

Another technique that necessarily involves the use of the left hand is *Glissando*:

All the string family instruments can perform this technique, which practically consists of sliding the finger and hand on the same string or two distinct strings from one point to another.

It can be done with the same finger or with two distinct fingers, one starting and one finishing.

In the score, it is marked like this:

 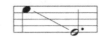

Let's see now the *Portamento*:

It is a technique that looks a lot like glissando; the substantial difference is that the glissando is a bit slower and the effect of the "smear" is evident.

Portamento generally has more of an expressive value, given by a faster passing from one note to another. I must say that violinists of the last century have abused it, using portamento everywhere, even in Baroque music.

Precisely for this reason, like vibrato, it is chosen in some way by the performer depending on the piece being played.

For this reason, it is very rarely indicated in the score.

Now, let's go over the *Double, Triple, and Quadruple Strings* discourse.

I have already spoken extensively about this speech explaining the individual instruments of the orchestra.

However, I would like to clarify and give you some more information that will undoubtedly be useful for you.

First of all, remember that only bi-chords allow two long notes to be heard simultaneously if played on adjacent strings.

For this reason, as I have already explained to you, since only two adjacent strings can play together longer, even the trichords and tetrachords will have to be divided, leaving the last or the last two notes to resonate more.

Attention to the dynamics!!!

This is a very important aspect.

A chord of three sounds to be played softly will necessarily be arpeggiated, obviously the same one of four sounds.

The more the dynamics increase, the more it is possible to "rip" the chord.

So paradoxically, a 4-note chord played strongly, essentially on the violin and viola, can also be played by ripping.

I showed you the example of Paganini's 14th Capriccio in the violin paragraph.

The left hand contributes a lot to the resolution of most musical embellishments.

In this context, we are talking about the *Trill* in a particular way since, as you know, it can have a different length.

A trill is practically the fast alternation of two fingers, usually at a pitch or semitone interval.

It can be played starting from both the upper and lower notes and can be of short duration but also long duration.

Depending on whether the duration is short or long in the score, it is marked like this:

The figure you see on the left is the execution of a trill respecting the alterations in the key of the tonality.

If you were to write a trill with different alterations, it must be marked as the last image on the right.

The trill is very effective when used in orchestral rows since it does not have a predefined rhythmic scan, unlike a soloist who usually feels quite defined when he plays it.

It is precisely this absence of rhythmic scanning that gives that fantastic effect in the orchestra.

P. Hindemith, Mathis de Maler

 Example n. 16

Another effect where the left hand is indispensable is the *Fingered Tremolo*.

It is basically like a trill; it differs from a standard tremolo because it is legato; that is, it is as if it were a trill whose interval goes beyond the second.

Then the bow is pulled as if playing a long note; the rest is done by the left hand.

It is an effect that is mainly done on a single string and respecting the maximum opening of the hand when taking an interval.

A double bass will never make a fingered tremolo of a fifth; a violin, for example, will.

So, the size of the instrument greatly affects the execution of this effect. So be careful when writing it.

The fingered tremolo is written like this:

It can also be done with a loose bowing, but the legate obtains the best effect.
It is undoubtedly an excellent effect with intense color. It was used a lot by Impressionist orchestrators, Debussy first of all.
This following example is from Debussy's "La Mer."

 Example n. 17

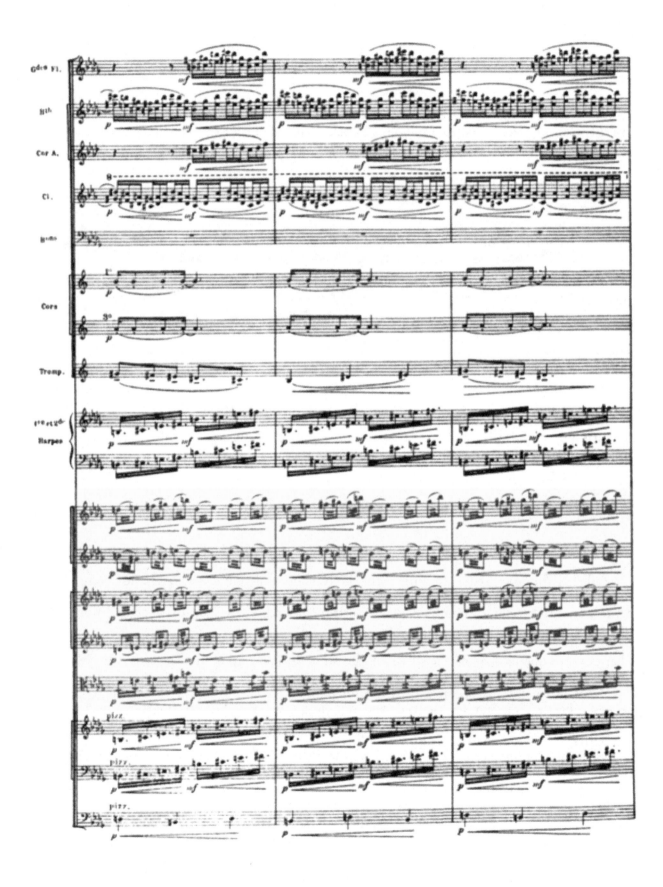

Legato is maybe the most important element only allowed by the left hand.
If I had to compare a stringed instrument to a wind instrument, I would say that the bow is the wind and the left hand is the real performer of the notes.
Indeed, it is.
Legato simply consists of playing several notes in the same bow without any other articulation.
The number of notes that can be played varies according to the speed of the piece and the number of notes itself.
Of course, you can feel the change in the direction of the bow. Still, the technique of string instruments allows you to make many notes tied in a single bow, especially if on a single string or adjacent strings .... let's think, for example, of a standard scale major or to an arpeggio.
Look at this example taken from Kreutzer's studies for solo violin:

R. Kreutzer, *Studio Capriccio n. 14*

Example n. 18

An essential timbral element in stringed instruments is undoubtedly the *Harmonic Sounds.*
The harmonic sounds that we can obtain from the family of strings are basically of two types:

1. Natural
2. Artificial

In both cases, it is indispensable to use the left hand.

Every sound we hear results from the superimposition of sounds superimposed on the fundamental sound.
A so-called "harmonics" sequence starts from the fundamental sound, giving rise to the sound under consideration.
In practice, the harmonic sounds on string instruments represent a bit of what the monochord of Pythagoras was.

A harmonic is obtained, given the string and brushing it (it is important! The string must be brushed and not felt) in specific points.
This is for the natural harmonics; for the artificial ones, instead, a finger touches the string (usually the first finger or the nut for the celli and double basses) and another finger placed immediately ahead (usually the 3rd or 4th finger) touches the string.
So, the first finger acts like a nut, also for violins and violas.
By applying the harmonic series to all the instruments of this family, it is possible to extrapolate each of these sounds that we do not hear with the eye we call "naked."
The mechanism works something like this:

Harmonic	Graphic	Section	Sound	Notation	Resulting Sound
1st Fund.		Complete	Unison		
2nd Harm.		1/2	1 Octave		
3rd Harm.		1/3	1 Octave + 1 Fifth		
4th Harm.		1/4	2 Octaves		
5th Harm.		1/5	2 Octaves + a Major Third		

In the graph above, the points where the rope is brushed are expressed by the red dot.
As you can see, if you brush the string in the middle, the resulting sound will be one octave higher; if it brushes a third, it will be an octave plus a fifth higher than the fundamental, and so on.

As for the artificial harmonic sounds, however, the discourse changes a bit: the mathematical aspect is always the same, but the technique for making it changes.
By artificial harmonic sound, we mean that harmonic sound which is not the result of the open string.
The sound is practically identical to the natural one; perhaps we say less "vibrant," but we are there.
The notation of artificial harmonic sounds is different since two fingers allow this technique.

As you can see, the note marked with the usual notation is the one that we press, and the note marked with the classic rhombus is the one that we must touch.
Artificial harmonic sounds require a particular hand opening because they hit both a nut and a touch with another finger.
They can be a fifth, fourth, major third, and minor third:

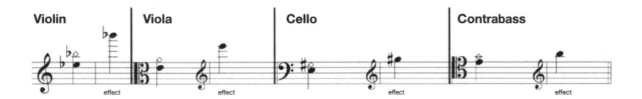

They are commonly referred to as "Flute sounds" as their timbre is similar to a flute or a piccolo.
Since they have this very particular timbre, harmonic sounds have been and still are widely used by contemporary composers.
Look at this example taken from Salvatore Sciarrino's 2nd Caprice for solo violin:

S. Sciarrino, Capriccio for solo violin n. 2

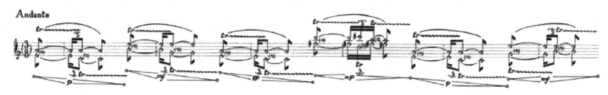

 Example n. 19

THE TECHNIQUE OF THE STRINGS (RIGHT HAND)

As I've already mentioned, the right hand is comparable to the wind for wind instruments.
This means that the actual sound production occurs through this hand.
As you saw in the previous chapter, the left hand contributes to the change of note frequency, but the real essential hand is undoubtedly the right hand.
The string family is so-called precisely because the means they use to produce sound is a bow.
Now here I am not going to tell you about the evolution of the bow; I have already talked about it extensively previously in this book.
The first thing to do to effectively understand how the bow contributes to producing sound and its potential is to study it in all its parts.

Here is a modern bow:

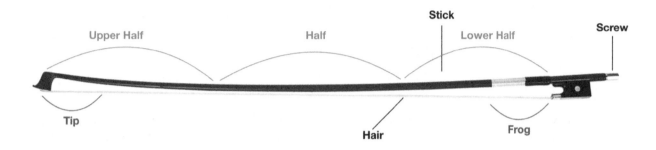

The bow you see here is the violin's bow, the longest among the family members.
I have already explained to you that double basses, for example, have a much shorter bow.
It is essential to know the various parts of the bow since they are linked to the various types of joints that a bow can make.
It is also always helpful to know the bow's division and for proper communication with the musicians that you will have to deal with when you have to concert or conduct your arrangement or composition.

Before proceeding with the bow potentialities, knowing a bow's direction is mandatory.

So, let's talk about what is commonly called *Bowing*.

A bowing can have two directions defined down and up.

This image will surely be clearer:

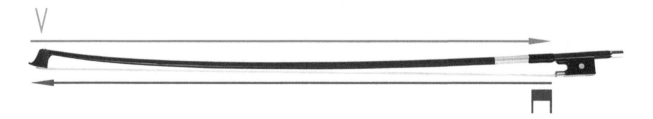

Remember that the symbols used for the bowing do not require you to draw the whole bow but simply indicate the direction that the bow must take, so a bowing can also start from the middle of the bow and not necessarily from the beginning of the horsehair.

In a passage without slurs, we play each note by changing the direction of the bow:

On the other hand, when you want to tie notes (for example, in a passage with expression slurs), all the notes are played in the same direction:

As I reminded you in the chapter on the left hand, there is no note limit to be done in a bowing ... it all depends on the passage's speed, of course, and on the length of the notes themselves in proportion to the tempo.

Before talking about what is commonly called bow stroke, we need to clarify a few things:
The bow is not a perfectly balanced instrument like a balance. Its center of gravity is shifted towards the frog, which means it is heavier at the frog.
This means that usually, the strongest dynamic bowings are performed downwards.
For example, the bowed instrumentalist usually starts it up when playing an upbeat note, an anacrusis, unless a sforzando is made on purpose.
Often, we can write two separate notes in the same bow just to allow the playing comfort to the instrumentalist.
The same is true if, for example, you have to produce two powerful and close bowings ...... they are often performed both down using a reprise of the bow.
In this regard, look at this example taken from Dont's 1st study-caprice:

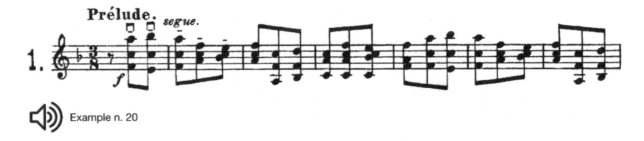

Example n. 20

As you can see, the composer indicates always using the down bow.

Now, let's get to the bottom of the right-hand technique by talking about *Bow Strokes*.
For bow stroke, we mean the way to use the bow.

Bow strokes are basically of two types:

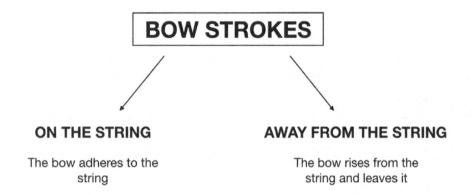

In the bow strokes on the string, the bow is in contact with the string without getting up from it.

I have already told you that the legato is the first bow stroke of this type.

If with the legate you incorporate all the notes in a bowing, the alternation of the bowings gives rise to the so-called loose bow stroke, also called *Detachè* in the culture of bowed instruments (often bow strokes are indicated in French).

This bow stroke is the practice of changing the direction of the bow at each note, and it serves to hear the articulation of each note.

It is a very versatile bow shot from all points of view: it can be performed in all parts of the bow and any dynamics, from pianissimo to fortissimo.

It is evident that the stronger the dynamics, the more it is performed towards the lower half of the bow.

Niccolò Paganini gives an example of detachè in his Caprice n. 16:

Example n. 21

The detachè is also widely used in the orchestra.
See its effectiveness in a very famous orchestral passage from Tschaikowsky's 'Romeo and Juliet':

Example n. 22

The opposite articulation of the legato is the *Staccato*.

The staccato is the execution of a very short sound without raising the bow. It is indicated with a dot above the note, and it is evident that, being short, the result will not correspond to the full length of the note.

 It can be performed by changing the direction of the bow or remaining in the same bow.

Another bow stroke deriving from the staccato is the *Martellato*.

As the term itself says, which derives from hammer, hammering, Martellato is a very dry staccato, similar to sforzato, and is a marcato bow stroke.
It is usually used in not too fast tempos to allow the performer to proceed with the sound's attack, which must be well defined.
It is usually indicated in four ways to distinguish it from the staccato.

 A very expressive and very dense bow stroke used by bowed instrumentalists also to provide further expressiveness to a legato bowing is the *Portato*, in French *Lourè*.
It is a legato bow stroke with a small separation between each note.

This allows, together with the vibrato of the left hand, to make a legato phrase much more expressive;
It is widely used in accompaniments and can be performed in all dynamics and bow directions.
It is indicated with a group of legato notes and a small line under each note.

Example n. 23

In particular, a very popular bow stroke in the orchestra is the *Tremolo*.
It is given by the rapid alternation of the two directions of the bow without ever leaving the string. It is indicated by small lines placed across the stem of the note.

Tremolo can be measured or unmeasured:

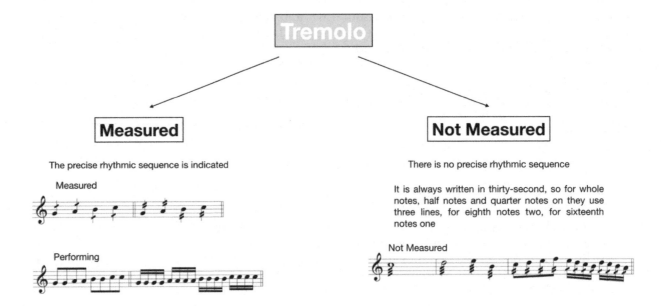

Measured

The precise rhythmic sequence is indicated

Measured

Performing

Not Measured

There is no precise rhythmic sequence

It is always written in thirty-second, so for whole notes, half notes and quarter notes on they use three lines, for eighth notes two, for sixteenth notes one

Not Measured

Look below: it is an example from Stravinsky's Firebird Finale.

 Example n. 24

The tremolo is often used to accompany the melody, and all the great Italian opera players make extensive use of it.

Let's now start talking about bows away from the string.
The most common bow stroke of this type is the *Spiccato*.
There are three types of Spiccato:

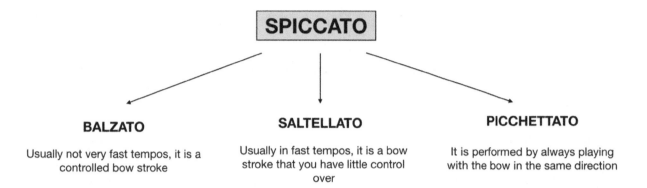

BALZATO

Usually not very fast tempos, it is a controlled bow stroke

SALTELLATO

Usually in fast tempos, it is a bow stroke that you have little control over

PICCHETTATO

It is performed by always playing with the bow in the same direction

Let's see them one by one
Let's start with the *Balzato*.

The Balzato is a bow stroke of which the performer has maximum control and is usually performed towards the lower half of the bow and at not very high speeds.
It is the spiccato bow stroke in which the note's duration is more significant given its execution in times that are not too fast.

You can find an outstanding example in the famous Eine Kleine by W. A. Mozart:

Example n. 25

The second bow stroke is the *Saltellato*.

As I have already anticipated, in this bowing, the control of the bow is less as it is usually used in relatively fast times; in fact, it is often used as a rhythmic accompaniment procedure in an orchestra with repeated notes.
There is little control because it is a natural rebound of the bow, thanks to the movement of the performer's wrist.

We can find an example of saltellato in the orchestral repertoire in Mozart's Overture of 'The Marriage of Figaro':

W.A. Mozart, Ouverture "The Marriage of Figaro"

 Example n. 26

Instead, I'll show you how it works on a solo instrument in the following example. Watch the final part of Ravel's Tzigane in the following example, here in the version for Violin and Piano;
It is fascinating because the bow player here starts from a controlled spiccato, and accelerating brings him to a saltellato.

Example n. 27

When the spiccato is in a single bowing, we talk about _Picchettato_.
In turn, the picchettato is defined as 'martellato' when the staccato is on the string, and 'flying' when the bow makes the spiccato, then moves away from the string.

In both cases, however, the notation is always the same.

N. Paganini, Capriccio n. 21

Example n. 28

Other bow strokes derived from the spiccato are even more complicated to control.
One of these is the so-called Gettato or _Jetè_ in French
As the definition says, the bow is literally thrown by exploiting its elasticity. Being elastic, it bounces, creating a series of very spiccato notes.
Precisely because the physical elasticity of the bow itself is exploited; it is a hardly controllable bow stroke.
Again, since the bow's physical properties and inertia and gravity affect, it is usually more easily performed using a down-bow. This does not mean that it cannot be done up-bow; on the contrary... it is correct, preferable, and more effective to do it down-bow.
It is also widely used in the orchestra for particular effects or strong notes of quick repeated notes.
An example of jetè in the solo violin repertoire is in Paganini's Caprice n. 9 for solo violin... in practice, the whole second part is based on the jetè technique.

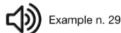 Example n. 29

A breathtaking orchestral example is from Stravinsky's Firebird.
Here the composer writes very clearly to throw the bow in the first and second violins, and I must say that the effect that comes from it, combined with the timbre of the mutes, is fantastic!

 Example n. 30

OTHER TECHNIQUES AND TIMBRES OF THE STRINGS

In this paragraph, we explore other techniques that we can do on string instruments both with and without the bow.

These techniques will inevitably give rise to new and particular widely used timbres that make this family even more enjoyable.

With this further informations, you will truly understand how expressive the strings are and how much they can make a composition or arrangement of a particular timbre effect.

The first I would like to talk to you about is the *Ricochèt* or arpeggiando.

Although this technique can be part of both bow strokes on the string and thrown, we must take it separately because the difference between the bow on the string and thrown, most of the time, is defined by the speed of the piece itself since, at high speeds, the bow also jumps due to its elasticity.

The technique in question is widely used, especially in violin literature, and a lot in the orchestra.

Many famous violin solos of excellent symphonic pieces have been colored with this technique.

One of them is from Rimskij-Korsakov's Capriccio Espagnol. Here the first violin uses the ricochèt a lot.

N. Rimskij-Korsakov, Capriccio Espagnol

 Example n. 31

And if we want to delve into the solo repertoire, then there is an embarrassment of choice, from Mendelssohn's Violin Concerto to pieces by Locatelli.

The following is the striking example of ricochèt: you can find it in Paganini's 1st Caprice for solo violin.

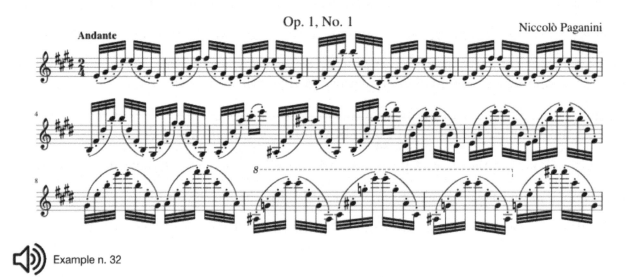

Op. 1, No. 1

Niccolò Paganini

 Example n. 32

The bow can change the instrument's timbre depending on where it rubs the string.
Usually, the bow is played in the center, between the bridge and the end of the keyboard, but it often moves to obtain different timbres.
The first situation of movement of the bow is when you play *Sul Tasto*.
Often composers indicate precisely this technique.
Practically the bow rubs the strings on the fretboard, then somehow approaches the neck.
The effect is very sweet. This happens because the harmonics are minor, making the sound enormously softer.

The technique is defined precisely *On the bridge* when the bow moves towards the bridge.
The resulting sound, changing the vibration point of the string, is very shrill and is often used with tremolo.

One of the most beautiful and particular rhythmic effects used today in the popular field, especially in folk music and jazz, is undoubtedly the *Chop* technique.

 Example n. 33

It is a relatively recent technique and has allowed bowed instrumentalists to use it as a real rhythmic instrument.
It is a rhythmic and percussive effect obtained by unusually pulling the bow.

The bow is not pulled perpendicularly to the strings as is always done, but with a mixed movement between up and down, back and forth, that is, along the length of the strings.
This technique is quite complex and requires a separate study.
You can produce real grooves built with pure rhythm and even ghost notes.
There are basically two types of essential chops that contribute to the formation of a groove:

- The Hard Chop (the hard one, accented), given by the movement of the bow at the extreme frog from above to hit the string;

- The Soft Chop in which the bow moves away from the string but is closer to it, thus creating a ghost note.

The chop is performed at the extreme frog of the bow, positioning the horsehair opposite the usual position to allow the percussive sound.
There are many chop variations, but it would take a book of its own.
You can also rub the bow along the length of the string, or it can strike the strings behind the bridge.
In short, it is an efficient effect.
A rhythmic and noisy effect, for example, can be found in the music of Astor Piazzolla. In many of his tangos, the violin often scratches behind the bridge. That is also a percussive effect, but the chop is more defined.

Chop is usually expressed with a rhythmic notation, and if you want to indicate specific ghost notes, they are written with 'x'

The bow can give a very particular effect when, instead of using it on the horsehair side, it is used in reverse, on the stick side.
This effect is called *Col Legno* (i.e., 'With Wood').
It is a very used effect.
Usually, you can pull the bow from the side of the wood (little used), but
On the other hand, it is very common to use the bow with wood by striking the string, just like percussion.
You can find a fantastic example of this timbre in the First Movement of the Planets op. 32 by Gustav Holst (next page).
Here the composer uses the wood of the strings to introduce the planet Mars and the result is a well-defined rhythm:

I. Mars, the Bringer of War.

Example n. 34

Like the wind instruments, the strings family also uses the *Mutes*.

As you know, the mute considerably lowers the dynamics of the sound, but as far as strings are concerned, it has more than a dynamic, timbral purpose.
The timbre resulting from the use of the mute is sweet and genuinely fascinating.

How does a mute on strings work????
In practice, the mute is a sort of "clothespin" that slows down the bridge's vibrations, so it is placed on the bridge.

There are different types of mutes for string instruments, and each mute, however, changes both the timbre and dynamic aspects.
They can be made of plastic, wood, or metal.

You must indicate the positioning in the score: 'with sordino' to put it on and 'without sordino' to remove it.

Now, let's talk about the most used technique on bowed instruments besides the *Pizzicato*.

The most common pizzicato is obtained using the index finger of the right hand without using the bow by plucking the string like a guitar on the fretboard. There are different types of pizzicato, and each has its particularity.

There are three types of pizzicato:

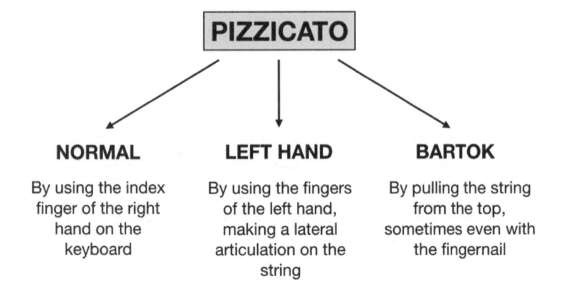

How do you indicate pizzicato in the score???

The abbreviation 'pizz.' simply indicates normal pizzicato.

A very famous example of a completely pizzicato orchestra is a polka by Johann Strauss Jr., whose title is Pizzicato Polka:

 Pizzicato with the left hand is indicated by placing a '+' on the note to be plucked.

Perhaps the most famous solo violin piece in the repertoire with left-hand pizzicato is variant 9 of Paganini's 24th Caprice:

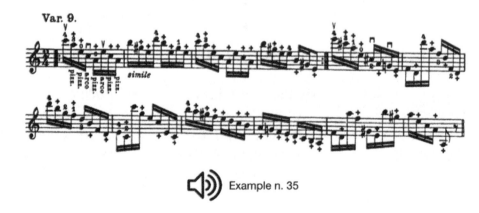

Example n. 35

Bartòk pizzicato is indicated as the sign of the nut of the celli and double basses in reverse.

Have you seen how many possibilities you have using bows?

They are certainly the most versatile family of instruments ever.

The use of strings in all types of music, obviously from classical to many sub-genres of popular music, is truly immense.

They are so important that they have also offered contemporary composers fertile ground for different timbres and effects.

Then being instruments without frets on the keyboard, the applications related to the glissando are innumerable.

This is why, even in applied music, film music, they play a fundamental role in describing the scene or image.

The advice I give you is to study them very well. If you can master the writing, I guarantee that the results that come out of your orchestrations will be incredible, whether you work with a real symphony orchestra or with plug-ins.

Knowing the strings well does not only mean learning how to write for strings, but you will realize that it will also mean managing the orchestra or the arrangement in general well.

Then reread and study all the paragraphs of this chapter several times to better master what you will write in the future.

SUBDIVISIONS OF THE STRINGS

I want to conclude this significant part of the book dedicated to strings with techniques mostly about composition and related to arrangement rather than organology.
Unless you work with a simple string quintet, the strings in the orchestra, as I have already mentioned, are divided into "rows".
There may then be further subdivisions within the rows, always considering the number of performers available.
The string splitting mechanism is fundamental when orchestrating an arrangement because the sound of a section can change dramatically by splitting the parts.
Let's see how this mechanism works.

Let's start with the *Tutti*.

It consists of making the section play all together, and it is the traditional subdivision technique of an orchestral string quintet so that each row will play a real part.

One technique used many times is the *Divisi*.

As the term itself says, it consists in dividing the rows into several real parts and indicating them specifically; in fact, we can have 'Divisi' a2, 'Divisi' a3.....etc.
It all depends on how many real parts the row has to play.
It goes without saying that to do a 'divisi', you must have a certain number of performers; you will never do it, for example, in a string quartet.

This technique is indicated in the score or above the part to be divided by writing 'div.' or directly 'divisi' when the division concerns, for example, two parts (usually the executors divide between music stands on the outside and music stands inside) which are divided by a few bars.
If you want, you can write more staves directly if the division exceeds two parts and is longer (I have already shown you the examples of Stravinsky or Tschaikowsky in the previous paragraphs).
This technique is very important, for example, to widen the voicings of a chord or to perform clusters or contrapuntal parts.
I also find it very useful for purposes strictly related to dynamics. It is evident that four violins will sound different from 16, both in timbre and dynamics. So, it's a great orchestral dynamics management instrument in this family.

Richard Strauss uses this technique divinely in 'Also Sprach Zarathustra'.
He plays on the use of a few music stands at the beginning to justify a more intimate sound .... gradually the other music stands are added, always divided, which accompany the melody of the first violins up to an immense orchestral sound of the strings in which they play all, but always with different real parts.

Another technique is that of using the *Soli* inside the section.
I have already told you about this speech in the previous paragraphs.
Thus, you can only use one family instrument to make one perform only.
The first instrument in the row usually performs it.
When there is only one, the other musicians in the indicated row will not play ...... they will resume playing as soon as they have the indication 'Tutti'.

See below this example taken from 'An American in Paris' by George Gershwin.
Here, the composer inserts a violin solo that dialogues with a viola solo then plays only the first violins' first music stand up to the 'Tutti'.

G. Gershwin, An American in Paris

 Example n. 36

A fascinating technique is that of the *Multiple Soli.*

What does it mean?

There are 'multiples soli' when only one instrument for each section plays a solo part, for example, a string quartet extracted from the symphonic score.

They are very effective because they allow the remaining family to accompany in some way and are indicated with Solo 1, Solo 2, Solo 3 ....

Look at this other part in George Gershwin's 'An American in Paris'.

Here the composer plays only a string quartet for two bars (2 violins, viola, and cello).

G. Gershwin, An American in Paris

Example n. 37

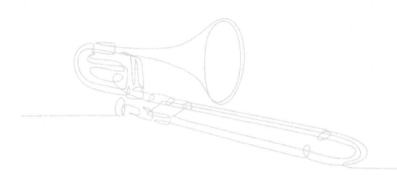

CHAPTER 3

THE BRASS FAMILY

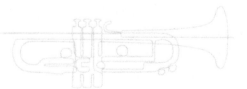

Commonly defined in popular 'BRASS', contrary to what their name explains, the brass family has more in common with the way they are played than with the material they are made of.

For example, transverse flutes or saxes are made of brass and yet are part of the wood family.

Or, the serpent, which in most cases is made of wood or, lately, carbon, is part of the brass family; in fact, it is somehow the ancestor of today's tuba.

What do I mean by this?

Therefore, the thing that unites these instruments is the mouthpiece they have to be played with, not the brass.

I have already explained the history of these instruments a little in this book. However, I must specify that they have had a crazy development over the centuries, both from an organological point of view and a common use point of view.

Let's say their rise began in the classical period, or even in the late Baroque, initially as instruments to be played outdoors (for hunting, for parades, but also in the church).

Despite being an ancient family, the brass instruments had their breaking point with the past and their development in the modern orchestra only in the nineteenth century or even, in some ways, even in the twentieth century. In any case, they are instruments that are constantly evolving.

Today's brass are completely different from the ancient ones of the Baroque period.

Everything has also evolved with the change in music and the musical composition itself. Still, this family of musical instruments has gone from a state of problematic execution to enormous freedom. All this is thanks to the new technological inventions that have led them to be free to play chromatically and perform all the dynamics.

While being very agile, we should note that agility decreases as the bore becomes larger. Therefore, a trumpet will undoubtedly be more agile than a tuba.

The range of the instrument and its sound volume obviously depend on the bore's diameter.

For example, a tuba has a less bright sound than a horn.

The trombone (I'm talking about the coulisse trombone) is less agile than a trumpet only because there are no pistons, so everything is regulated by using the coulisse.

The brass instruments are many and different in shape and size, but usually, the most used in the orchestra are the horn, the trumpet, the tenor trombone, the bass trombone, and the tuba.

Obviously, these are not the only brass.

Let's take into account, for example. In a typical wind band (a fantastic formation that I adore and with whom I grew up in my country), the types of brass that are used go beyond those of the usual symphony orchestra or the brass used in pop or jazz (flugelhorns of different sizes, euphoniums, etc.). This book will examine the most used brass in the popular area, coinciding with today's symphony orchestra.

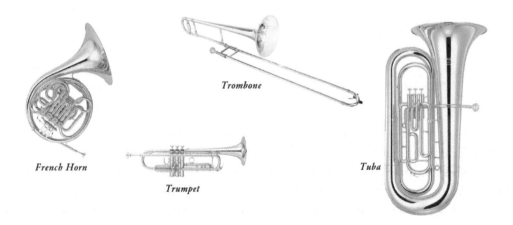

Trombone

French Horn

Trumpet

Tuba

Brasses are composed of two types of substantial tubes called Bore:

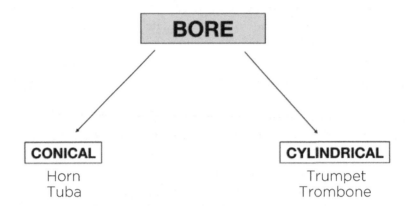

The bores of the trumpets and trombones are cylindrical.
Instead, those of the horns and tubas are conical (obviously not all, but mostly)
Both transposing and non-transposing instruments characterize the brass family.
Unlike the strings with only the double bass as a transposing instrument, the brass instruments have different instruments with different transpositions.

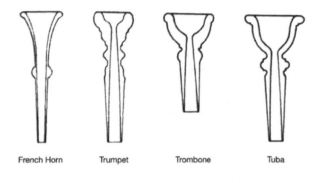

We said the mouthpiece!
The mouthpiece is the fundamental element of this family of instruments.
However, each type of instrument has a different mouthpiece. This is important for the nature of the instrument itself, its range, and, even if not so much, its timbre.

However, these instruments used only the bore in ancient times, so they were limited to the tonality they were made. Now, thanks to pistons and valves, all brass instruments are versatile and capable of performing the full chromatic scale in practically all their ranges.
Let's see what has changed and why.
I'll quickly explain how brass works:

The basic principle of brass is based on harmonic sounds.

The above is the C harmonic series.
In brass, the so-called "natural" instruments base everything on this principle.
In fact, until 1800, horns and trumpets, which were still very common, having no pistons or valves, could in practice only play the sounds related to the harmonic series of the root note on which they tuned them.

By blowing, the performer produced the root, then by blowing harder, he produced the other harmonics. If the instrument was in C, the performer could practically only play these sounds. They took all these notes by changing the position of the lips and controlling the breath.

Obviously, this stratagem was very reductive.

- First of all, as I told you, the notes that they took were few, and there were many unplayable ones;

- Then, the intonation of harmonic sounds is not perfect since our tempered system is essentially based on real pitch corrections ...... so in addition to being few, many notes were also out of tune;

- Furthermore, the root note, called Note Pedal, is not so easy to take. Beginners struggle a bit.

And here come the valves or the pistons!!!
The pistons were born from the need not to change the so-called *'Crooks'*.
What are these Crooks?
They are additional curved bore pieces that, in the classical period, were added manually by the performer.
Pistons solved this problem.
They are three other small, added, permanent pieces of pipe activated through valves that you press.
In this way, the length of the tube increases, and in ancient times the thing was only available with the crook change.
In the following image, taken from an acoustic text of brass instruments, on the left, we have the piston open, then in its natural position, on the right, the one pressed, closed.
You get a greater air column length by pressing the piston, so the sound changes.
Note, from the arrow, how the direction of the air inside the bore also changes.

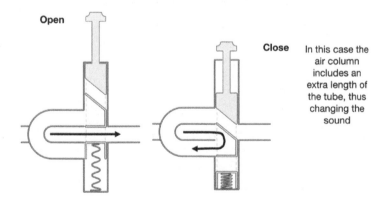

This mechanism has practically revolutionized everything in this family, a bit like the keys in the woods have been.
On the other hand, the trombone has a different mechanism: it uses the coulisse, and I will talk about it in detail in the following chapters.
This family is waiting to be discovered. You will realize how important these instruments are for arrangement and composition. Above all, you will understand, during these chapters, their potential, how to use them as you please in the orchestration.

THE FRENCH HORN

Born from the hunting horns of the Baroque period, today it is called the French Horn, even if it has nothing of French.

Anyway, they called it 'French' because they indicated the score in French; however, we are interested in the instrument and not the exact origin of its name.

Here I will not talk about all natural horns. There are different sizes (it all depends on the number of crooks that the instrument has), but I will talk specifically about the horn cut in F, which is practically the most used in orchestras: the modern horn.

Today, the modern horn is formed by adding a further round of pumps giving life to what we refer to as a double horn.

This allowed for the more effortless playing of high notes, given that a lot of contemporary music often uses the horn in high ranges.

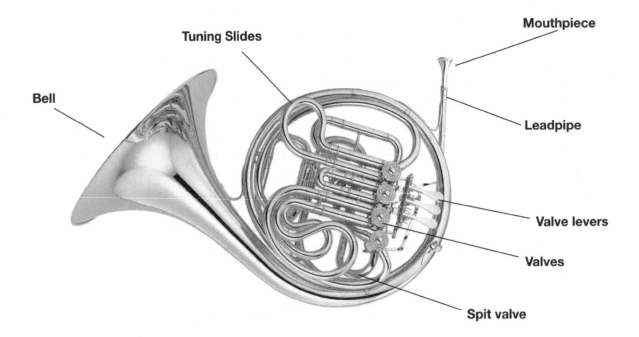

The horn has a vast range.

This is an important element that, also linked to its timbre, often brings this instrument even beyond its use in brass, also using it with the wood section.

If you notice, in the scores, the horn is the first instrument inserted between the brass instruments, immediately below the woods.

This happens because it is a somewhat 'hybrid' instrument, which acts as the glue between the woods and the brass section.

For this reason, the French horn is also present in a classic wood quintet, although it does not belong to that family.

Below you see the range of the modern double horn.
I brought the range back to real sounds, that is, those you can actually hear.

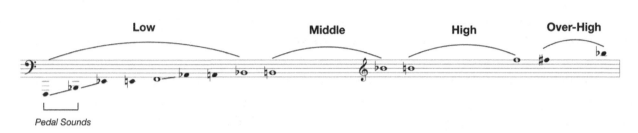

From this image, it is immediately clear how wide the range of this instrument is.
The nice thing about the horn is that it produces a beautiful sound in all the registers, although, as in all brass, the best registers are in order, the middle and the high, the low and the upper are often weak.
Like all instruments of this family, the horn uses pistons to lengthen or shorten the bore.
So, let's see what the Positions are:
A horn's positions are 7, a bit like other brass instruments.
The combination of the piston pressure gives these positions.

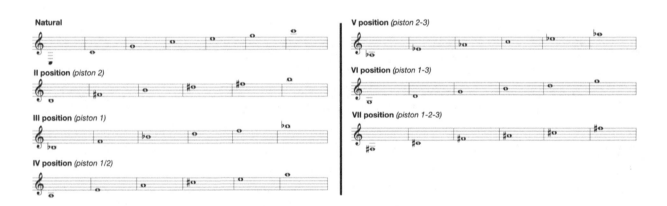

In this image, you can see the notes you can take depending on the position of the pistons.
Now let's see how a Horn is written.
So, let's talk about its notation.
First, we should immediately note that the Horn is a transposing instrument: in F.
It is written in the treble clef and, at times, for the low notes, also in the bass clef.
Transposer in F means that the effect obtained from its writing in F is a fifth below the written note.
In practice, if we wanted to get a middle C on a horn, we would have to write a fifth above the real sound, then a G on the second staff.

Let's define horn writing well.

We must write this instrument a fifth above the real key of the piece, of course, but it is not enough to write a fifth above.

First, you need to change the key signature.
How should this signature be changed?
Having to go a fifth above, obviously just move a fifth in the circle of fifths:

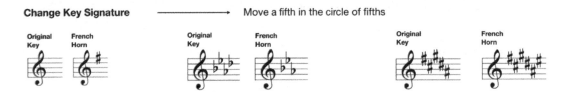

Write the whole fifth above paying attention to transient alterations

Being a transposing instrument, when reading the score, I suggest you use the Mezzo-Soprano clef (going one octave down then to get the right frequency) or read two staves or two spaces below.

In the example below, I show you the solo of Tschaikowsky's fifth symphony:

 Example n. 38

Above is the real sound that you hear, and below as you will find it written in the score.
Often composers omit the key signature in the horn part by adding the current alterations.

Today the horn is widely used in all symphonic areas, especially in film music, where they often use even 6 or 8 horns playing in unison.
The resulting sound is fantastic whether they play soft or loud.
Let's say that the horn has a lovely and muffled sound when played softly, and in the forte, the brass in it comes out.
The substantial task of the horns in the orchestra is to support harmony. In fact, there are four horns in standard symphonic orchestras, and in any case, at least in pairs.
Usually, the acute parts are assigned to the 1st and 3rd horn and the low parts to the 2nd and 4th
In the following example, I'll show you how the entire horn section sounds great both in unison and harmony.
The example you will see now is the beginning of Mahler's Third Symphony.
Here the horns are even 8!!!!

In the first part, they all play strongly and in unison, then they divide, creating very effective movements within the score.

 Example n. 39

Thanks to its tonal versatility, the horn is one of the most used brass for effects.
The particular effect that the horn can make and distinguishes it is the closed and open sound.
They are very interesting sounds that greatly expand the tonal possibilities of the brass section, so the mixture of colors.

Closed sounds are also called *Bouchès Sounds*. They are obtained by inserting the hand into the pavilion. They have a soundless and nasal timbre.

The difficulty is that when you put your hand inside the bell,
the sound goes down by a semitone, as the tube is shortened, so the horn player has to read a semitone above. The notation of closed sounds is made explicit by a sign + above the note

On the other hand, *Open Sounds* are nothing more than the usual sounds emitted by the horn without intervention.
We can do other particular tones with this instrument: for example, the so-called *Echo Sounds*.
They are very similar to closed sounds. The difference is that the hand does not close the whole bell. It leaves a chink open, which is why they have a delicate and sweet sound as if it were in the distance.

The notation is made explicit by a sign above the note. ⏀

We can mix these timbres during the performance, so the horn in the same measure can perform the combination of techniques.

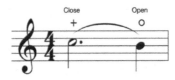

The horn can also play trills and frullatos, but you have to be careful with the trills; they can't all be performed.
On the other hand, the frullato technique is simple to make and can be done with both the tongue and the throat. It works best in the mid-high register.

As you have noticed, the horn is a fantastic instrument, very versatile, and with a changeable and unmistakable timbre.
Now, of course, I have limited myself to explaining its technical characteristics, but in the orchestration phase, the horn is vital for the orchestra's timbre.
Beyond the examples I showed you, in which the horns still excel, this section has an excellent function of doubling many parts of the orchestra, both solo and all together, giving more body to the sound without coloring too much and invading the terrain of others, especially when used in mezzo-forte dynamics.

THE TRUMPET

The trumpet occupies the soprano position in the brass family; therefore, according to the principle I told you about in the previous chapters, it is the most agile of the instruments of this family.
It has a similar historical derivation to the horn, but it was particularly distinguished thanks to its shape.
The modern trumpet, the one we see today, appears in this way already in the Middle Ages, obviously without pistons, as a natural instrument and has practically invaded all armies in the military.
However, we can say that it is one of the longest-lived instruments (think of the Egyptian Trumpets of thousands of years ago!)

This is the Modern Trumpet:

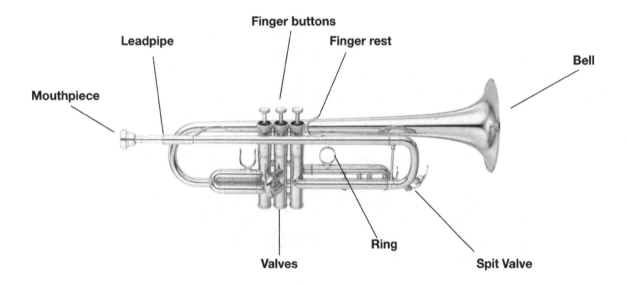

Here I will tell you about the trumpet in B flat, which is the most used in both classical and jazz.

Trumpets are many and of different cuts. I'll show you just a few more common ones.

Look at the image in the following page:

D Trumpet

C Trumpet

B♭ Trumpet

E♭ Bass Trumpet

B♭ Cornetta

B♭ Flugelhorn

The trumpets in B flat, C, and D are very similar.
There is also the Low Trumpet, cut in E flat, the Cornet in B flat, and the Flugelhorn in B flat, which are the most used among the instruments of this type.
In the orchestra, you will rarely find them all.
Let's say that generally, the trumpets in B flat are used (first of all) together with those in C and D.
For example, we can find the entire types of trumpets only in symphonic bands.

The trumpet in B flat does not have an exaggerated range, just over three octaves. The best register is always the medium, even if, in the jazz area, the first trumpets are very specialized in over-pitched sounds, even going beyond the normal texture.

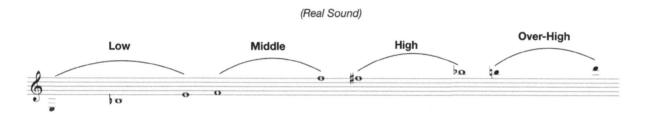

Like the other brass instruments, the trumpet also has different piston positions.
The positions of the fingers on the pistons that a trumpet has are 7.

In the following image, I show you all seven positions:

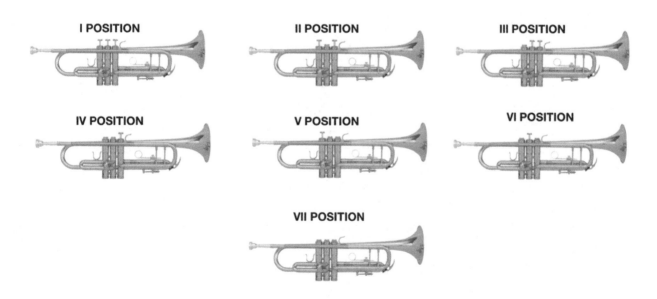

In the following diagram, you will see the entire chromatic range of the trumpet in which the Roman numeral indicates the natural harmonic and the Arabic number the combination of the pistons:

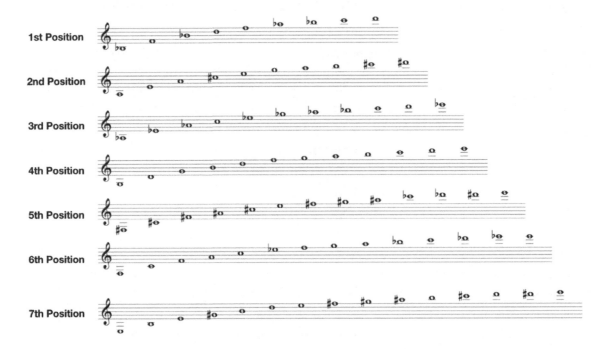

I'll show you an example below.

Here, I represent harmonic sounds that are taken in various positions.

It starts from the 2nd harmonic (the root would be one octave below) up to the 16th

The Trumpet is a transposing instrument; the one I'm talking about is in B flat.
This is essential since everything starts from here.
It is written in the treble clef, and being an instrument transposed to B flat, the effect you will hear when you see a note written in the trumpet staff is a tone below the note written in B flat.

It is therefore essential for those who write and orchestra, before reading, the writing of the trumpet: it must be written a tone above the real key of the piece.
Let's go step by step because it is not enough to write a tone above.
The fact that the trumpet is all written one tone above in practice reads a key above the real key, so the arranger/composer must write the trumpet staff in this way:
First, you need to change the key signature and, going one tone above; then, you must move two fifths in the circle of fifths:

Change Key Signature ⟶ Move two fifths in the circle of fifths

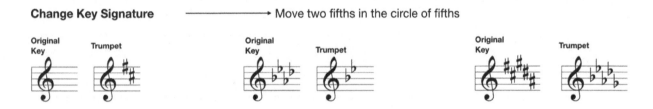

Write the whole music a tone above paying attention to transient alterations

In the reading phase, on the other hand, when we are conducting one of our scores and therefore what a trumpet player does when he reads, we can use the tenor clef to read a tone below:

From the point of view of use, we could open an infinite chapter on this instrument.
Being very old, over the centuries, it has been overused in many different areas.
Today it is the basis of symphony orchestras as it occupies the position of the soprano of the brass family. Usually, a regular symphony orchestra starts from a number of 2 or 3 trumpets, up to 4 or even 6 trumpets in some scores of Holst or Mahler. It is a pivotal instrument in the popular area, especially in jazz: a regular Big Band has 4 trumpets, so you can understand its importance. The function of the trumpet is essential in both the symphonic and jazz area. In addition to being an excellent doubler for other orchestral instruments (violins, oboes ...... it depends on the color you want to achieve by orchestrating), they are often used in unison to determine a specific melody or counter-melody. Below is an example from the 4th movement of Beethoven's Fifth Symphony. Note how the Trumpets, in this case in C, double the parts of the strings to give more dynamic support in the first part, then give the harmonic support to the theme together with the Horns in C, which practically double the part of the trumpets.

Example n. 40

Trumpets can also have a function of harmonic support above or with the horns and are fantastic when they express a theme in unison, especially in forte dynamics.

They excel in orchestral color.

Think, for example, of the opening credits of Star Wars composed by John Williams: there, the trumpets all play in unison and dominate the full orchestra in forte dynamics.

 Example n. 41 *J. Williams, Star Wars Main Titles*

Very often, the trumpet in the symphonic context has a solo role.

In the following example, you will see the beginning of Gustav Mahler's Fifth Symphony.
The trumpet opens the symphony by itself.

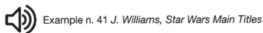

 Example n. 42

In the popular area, trumpets, in addition to classic functions, also have a solid rhythmic role, especially if you play in the Big Band section whether they are harmonized or not.

However, there is one important thing to specify (as I mentioned earlier): the trumpet players of a big band's section, especially the first trumpet, are usually more skilled in the acute range of the instrument.

The first trumpet reaches a range that a common classical trumpet player does not do in these areas.

I want to linger a little on some issues related to timbre, perhaps removing something from the general timbre of the brass, but I find this aspect truly essential for trumpets.

We assume that the trumpet can play from pianissimo to fortissimo, making the vibration of the brass truly felt.

Like all mouthpiece instruments, the trumpet can vibrate thanks to the combination of the pulse of the lip and the movement of the hand on the piston.

You should note that the trumpet cannot put its hand in the bell as the horn does. I say this because, theoretically, it would seem that the trumpet cannot make open or closed sounds..... but it can! It can also do the glissando with a quick slide of the lip; however, it is an effect that you should not use a lot, a bit like in horns, since it is not exactly the classic glissando that you can do, for example, with a bowed instrument.

The brass family, particularly the trumpet, has numerous Mutes that change the sound, and we use almost all of them.

Every arranger/composer needs to know the sound of these mutes, many of which are used in jazz.

The trumpet and the trombone are the two instruments that can "wear" more mutes, unlike the horn and the tuba, which are limited to a mute.

Look in the images below how many mutes a trumpet can wear:

 Example n. 43

STRAIGHT

It has a metallic and muffled effect

 Example n. 44

HARMON or WHA-WHA

It consists of two parts: the mute and an internal funnel. This tube can be somewhat controlled, producing very different colors. The right hand is used to produce the classic "Wha-Wha" effect and is indicated with a '+' for the closed hand and 'o' for the open one. It is widely used in jazz music

Example n. 45

CUP

Widely used in jazz music. It can be open or closed, giving the instrument a very nasal sound

 Example n. 46

WHISPER

Literally from English "whisper", it is the sweetest of all and when played softly it is almost imperceptible

 Example n. 47

PLUNGER

It is a mobile mute that the performer has in his hand and uses it by moving it towards or away from the bell. Also, in this case the notation '+' and 'o' are used.

BUCKET

It is the only one does not fit into the bell, but is attached to it

SOLOTONE

Very similar to the Harmon, it has a very nasal sound like a tele phone or an old radio

VELVET

It is basically the same as the Bucket

About trills, tremolos, and frullatos, the trumpet applies the same rules as the horn.

THE TROMBONE

This chapter talks about the trombone, or rather the trombones.

I use the plural because I will talk about two different trombones, the Tenor Trombone and the Bass Trombone. They are practically the most used in both orchestral and jazz areas.

The trombones are a real family (from the Alto trombones to the Cimbasso).

However, we don't need to talk about the whole family, although the conversation is always interesting. The Trombone is one of those instruments that haven't had many modifications, apart from the pistons one. In practice, it appears today more or less as it was in the Renaissance.

It already appeared in the organological works of Praetorius at the beginning of the 1600s, and it remained the same. This is because it was born as a chromatic instrument, so it has remained ......not only......it is a versatile instrument, excellent both to be played alone and in section. It also has considerable dynamic possibilities and a vast range. Perhaps its name derives from that of "big trumpet". The peculiarity of this instrument is undoubtedly the Coulisse, which is the system that allows the performer to lengthen and shorten the tube as he likes and to tune perfectly. For this reason, it was also called, in Italian, 'Tromba da Tiro' (because they pulled the coulisse). Most of the bore of the trombone is cylindrical. It becomes conical at the end, and the bell is smaller for the altos and tenors, but it widens so much starting from the bass trombone to allow the good resonance of the low frequencies. Although we used three types of trombones in orchestra, Alto, Tenor, and Bass, I will talk about the last two, which are widely used in all popular languages, especially in jazz.

Here is a Tenor Trombone:

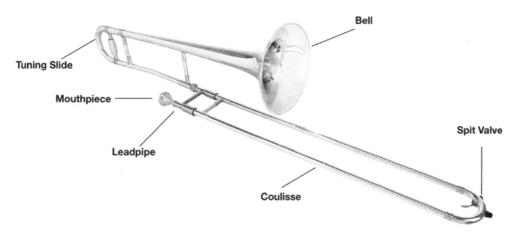

However, this is a Bass Trombone:

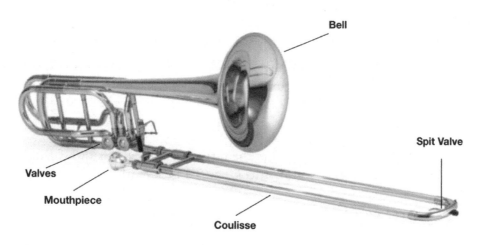

As you have noticed, there are some substantial differences, starting with the size of the bell. Also, note the crooks and additional valves.

Let's now see the range of these trombones.
As I told you, the trombone has a considerable range, and the coulisse helps a lot in compiling the chromatic scale:

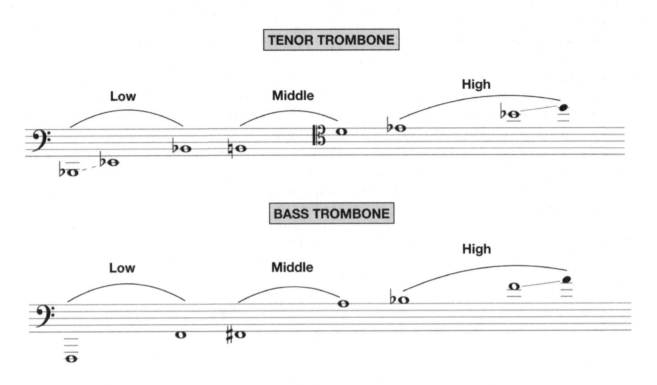

Like all brass instruments, the trombone also has seven positions, and the position of the coulisse defines them:

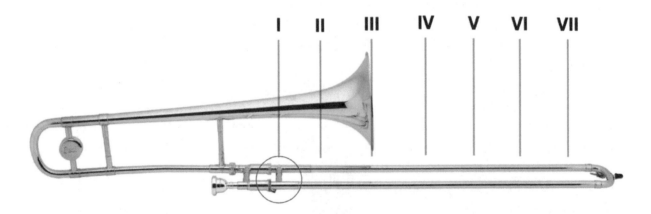

The reference point is the part circled in red that the instrumentalist holds in his hand.
Each of the seven positions, from B flat in first to E natural in seventh, lowers the note by a semitone compared to the previous one.
The maximum extension of the coulisse is in the seventh position.

The roots of each position are called pedal notes, and we do not use them much anyway; we can produce the same notes in different positions since they coincide with the harmonic series created.
It is interesting to see the Harmonic Table of the Trombone.
I only report the tenor trombone for a fundamental reason: in practice, the Bass Trombone, usually cut in F, does not have seven positions but six. In fact, it lacks the fifth. The reason is quite simple. The coulisse used for the bass trombone is the same as the tenor. The substantial difference lies in the distance between one position and another. In the tenor trombone is about 8 centimeters, while in the bass, it reaches 12 centimeters. So, the difficulty of extending the arm is greater.

SOUNDBOARD - Tenor Trombone

As for the notation, the trombone, despite being cut in B flat the Tenor and F the Bass, is not a transposing instrument, so you will write and read exactly the notes you write and hear.
To avoid excessive ledger lines, we write it in the bass clef in the standard register and the tenor clef in the high register. The use of the trombone is extensive: in ancient times, they used it in many areas (military, ecclesiastical, party ....)
Today it is an instrument of fundamental importance since it covers the bass or medium-bass role of a brass section both in the orchestra and popular music.
It is a very used musical instrument both in symphonic and popular areas, and it is fundamental in jazz. As it is very versatile, it is used both alone and in section: in big bands, there are usually 4 (which can be three tenors and a bass, or sometimes even an alto, two tenors and a bass); in the symphony orchestra 3 (2 tenors and bass or alto, tenor and bass - it all depends on the compositional and orchestration needs of course). The function of the trombone in the orchestra is usually that of harmonic support. Still, it is also very useful to produce counterpoints, counter-melodies, and doubling of other parts. About the timbres, I must say that it can play from pianissimo to fortissimo, and its timbre can easily go from sweet to metallic given by brass.

In the following image, I bring you the beginning of the 4th movement of Schumann's Third Symphony.

Here the composer composes a real choral for three trombones (an alto, a tenor, and a bass).

They are usually written on two staves, the first two in the alto clef on the first staff and the bass separately on the second.

If you listen to the pianissimo of this instrument in this context, it is truly fantastic and hypnotic. Then, in this case, the mixture with the bassoons and the horns is masterful.

IV.

R. Schumann, Symphony n. 3 - IV mov.

 Example n. 48

You can make super cantabile passages with the trombone; in fact, you can perform the vibrato thanks to the back-and-forth movement of the coulisse.

Even the trombonist cannot put his hand in the bell as the horn, but it can use practically the same types of mutes as the trumpet.

The presence of the coulisse is important.

It facilitates many things but makes others complicated.

There are, therefore, some particularities to keep in mind for the trombone.

Like all instruments of this family, it can easily reproduce quartertones aided by the coulisse.

It perhaps allows one of the typical effects of the trombone and that everyone reconnects to this instrument: the glissando, which is very effective and straightforward to do.

You can find a famous example of glissando in Igor Stravinsky's 'Pulcinella'. Here the trombone plays alone in a dialogue with the contrabass.

Stravinsky comes out a little from the classic style of this composition using the glissando, which is impressive anyway.

 Example n. 49

I. Stravinskij, Pulcinella

However, this instrument has limitations.

For example, the double and triple staccato is less effective than on the trumpet and horn, obviously considering the size of the mouthpiece.

The actual legate is slightly difficult to do, but there are gimmicks.

Perhaps the trombone is one of the few instruments that does not have a proper legate.

When two or more sounds are not harmonics of the same root, the performers are forced to make a sort of staccato-legato with a light flick of the tongue, sustaining the sounds until the end to make the detachment of the notes imperceptible.

When the trombone is in high positions, it is slightly easier to get a legate since there are many notes in common between the various fundamentals.

So, in a nutshell, the greater the distance of the drawstring between one note and the other, the more difficult it will be to make a good legate.

As for the trills, we can closely connect the discourse with the legate.

Unfortunately, we could also say that the coulisse trombone does NOT have trills since the nature of the grace notes is precisely the rapid alternation of two notes.

You can make different trills using the lip, and the bass trombone, for example, can use the valves of the crooks.

But basically, I always avoid writing trills for this instrument unless I want an exceptional effect of its own.

THE TUBA

The tuba is the last of the brass I talk about in this book.

Like the double bass in the strings and the contrabassoon in the woodwinds, it is the extreme bass of the family.

The tuba is probably the youngest instrument of this family.

As we know it today, we find it towards the end of the 19th century.

Despite the various types of tubas, today, the instrument is not transposing. The words F, E flat, B flat, etc., refer exclusively to their range.

Most of the tubas seen today in the orchestra are in C or the double bass in B flat since they can better intone the notes of today's orchestral repertoire.

The tuba bore is conical and can use both pistons and rotary cylinders, and, of course, it is the brass family instrument with the largest bell and mouthpiece.

Here is the modern tuba:

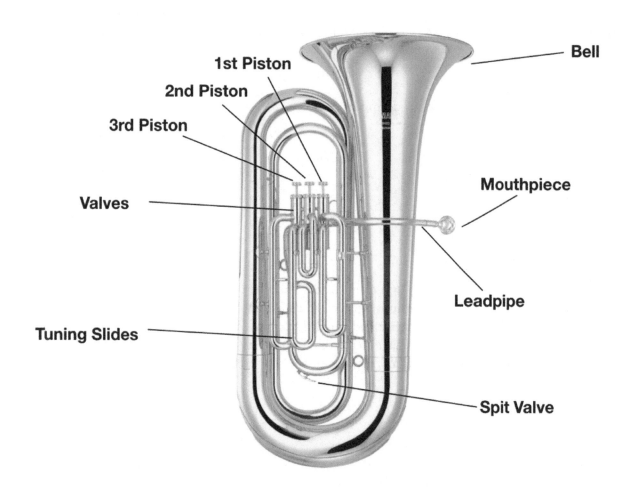

Like all brass instruments, the tuba is also somehow part of a family.

There are many types of tubes:

Euphonium   Bass Tuba in F   Contrabass Tuba   Sousaphone

The tuba has a large enough range considering its size:

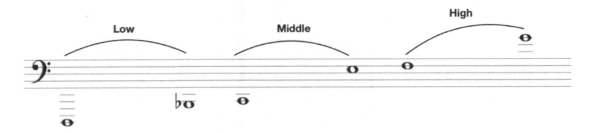

In the low register, the tuba has a hefty and deep sound, and due to its size, it is a bit slow.
It is very agile and powerful in the medium register, which is very soft and round.
However, the higher you go, the more tense and small the sound is.
Regarding the positions, I propose an image that will be very clarifying.
In the following image, you see the chromatic range of the sounds of the tuba:

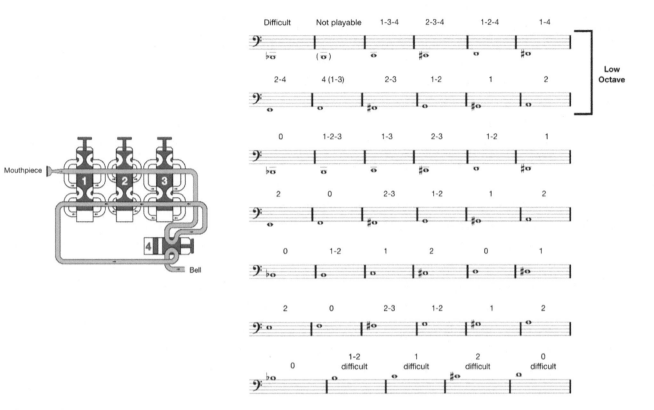

In this image, you can often see the number 4.

You will wonder how it is possible given that there should be three pistons?

For a bass instrument like the tuba, the situation changes a bit.

The valves of (virtually) all instruments in use today are configured in the same way: the second valve lowers the pitch by a semitone, the first valve lowers it by a tone (2 semitones), the third valve lowers the pitch by one and a half tones (3 semitones).

If there is a fourth valve, you can lower the pitch by 2.5 tones (5 semitones).

Practically, the fourth valve is used alone to replace the 1 + 3 combination and can be designed to provide the 33.8 cm (in the case of the one-meter instrument) needed to lower the pitch by a perfect fourth (5 semitones).

Furthermore, you can use the combination 2 + 4 as a satisfactory alternative for the complex combination 1 + 2 + 3. This means that the fourth valve is the best solution to perform well a chromatic scale in the low register. The image on the right will make you understand the usefulness of the fourth valve.

The 4-valve + crook tuba could theoretically use as many as 32 positions. But given that many sounds are in common, 13 are used.

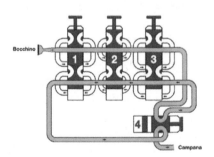

Look at the harmonic table of the positions of the tuba:
(The root is excluded in this table, starting from the 2nd harmonic)

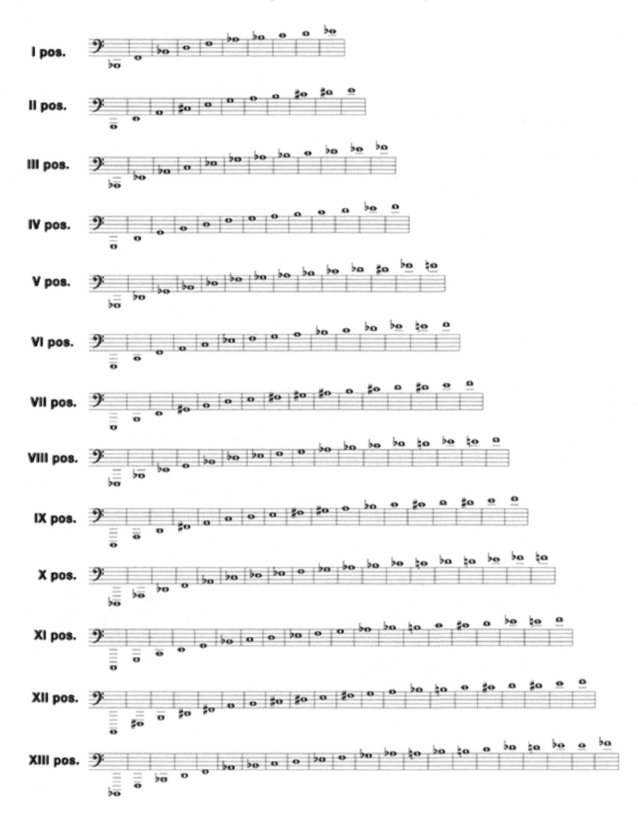

As I have already anticipated, despite different Tubas, in various models, today, the instrument is not a transposer. I have already told you that the wording B flat, F, etc. refers exclusively to their range, and it is always written in the Bass key.

The tuba completes the brass range perfectly. In fact, having a round sound full of harmonics is an excellent instrument for emitting the fundamentals of the chord in the section.

Look below for this example from the beginning of Mussorgsky's "Pictures at an Exhibition" orchestrated by Ravel.
The tuba defines the fundamentals by doubling the Third Trombone to the lower octave. Here, when the tuba enters, it gives a lot of depth to the brass section.

M. Mussorgsky, Pictures at an Exhibition

 Example n. 50

Its primary use is in the orchestra, although there are situations in which it plays alone.
In the "Pictures at an Exhibition", Ravel himself leaves the Tuba playing alone: the sound is very tied, very soft, and binds very well with the low register of the strings. (next page)

4. Bydło

M. Mussorgsky, Pictures at an Exhibition (orch. Ravel)

 Example n. 51

In the popular area, it is little used, but it has a strong presence in symphonic bands (even as a sousaphone) and scanned the bass in the first Dixieland orchestras.

In these contexts, the Sousaphone marks the rhythm of the bass on the first and third quarters, typical of the ragtime style.

The tuba can play from pianissimo to fortissimo, and its timbre can easily pass from sweet to full-bodied, and it can vibrate as in all brass.

Given its size, it can only use one type of Mute, usually a Straight model, which, however, being large, needs some time to be inserted, so the insertion speed of a mute is not, for example, like that of a trumpet.

The peculiarity that you immediately see at first glance is undoubtedly the size of the instrument. The bell stands out within the orchestra.

Technically, the double and triple staccato is less effective precisely because of its size.

It can make excellent ties and execute very vigorous attacks.

The sforzandos of Tuba are fantastic, even the sforzandos that go straight to the pianissimo.

It can do the Trills, but they are little used in orchestral literature. However, they can also be effective thanks to the cylinders, and finally, like all brass instruments, the Tuba can perform the Frullato technique.

THE BRASS TECHNIQUE

The technical possibilities of the brass family are endless.

The brass technique is basically the same for everyone, so much so that in many conservatories globally, the trumpet degree is still referred to as trumpet and trombone, as if they were two identical instruments, and we know very well that they have many differences. However, the whole brass technique is influenced by their size (this is a speech that we can say about all musical instruments). I have already shown you how the articulations of a double bass are not those of the violin, for example. It will be the same for the woods. The part certainly in common is the production of sound: this is obvious since the element that allows this procedure is the mouthpiece, and basically, the blowing technique is the same for all brass instruments, obviously always taking into account their size. Lower is the sound, the lips are always more relaxed, and they are tense the more acute the sound is. The first essential technique is the dynamics related to the register. I want to clarify this aspect because it has a considerable influence on all attacks and joints. The lower the sound, the harder it will be to make an attack that is too soft or excessive sforzando because the lips are very relaxed.

On the other hand, in the high register, gentle attacks and controlled joints are more difficult only due to the tension of the lip. So, in a sense, it all depends on the tension or relaxation of the lips.

As you have seen in the previous chapters, the register in this family is large, so you can easily do the articulation games between the various brass instruments. Unlike woods, brass needs more breath to play. This dramatically affects the phrasing. Be careful of the writing!

Although we write the phrasing like woodwinds, the whole sentence in a single ligature, brass instruments paradoxically need more pauses to play a phrase, especially in pieces with strong and particularly slow dynamics. There is also the so-called 'circular breathing', a technique that not everyone knows how to do and consists of moving the cheeks' muscles while playing to fill them with a small reserve of air. While playing, cheeks are then squeezed to let the air into the bore while continuing to breathe through the nose. This is a highly complex technique, but it is impressive when done right. All the instruments in this family are very versatile for any attack.

However, the attack that divinely distinguishes this family is undoubtedly the Forte-Piano or sforzando. These attack types often form the basis of the articulations of many jazz compositions.

The sforzando with an added crescendo is then even more effective. In fact, many compositions for big bands are all based on short attacks, with sforzando or without a crescendo.

This practice is widely used in medium or fast pieces, but we can use it in any piece if musically it is possible. The backgrounds of many songs of this speed support the solos of the leading instrument at that precise moment, and the effect is fantastic.

Big bands widely use short, punchy, sforzando attacks with or without crescendo:

The articulation of the notes with the brass is very well defined. Even in piano, it is very delicate without making the brass sound too loud.

The example below is from the last bars of the First Movement of Mahler's First Symphony. Notice how these articulations of the seven harmonized horns bond very well with the woods.

G. Mahler, Finale Symphony n. 1 – 1st mov.

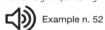

Example n. 52

We should well define the situation related to double and triple articulation about articulations.
This is because, as I have already explained to you before, the ease in performing the double and triple blows is directly proportional to the size of the instrument.
So, a tuba will never do a triple articulation as fast as the trumpet does.

To obtain a double articulation, the performers use the syllables "Ti-Ki" or "Tu-Ku"

The performers use the syllables "Ti-Ki-Ti" or "Tu-Ku-Tu" to obtain a triple articulation. Some prefer "Ti-Ti-Ki" or "Tu-Tu-Ku"

The example below shows the triple articulation of the trumpet in Rimsky-Korsakov's Sheherazade:

N. Rimskij-Korsakov, Sheherazade

 Example n. 53

It's all a mechanism dictated by the language, and the result is excellent, especially with smaller instruments in brass.

The agility in performing double and triple articulations, as I told you, also depends on the size of the instrument.

In this regard, I bring you under this other example from Sheherazade by Rimsky-Korsakov.

Notice how quickly the trumpets and horns play the staccato notes. In fact, in this step, they harmonically fill the snare drum roll. The effect is amazing!

N. Rimskij-Korsakov, Sheherazade

 Example n. 54

Legato is possible in all brass.

The only problem somehow is the trombone.

I have already told you about this problem: the trombone can only perform a real legato between the same harmonic series notes.

However, I have already explained the trombonists' trick to make the legato even between notes of different harmonic series, even if paradoxically, it is fictitious.

In the following example, I bring you the famous trombone solo in the Tuba Mirum of Mozart's Requiem. If you listen to it, you will realize how the legato still performs well, despite the difficulty associated with the coulisse.

 Example n. 55

I summarize the discourse on the glissando a bit because I have extensively talked about it in the lesson about the single instruments.

I decided to tell you about it first because while the glissando is an effect that all brass can do, it's not a real glissando.

The glissando that we do with the mouthpiece is usually of the lip.

The only brass that makes an effective glissando is the Trombone. This is because the coulisse allows you to gradually switch from one harmonic to the other, creating an excellent glissando effect.

In the lesson about the trombone, I showed you the example of Stravinsky's Pulcinella.

If you listen to a glissando made, for example, with a trumpet, the effect is absolutely not the same.

The one with the trumpet will not be defined as the trombone.

Many times, composers prefer to write fast arpeggios that can approach the effect of the glissando even if it is not really a glissando.

Mahler gives an obvious example of this writing in his First Symphony by writing a very fast arpeggio to the horns:

G. Mahler, Symphony n. 1 – 1st mov.

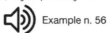 Example n. 56

The simple articulation in brass is made using two syllables:

HARD ATTACK ⟶ *syllable "Tu"*

SOFT ATTACK ⟶ *syllable "Du"*

In the jazz area, the articulations are truly varied, perhaps because a little dictated by the swing trend of most of the songs, but also for a real question of tradition, especially in the arrangements for big bands, where four trumpets and four trombones play and always alternate.
Here are the most used articulations:

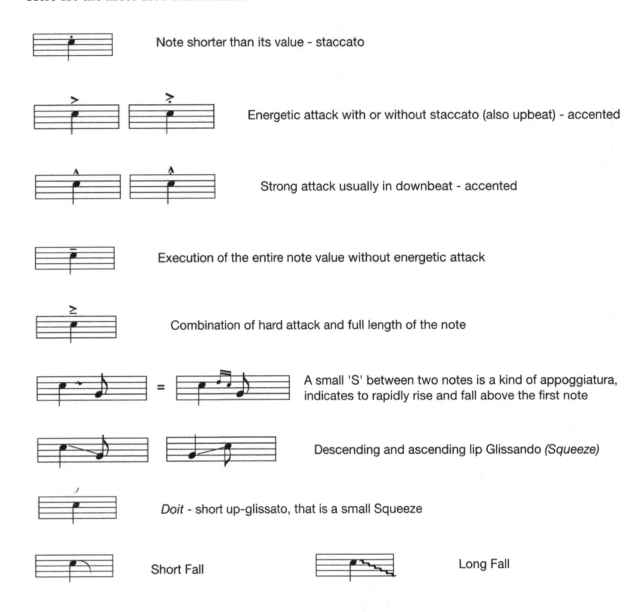

Note shorter than its value - staccato

Energetic attack with or without staccato (also upbeat) - accented

Strong attack usually in downbeat - accented

Execution of the entire note value without energetic attack

Combination of hard attack and full length of the note

A small 'S' between two notes is a kind of appoggiatura, indicates to rapidly rise and fall above the first note

Descending and ascending lip Glissando (Squeeze)

Doit - short up-glissato, that is a small Squeeze

Short Fall

Long Fall

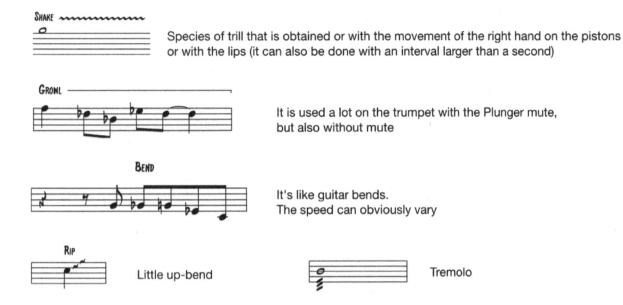

SHAKE

Species of trill that is obtained or with the movement of the right hand on the pistons or with the lips (it can also be done with an interval larger than a second)

GROWL

It is used a lot on the trumpet with the Plunger mute, but also without mute

BEND

It's like guitar bends. The speed can obviously vary

RIP

Little up-bend

Tremolo

The knowledge of brass is essential regardless of the musical genre that you arrange.

I find them essential, especially in pop and jazz.

Now the brass instruments are not those of 200 years ago: at the time, the composers were a little reluctant to write for this family just because maybe they didn't see the technical improvements willingly, but luckily, history has shown us much more.

There are no symphonic pieces in which brass do not play a role today. This is undoubtedly thanks to technical improvements, but above all to the fact that at the beginning of the twentieth century, they already had a respectable position.

Knowledge of musical instruments is essential to color the orchestra well, and the brass can only improve and color your ideas better.

SUBDIVISION OF THE BRASS FAMILY

This paragraph will quickly show how the brass family in the score is usually divided.

Like woodwinds, brass also have many parts for each type of instrument in the family, and as a result, in most cases, they are coupled into a single musical staff.

When the score is symphonic, and the brass parts are represented by several family instruments, we usually proceed by range, with a slight difference: the horns are placed before the trumpets.

The reason lies in the fact that the horn has a precise glue function between the section of the woods and that of the brass.

Apart from this, which is more about writing a score, you should know that:

When instruments are single, they are indicated with a number (Trumpet 1, Trombone 2, etc.)

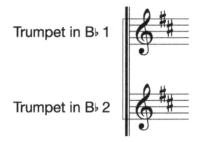

When they are paired, they are usually in a single staff (Horn 1,2 or Trumpet 1,2)

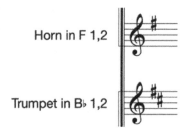

When there are more instruments, the staves are usually divided, trying to keep a coupling.

For example: if I have four horns, they are usually written in two staves with the division Horn 1,3 and Horn 2,4. This is because, as I have already told you, the first and the third horn are usually the ones that make the sharper parts.

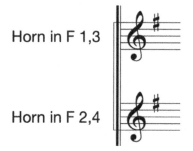

If we have three trumpets instead, usually the first two are coupled, and the third goes on a separate staff,

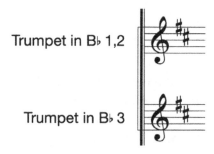

or if the part of the first trumpet is particularly different from the others, we write it on a single staff and the second and third on another.

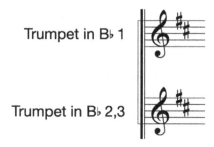

The trombones are usually divided into two staves: on the first, there will be the tenors, also coupled, and on the second, the bass trombone.

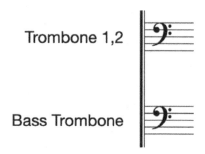

The tuba is usually written by itself, or you can dedicate a staff by pairing the tuba and the bass trombone since, as I have already explained to you, the bass trombone often doubles the tuba higher octave.

Bass Trombone
Tuba

Sometimes trombones can also be written individually if an alto is played in an exceptionally high register.

When there are less used instruments, such as cornets, or flugelhorns, or euphoniums, they usually queue up to the family they belong to, following the range they have.

When the instruments play a unison in the same staff, we explicitly express it with the terminology A2 or A3, depending on the number of players present in that musical staff.

1.2.3.4.5.6.7.8. Horn in F.

Here Mahler, in his third symphony, using eight horns in unison, in the beginning, puts them all on one staff and specifies by writing "A8".

Keep these things in mind because they will benefit you both when writing and reading the score.

CHAPTER 4

THE WOODWINDS FAMILY

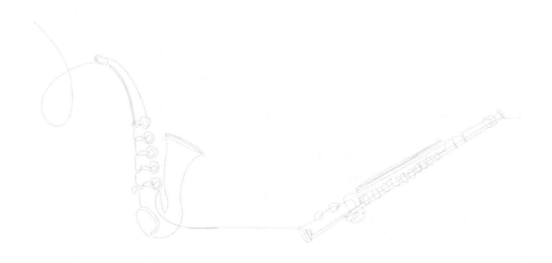

Each section has its sonority in the orchestra, its purpose, and the woodwinds look for their purpose in color.

The brasses are the bright ones, the strings give homogeneity, the woods are absolutely the color.

As we have seen with the brass family, even the term "wood" may be a bit obsolete as not all instruments in this family are made of wood.

Indeed, the cause of all this is historical: in ancient times, the instruments of this family were all made of wood.

Today, the main components of this family are made of wood, but for example, the saxes are made of brass, the transverse flutes can even be made of platinum, gold, or silver, although there are still some flutists who use the wooden transverse flute (I am excluding in this context the baroque flute or the recorders: I will talk about the modern transverse flute)

You will ask yourself: why are saxophones made of brass?

A cause is also found in the historical period in which the sax was born: in the 19th century.

They have been classified as woods because, as I will show you in the course of this chapter, they have much more in common with this family than with brass, which, as I have already explained to you, are united by the presence of the mouthpiece.

So, if for the brass that was the typical apparatus, it will be the reed for 99% of the woods.

I say 99% only because the flute is not a reed instrument and is practically the only wood to be blown on the edge.

I already told you about the history of woods in the first chapter of this book, so I won't talk about it now except by hinting at something.

It is undoubtedly a very ancient family that saw its present completeness only starting from the 19th century.

Today, in the complete formation of the symphony orchestra, the woodwinds are coupled. Obviously, the woods have many scores with a single instrument, but the full symphony orchestra provides them coupled.

Why are they paired?

The answer to this question is quite simple and must be sought in these instruments' primordial function.

Their original function was basically to play the melody.

Going back from the time of Giovan Battista Lully and beyond, melodies were often written in third or sixth intervals by the same type of instrument, so having a couple of oboes made sense.

So, adding a couple of instruments of the same type was almost a natural step in practice.

The beautiful thing about woods is that they are incredibly agile instruments, and this makes them fundamental not only for the timbre but also for the virtuosic aspect they have: they can do legato, staccato, make fast runs, vibrate (however, today, the clarinet is often used in flat, without vibrato, even if technically it can do it - I will talk about it in the paragraph of the technique).

In this paragraph, I will not tell you about all the woods .... there are so many!

As I did with the brass instruments, I will limit myself to explain those most commonly used in the symphonic and jazz or popular area in general.

I will talk specifically about these: the flute, the oboe, the clarinet, and the bassoon (in the photo, they are not in scale .... the bassoon is much big in proportion!)

Transverse Flute   **Oboe**   **Clarinet**

Bassoon

During this chapter, I will show you each of the families of this fantastic orchestra section. We will also talk about families because each instrument is part of a real family.

So, as I mentioned a little while ago, we can divide woods into two significant types. See the graph below:

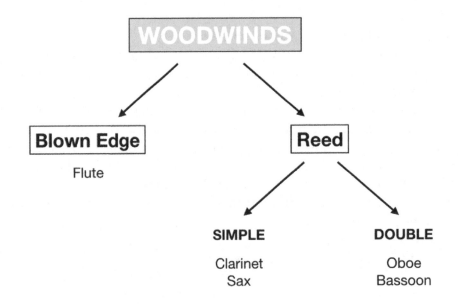

Technology has also done a lot for the woods, allowing them to become more and more agile and very useful in the orchestral and solo field.
The pistons made the revolution in the brass family, so the keys made it in the woods.

The key mechanism has opened up an entire world for these performers.

In addition to the perhaps six initial holes of an instrument, the keys have always been added somehow.

If you think, there are only ten fingers ...... I say only ten because the keys have allowed us to lengthen the instrument's register and perform things that were practically impossible without them before.

Modern woods have undergone several changes related to the keys.

There are still woods that are not so similar from the point of view of the keys: for example, in Germany, they use slightly different clarinets than in Italy.

The instrument is always the same, but I'll explain this speech better.

A great and important revolution on the keys was made by Theobald Böhm, a great virtuoso of the 19th-century flute, who made improvements that everyone could then use.

Böhm realized that he could only achieve the purity of the notes he desired by using a flute with large holes to eliminate the impurities of the sound.

Without now explaining to you all the creative process of Böhm, he basically invented a series of ring keys thanks to which the finger, covering a hole, pushed a ring simultaneously, putting into action another key that covered a different hole at a certain distance.

Thanks to this system, the fingers could close holes even larger than their reach, so it was no longer mandatory to bring those holes closer or smaller to fit the hand's fingers.

Böhm's system has revolutionized all woods.

Another system was that of Muller.

What did? He built a clarinet with 13 keys, new pad types, and ciliated holes.

Ultimately, for example, in modern clarinets today, we have instruments of 17 keys and 6 rings that help control 24 holes. They are used in all West except in German countries where the 13 keys Muller system is used, and the positions are slightly different.

Perhaps the most important key that woodwinds have, except for the flute, which does not have one, is the so-called Register Key, which breaks the series of harmonic sounds in practice.

The register key allows all woods to octave, so using it, the sounds of 100 Vibrations will become 200. This is possible for all woods except the clarinet, which triples the vibrations with the speaker. Suppose the chamber is emitting 100 vibrations with the register key. In that case, we go to 300, passing, for example, from a C to a G and the flute, which does not need a register key as it octaves using hyper-insufflation, thus going to the acute octave.

Some keys then allow the woods to play trills otherwise impossible to do.

Being such a various section, they always discuss the classification of these instruments.

I have already explained the problem of the generic classification of musical instruments in the first chapter of the book, but for woods, the matter becomes even more complex.

For sure, they are aerophones......and we are sure!

The classification problem is related to the transposition, the bore, the families themselves, or the type of reed.

Now, this is a bit marginal, but, as we did with brass, I'll show you the types of bore, which in this case we will call the tube shape or bore, of these instruments.

As in brass, the tube shapes used for woods are two:
Conical and cylindrical.
All the double-reed instruments are conical in shape, therefore the oboe, the bassoon, and the saxophones (which are single reed)
The chambers of the flute and clarinet are cylindrical.

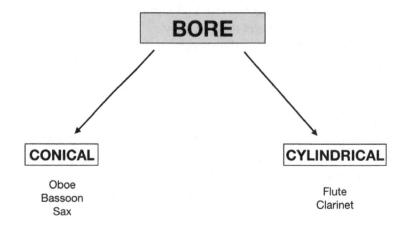

Woods can also be transposing instruments or not. In this regard, look at this diagram:

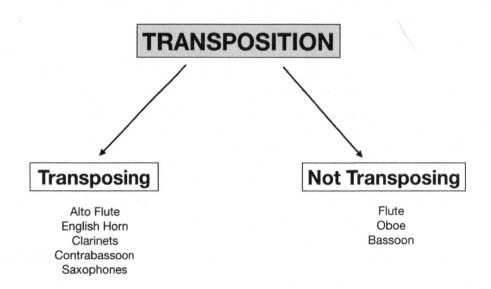

Woods are very complex instruments and all to be discovered.
The work we will face in this chapter will be a lot, but it will be enjoyable.
So, get ready because there are many kinds of woods, and above all, they have an incredible potential that far exceeds that of brass.

THE FLUTE

You can notice right away that the transverse flute is the only one of the wood family, first of all, not explicitly made of wood and above all not being played through a reed, be it single or double, but from a lateral mouthpiece.

Also, his belonging to this family is historical.

Here, I am talking to you about family as I also did with brass because there are many flutes of different sizes.

Here are the main flutes:

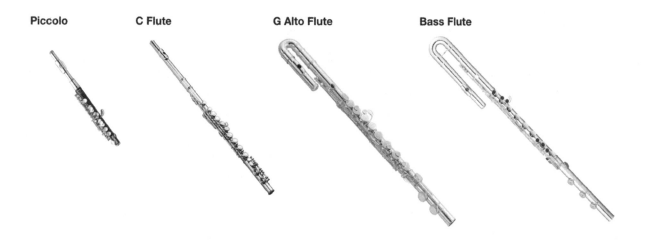

| Piccolo | C Flute | G Alto Flute | Bass Flute |

They are not even everyone. The contrabass flute is missing.

In this book, I will only talk about the flute in C and the piccolo.

I will also mention the Alto flute, mainly for its sonority. Still, basically, we will talk about the first two, which are now fundamental for the entire woodwind section.

The piccolo is not always used. It is usually used in huge ensembles to add a further range to the orchestra with the color of the woods.

I think everyone knows the flute, partly because the recorder has accompanied many of us to study music.

The flute I am talking about is in practice the ancient recorder which is then the direct descendant of today's transverse flute.

The flute's history is truly very ancient: it can already be found in many musical iconographies of the 1400s.

However, I do not want to go back in time. I just give you some words to make you appreciate this instrument better.

Initially, it was a musical instrument made of a single piece, so they could not tune it: perhaps, for this reason, there were many and of different sizes, and they got cylindrical bore.

The first mention of a complete family of flutes appears in Agricola's treatise on organology.

Obviously, we are interested in today's flute and the instrument we know today is the result of many passages that now I'm not here to tell you precisely.

However, we must say that the flutes, oboes, and bassoons were the first to be admitted to the orchestra.

The flute of today is not the flute of the past.

When he spokes of the flute, Bach himself referred to the recorder.

The transverse we have today is the one deriving from the so-called Böhm flute, a very important flutist who practically invented the ring key system that we see today on many woodwinds.

Let's say these flutes were adopted in the mid-19th century, so quite recently.

The position of the other flutes that I showed you earlier takes place with Berlioz and Wagner, especially the piccolo.

On the other hand, the alto flute is less used. Still, Stravinsky used it extensively, using it a lot in its intermediate register, therefore only for purely color purposes.

So, let's go to the discovery of this family.

Let's see which parts the instrument is composed of:

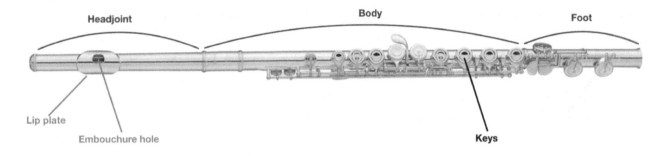

The flute is divided into three parts:

- the headjoint: where the embouchure hole is present

- the body: where most of the keys are present

- the foot: the final part

In the following image (next page), I will show you how a flute works, highlighting the keys and functions of both hands:

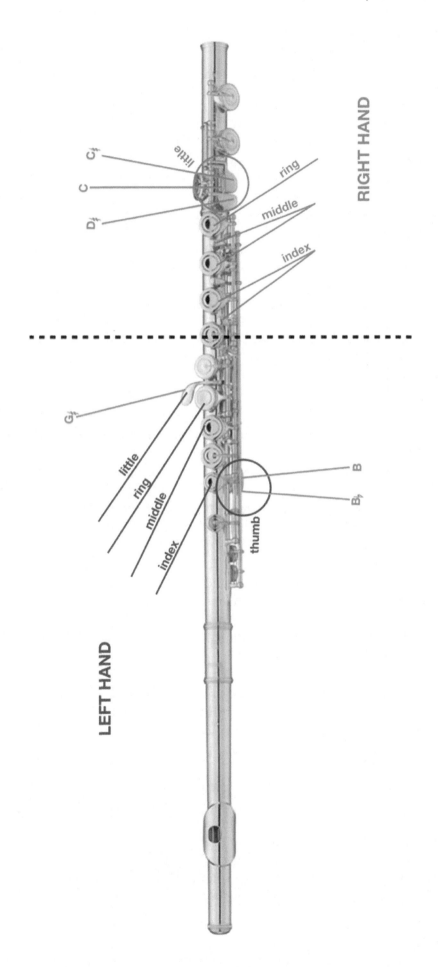

Here is the range of the soprano transverse flute in C:

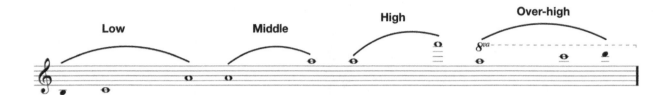

Understanding the range of the flute is very important for writing, especially because of the problems related to the register.

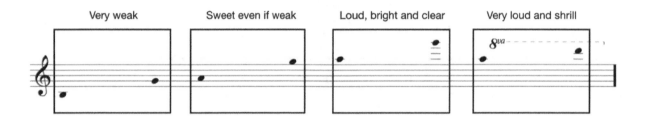

As you can see from the image above, the flute is very weak in the low register; in an orchestra, one would hear very little.

For this reason, most of the orchestral literature sees the use of the transverse flute in its medium-high register.

However, this instrument is very important today. Its use is of primary importance and being the soprano of the woodwind family in the orchestra, it often leads the entire section.

It is also widely used in jazz.

In Big Band, it is critically important to give a distinct color to an arrangement. In fact, the Big Band's Primo Alto (sax) frequently plays the flute and changes it, if necessary, with the sax.

Thanks to its incredible agility, it is an excellent solo instrument and is perfect for coloring the orchestra's strings section.

However, we must be careful when using the flute, especially from the point of view of register and dynamics.

The two are directly proportional.

Together with the sound volume, the timbre changes according to the register.

If you try to listen to a flute playing in the low register in the middle of the orchestra, as I told you before, you will probably not be able to hear it since it is practically deaf in the low register or the lower middle part. On the other hand, in the acute, it is very bright on the high note and should only be used in the "fortissimo" for the upper register.

As we have already seen with brass, the size of the instrument affects its ability to perform different articulations. For this reason, the flute is, together with the violin, the most agile instrument of the entire symphony orchestra.

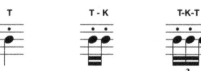

The staccato is excellent. In fact, it is often used double and triple articulation. It is obtained with a slight flick of the tongue while pronouncing the sound "T". Instead, the double staccato is performed alternating "T-K" and the triple "T-K-T", a bit like in the brass technique.

In the following example, I'll show you how Beethoven uses the flute in this excerpt from the Lenore Overture. In practice, he gives the instrument the main theme in solo accompanied by a subdued tremolo of the strings.

Note also the different articulations of the flute. Very clear.

L. van Beethoven, Ouverture Lenore n. 3 op. 72

 Example n. 57

Legato is very effective but beware of too-long phrases.
I want to clarify this aspect because the flute needs a lot of breath to be played, so you have to give the performer time to breathe.
The dynamics it can do are perfect: it can easily pass from pianissimo to fortissimo and make excellent crescendo and decrescendo, but always pay attention to the register in which they are used.
We can do practically all trills and tremolos except these:

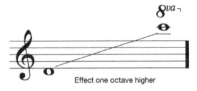

Let's now see the *Piccolo*.
From the morphological point of view, it is the same as the flute.
It has smaller dimensions since its range is more acute than a flute.

It is a transposing flute: the effect note is an octave up:

It has a very similar range to the flute: it starts only from the D above the central C, obviously with an octave effect above,
The Piccolo is an instrument that doubles the flute very well and gives a complete sonority to the section.

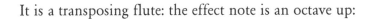

Effect one octave higher

Its registers are very similar to those of the flute:

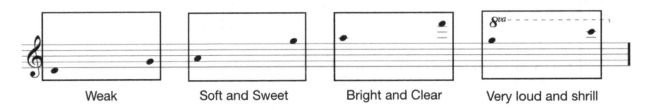

| Weak | Soft and Sweet | Bright and Clear | Very loud and shrill |

They define this instrument 'Ottavino' only in Italy, in all other parts it is called 'Piccolo';
It is very biting in the acute register, you have to pay attention to the writing of the dynamics, and it is excellent both alone and to increase the wood family in the acute range.

The following example is from 'La Gazza Ladra' by Gioacchino Rossini.
Here the piccolo is alone, and its sound is very close to a whistle.

G. Rossini, Ouverture "La Gazza Ladra"

 Example n. 58

In this other example, taken from Rimsky-Korsakov's Shèhèrazade, the piccolo doubles the flute to the higher octave.

Note his agility even in fast staccato.

Example n. 59

I now also mention the _Alto_ of this splendid family.

I like it very much because its timbre is intense.
It has a slightly longer and thicker tube than the regular flute and can be straight like the soprano flute or curved like the bass.
Here is an image of the curved one, but straight ones are more common anyway.
It is a transposing flute, in G, so the effect note is a fourth below the written one:

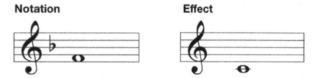

As we have seen for the other transposing instruments, it is necessary to follow exact rules: for writing, move one position to the left in the circle of fifths and write everything a fourth above, paying attention to transitory alterations. I recommend using the baritone clef for the reading, then going an octave below to hear the right frequency.

Here is the range of the alto flute:

And these are its registers:

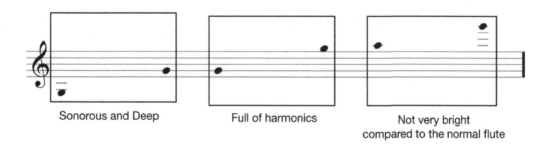

Sonorous and Deep   Full of harmonics   Not very bright compared to the normal flute

Stravinsky gave a lot of space to this flute in his 'The Rite of Spring', also assigning solos.

THE OBOE

Like all woodwinds, the oboe is also part of a family of instruments, in this case with double reeds.

Contrary to what many think, it is an instrument of even medieval derivation. It derives from the medieval Bombarde and Ciaramellas, wooden double-reed instruments with six holes and a single key.

The real appearance of the oboe dates back to the court of Luigi XIV in the mid-1600s, therefore in a decent setting, contrary to what happened with the bombards, which were played more outdoors.

Obviously, it wasn't today's instrument: it only had three keys.

For over a century, the oboe was considered the prince of the woods and was used to double the violins, then, as it gradually took on a not indifferent solo role.

The keys certainly helped this whole principle.

In this chapter, we will have the opportunity to see everything related to the technique and use of the oboe, both in a solo and orchestral context.

It is not a very used instrument in jazz but very useful for symphonic orchestrations, including jazz style.

The color that the oboe gives is unmistakable, and I believe, irreplaceable even when it doubles other orchestral instruments.

It all depends on the reed, an essential and delicate instrument element: you need to have great control of it!

Oboe

English Horn

Good use of the reed allows oboists to make tied and very long phrases thanks to the ability of good performers to release the air slowly; this aspect gave the oboe its "lyrical" role in the orchestra.

The oboe that they regularly use in the orchestra is the soprano. But you can also find the oboe d'amore (transposer in A), the English horn (transposer in F), the bass oboe, and the more recent Heckelphon, a sort of oboe baritone invented by the German Heckel at the beginning of the 20th century.

This book will deal only with two family instruments: the oboe soprano and the English horn. I will speak only of these because the others are little used, unlike these two, widely used in an orchestra.

As I told you, the first is the soprano (the classic oboe), and the second is a transposer in F: an oboe cut a fifth below. I'll explain both of them and highlight the differences between them.

However, let's begin to see the morphology of the oboe family, how the instrument is made, and what its characteristics are:

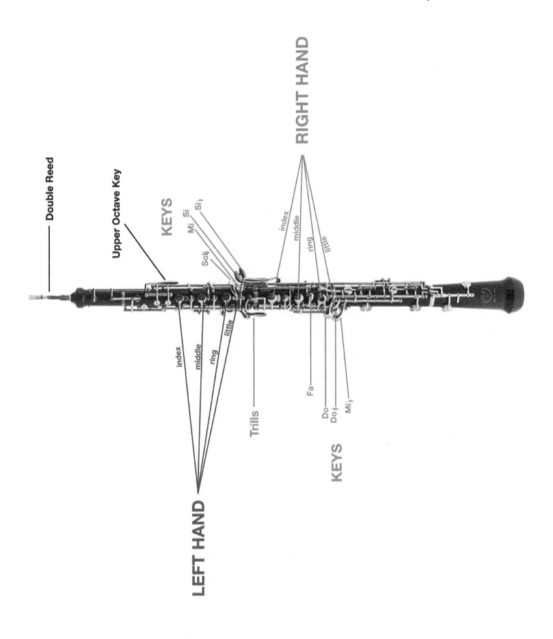

Double Reed

Upper Octave Key

KEYS

RIGHT HAND

LEFT HAND

Mi♭ Si♮ Si♭

Sol♮

index middle ring little

index middle ring little

Trills

Fa

Do♮ Do♯ Mi♭

KEYS

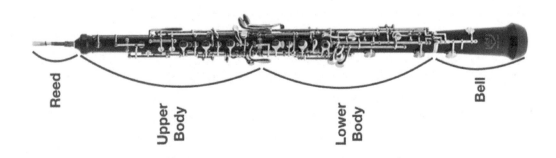

Reed

Upper Body

Lower Body

Bell

The oboe comprises four parts:
the upper part is occupied by the double-reed, then we have two elements with holes and keys (one occupied by the left hand and one from the right) and finally the bell, from which comes out the sound.

The range of the oboe is quite broad:

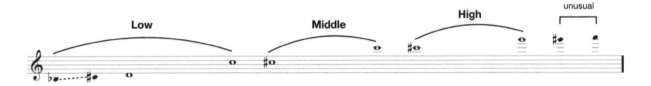

And, like all instruments, there are registers where the instrument sounds best.

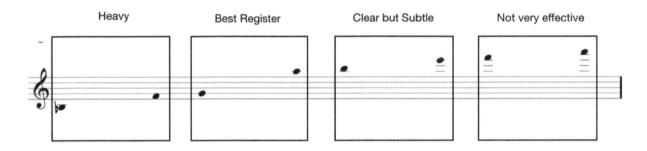

Unlike the flute, the oboe becomes a little shrill and less penetrating when it goes high.
On the other hand, in the low register, it is very heavy, and it is better not to write in piano dynamics. The last A of its range is hard to produce. It is better to stop at the Fa or the most at the G, so we can say that the best register is the medium-high one.

As I mentioned earlier, the oboe is a musical instrument widely used in the symphonic area, both solo and ensemble, but rarely used in jazz.

The example below is taken from the beginning of the second movement of Brahms' violin concerto, in my view, one of the most beautiful oboe solos written!
Note how only woodwinds with horns (treated as woodwinds) play in this part.
The flutes play in a low register to leave room for the oboe solo that performs this beauty in its best register and unique lyricism.

J. **Brahms,** Violin Concerto op.77 - II mov.

Example n. 60

The timbre of the oboe is very clear and decisive. It is used a lot for solos, being a very lyrical instrument.
It has a very heavy timbre in the extremely low register; for this reason, it is often replaced by the English horn and is very stunted in the very high register, unlike the flute, which becomes very bright.

The oboe has a great deal of freedom of articulations: they can all be done, thanks also to the keys, of course.
The legato of the oboe is inimitable and amazing, and the staccato is very effective even if double or triple articulations are never used.

In this regard, I would like to bring you this very famous example taken from Rossini's 'La Scala di Seta' Ouverture.
In this piece, the oboe does a very lyrical solo at the beginning, but I am showing you a quick and detached extract .... in addition, the entire section of the woodwinds accompanies the oboe.

G. Rossini, Ouverture "La Scala di Seta"

 Example n. 61

Trills can be played practically all, except between B flat and low B natural.
On the other hand, Tremolos should not be made wider than a fifth and, in any case, avoid them in the high register of the instrument.

The other instrument of this family that they use today is the *English Horn*.
The soprano oboe is the one that has the range more towards the top, but the other oboes widen the range towards the grave.
The English horn is practically the alto instrument of the oboe family.
The bore of the English horn is conical like that of the oboe.
In fact, from an organological point of view, they are the same, but the English horn is slightly longer as it reaches lower notes than the oboe and the mouth of the reed is not straight but slightly curved.
In addition, the bell is slightly different: it is a little more rounded (called the love bell), which gives the English horn a warmer and more melancholy sound.

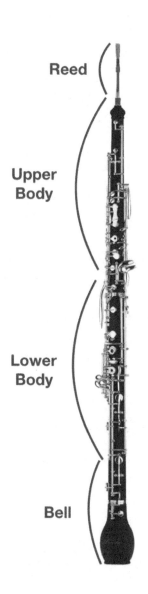

Reed

Upper Body

Lower Body

Bell

The range of the English horn is similar to the oboe but starts from the lowest:

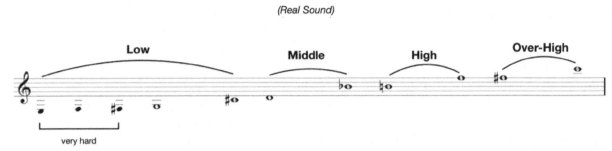

The register also closely looks like the oboe in rendering: like the oboe, the sound of the English horn becomes thinner the higher you go.

However, we must specify that in its best register, the English horn is of great accounting, very intense and ideal for melancholy solos:

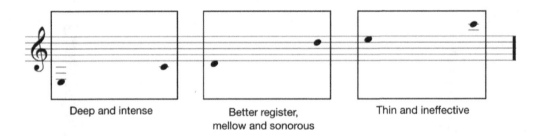

| Deep and intense | Better register, mellow and sonorous | Thin and ineffective |

We must necessarily consider the notation of this instrument because it is a transposing instrument in F.

It is written in a violin key, and, as it was for the French Horn, the effect is a fifth below the note written in F.

Consequently, the writing will be different from listening to the note.

We must write the English Horn a fifth above the real key of the piece, so we have to do the same procedure as the French horn:

Change Key Signature ⟶ Move a fifth in the circle of fifths

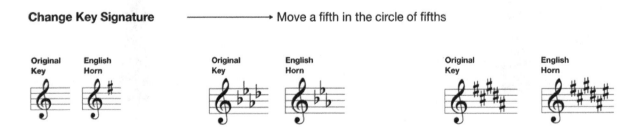

Write the whole music a fifth above paying attention to transient alterations

The reading will consequently be transposed:

Being a transposing instrument, when reading the score, I suggest you use the Mezzo-Soprano clef (going one octave down then to get the right frequency) or read two staves or two spaces below.

The English horn is an instrument of incredible lyricism.
How can we forget the fantastic solo of the English horn in the second movement of Ravel's G piano concerto?
Or the famous solo in the second movement of Symphony n.9 "From the New World" by Dvorak.
As you can see, it is used a lot in the adagios of the various compositions because of its melancholy and sweet nature.

 Example n. 61b *extract from "New World Symphony" by Dvorak*

THE CLARINET

Certainly, the youngest of all woods, at least as it appears to us today, the clarinet still derives from the transformation of the Renaissance "cennamella" or the French Chalumeau.
The one who made these transformations was Johann Christof Denner between the end of the seventeenth and the beginning of the eighteenth century.
Then they built clarinets of various sizes.
The clarinet is the progenitor of an immense family that has constantly expanded over the decades.

Here is the whole family of the most used clarinets:

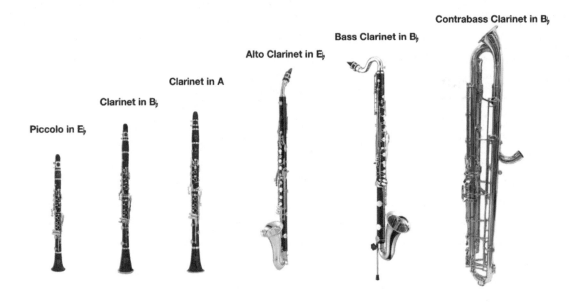

Obviously, I will not tell you about all of them, but about those most used in the symphonic and popular area.
Let's say that the clarinet is now the principal instrument of the symphonic bands, so in that context, we could easily find all the family instruments.
The first instrument to be added was the bass clarinet, one octave below the normal; Adolphe Sax designed the current model in 1836, hence also its saxophone bell shape.
There were already Alto clarinets at the end of the 1700s, and the most recent of all is undoubtedly the Contrabass. The clarinet is usually built with ebony with the simple reed and is now an integral part of the woodwind family in a symphonic orchestra.
It is also widely used in the jazz environment, like the flute in big bands.
Being a simple reed instrument, therefore very similar in tone to the Saxophone, it often replaces some saxophone to obtain different timbres in big bands. As you have seen, there are a lot of clarinets, and since they all use the same positions, clarinetists can play all the instruments of the family. The various clarinet types (E flat, B flat, A...) depend on the size of the instrument.
As I already told you at the beginning of the book, most of the improvements have been made by using the keys. After Böhm's fantastic invention of ring keys, the clarinet today has from 17 to 18, although, as I have already told you, in German countries, they also use the MÜLLER method, with 13 keys. Regardless of this, in this chapter, I will limit myself to talking only about the B flat clarinet and the bass clarinet, which are the most used in orchestra and big bands.

Here is the modern clarinet (next page):

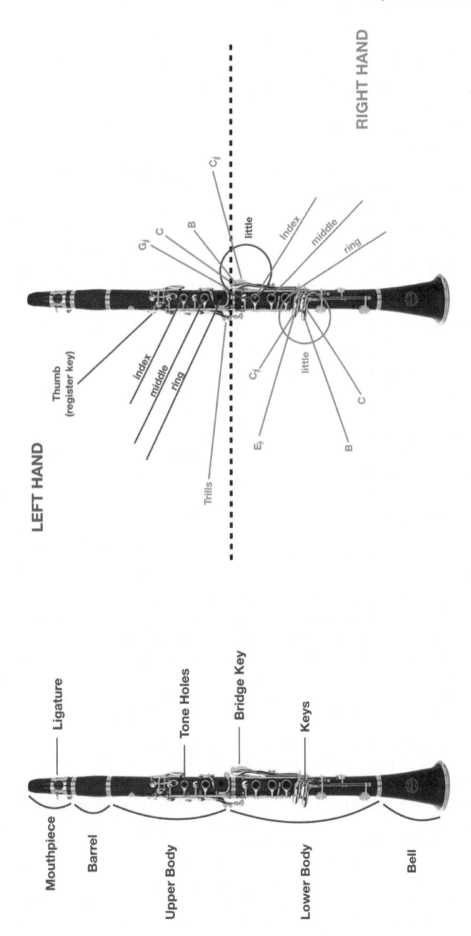

RIGHT HAND

LEFT HAND

C♯

C

B

G♯

little

Index

middle

ring

Thumb
(register key)

index

middle

ring

Trills

E♯

C♯

little

C

B

Ligature

Tone Holes

Bridge Key

Keys

Mouthpiece

Barrel

Upper Body

Lower Body

Bell

As can be seen from the image, the parts that make up the instrument are 5:
The mouthpiece, where the reed is inserted and tied with screws;
the barrel, so-called because of its barrel shape, between the mouthpiece and the upper body;
the two bodies, upper and lower, with holes, keys, and the bell.

The clarinet has a considerable range:

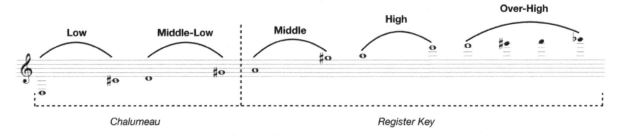

The register of the instrument is very particular:

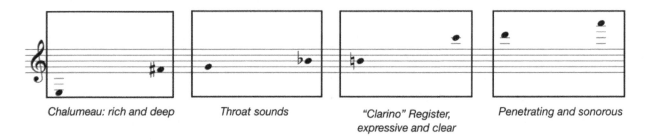

The low register is called Chalumeau and is very rich in harmonics.
The 'clarino' register is the best, most precise, and most expressive.
Even the clarinet in the upper note has an excessively pungent sound and should be played in forte dynamics.

The clarinet is an instrument that, immediately after its rise, had a great fortune and great use.
In fact, despite being the latest addition, it is now an integral part of the woodwinds in the orchestra.
Thanks to its agility and timbre peculiarity, it is also widely used in jazz.
Just think of the figure of Benny Goodman, a great jazz player of the last century, who raised the clarinet to the Olympus of jazz.
This instrument binds very well in the jazz area, both as a register, as a range, and as a timbre which, in this context, is, however, a bit modified by the performer, making the sound a little more scratched and shriller.
The clarinet is used a lot in the orchestra: it is an excellent solo instrument and perfect for adding color to mid-range melodies.
The example below is from Rimsky-Korsakov's Caprice Espagnol.
Here the composer uses a Clarinet in A in solo for obvious reasons related to the key of the piece, which is in A major;
his timbre stands out within the entire orchestra:

The clarinet is a very agile instrument to do many articulations.
It has a very good staccato but is not as clear as the oboe.
In fact, they don't use so much double and triple articulation.
Legato is very effective. But pay attention to sentences that are too long, a bit like we have seen for the flute.
Let's say that double-reed instruments have more ease in making particularly long sentences.

One thing that best distinguishes the clarinet is certainly its dynamic capacity.
In fact, its dynamics are fabulous.

 Example n. 62

N. Rimskij-Korsakov, Capriccio Espagnol

It can start from 'nothing' in a whisper, growing a lot and returning to 'nothing'.

Practically, all trills and tremolos can be done, even if those with wide intervals are more complicated using the notes above the staff.
An excellent effect is the glissando, even if it is very complicated in the passage from the chalumeau register to the 'clarino'.
It is also excellent in carrying out small bends.
Gershwin gave us a very famous example of glissando in his 'Rhapsody in Blue':
it is perhaps the most famous solo clarinet intro of the 1900s.

Here, after a trill, the clarinet player performs a beautiful solo glissando.
This gives the piece a decidedly jazzier color.

RHAPSODY IN BLUE

GEORGE GERSHWIN
Scored by Ferde Grofé

Example n. 63

170

The Clarinet in B flat, being a transposing instrument, must be written one tone above the real key of the piece:

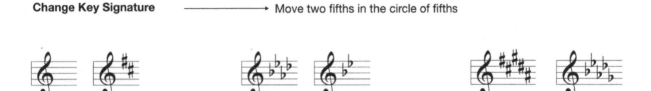

Change Key Signature ──────────→ Move two fifths in the circle of fifths

Write the whole music a tone above paying attention to transient alterations

Consequently, the reading will be similar to that of the trumpet in B flat: Written one tone above, the staff should be read using the Tenor clef.

The *Bass Clarinet* is also a transposer in B flat written in the treble clef. Its register is one octave below the B flat clarinet and is written as the tenor sax, a major ninth above moving forward two positions in the circle of fifths:

Real sound   Transposed Note

Up a 9th major

The range of the bass clarinet is also wide:

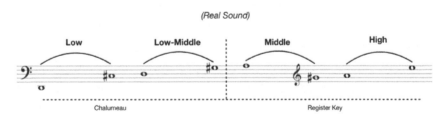

(Real Sound)

Low   Low-Middle   Middle   High

Chalumeau   Register Key

I reported the real notes to make you understand the frequency of the sounds of this instrument well.

As for the register, however, the bass clarinet has an intense sound in the chalumeau register and is excellent for doubling the bassoons in this register, thus giving body to the entire section of the woods.

It is very lyrical in the clarino register; it is often also used as a soloist in this context. On the other hand, the high-pitched sound is a bit thin because it somehow approaches the medium-low register of the B flat clarinet.

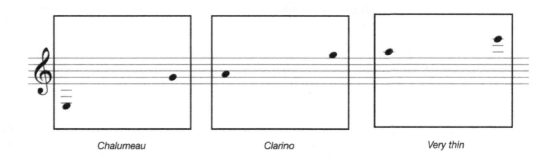

| Chalumeau | Clarino | Very thin |

The following example I bring you is from INSIDE, my Serpent and Wind Orchestra concert (next page).

I have deliberately given the bass clarinet a rhythmic groove that carries the whole orchestra forward, accompanying the oboe's solo and then the soprano sax.

In addition, I also wrote a low C, so in the extreme low register .... that note gives the groove a lot of depth.

INSIDE
- *Spirit* -

A. Girardo, Concert for Serpent and Winds Orchestra - I mov.

 Example n. 64

Shostakovich, for example, inserts in the V movement of his Eighth Symphony, a very effective and long bass clarinet solo accompanied only by a light pizzicato of the strings, making it then dialogue with the violin solo, therefore an instrument that is precisely the opposite, both in terms of tone that as a register.

Example n. 65 *Shostakovich, Symphony No.8 In C Minor, Op.65 - V mov.*

The Bass Clarinet should be written a ninth above the real key of the piece, in practice like the Tenor Sax:

Change Key Signature ⟶ Move two fifths in the circle of fifths

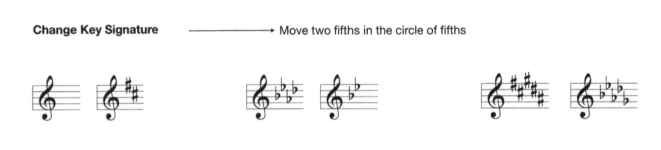

Write the whole music an octave and a tone above paying attention to transient alterations

Concerning the reading, since it is written a tone above, the staff should be read using the tenor clef and down an octave:

THE BASSOON

The bassoon is basically the bass of the woodwind section, together with the contrabassoon.

In practice, it could be part of the oboe's family: firstly, because the bassoon is also a double-reed instrument and secondly because it has a history very similar to the oboe.

For convenience, I could describe the bassoon as a large oboe intoned a twelfth below and up to B flat1 thanks to a U-folded reed and a parallel ascending tube on which two thumbs control the holes and keys.

However, the bassoon is also very old: it can even be traced back to the Renaissance Dulciane.

Being a large instrument, the holes should be too large for the fingers.

They found the solution by reducing the size of the hole by drilling the holes at a 45 ° angle with a considerable thickness of the wood.

This aspect allowed the bassoon also to have a characteristic sound thanks to its conical bore.

Dulciana

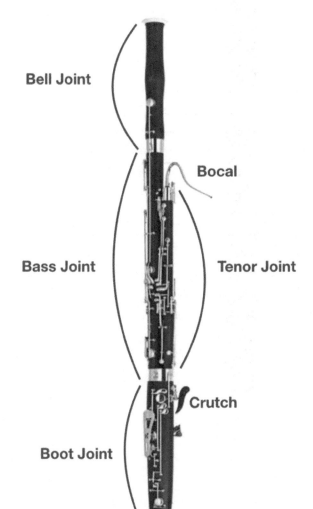

Bell Joint

Bocal

Bass Joint

Tenor Joint

f **Crutch**

Boot Joint

It is usually made of maple wood and has played a fundamental role in the modern orchestra, but it was considered indispensable in the early Romantic period.

The Bassoon, therefore, with the contrabassoon, which will be the two instruments I will talk about in this chapter, complete the range of woods, giving this section a unique and irreplaceable tone and color.

First of all, being a demountable instrument, like all woods, it has its specific division:

It is divided into three parts:

The upper part is the bell from which the sound comes out.

The central part is the instrument's main body, with some holes and keys operated by the left hand and the allocation of the fin for insufflation.

The lower part, used by the right hand, also has holes and keys.

In the following image, I show you the bassoon taken from both sides, just to get a clearer idea of its use:

LEFT HAND　　　　　　　　　　　　　　　**RIGHT HAND**

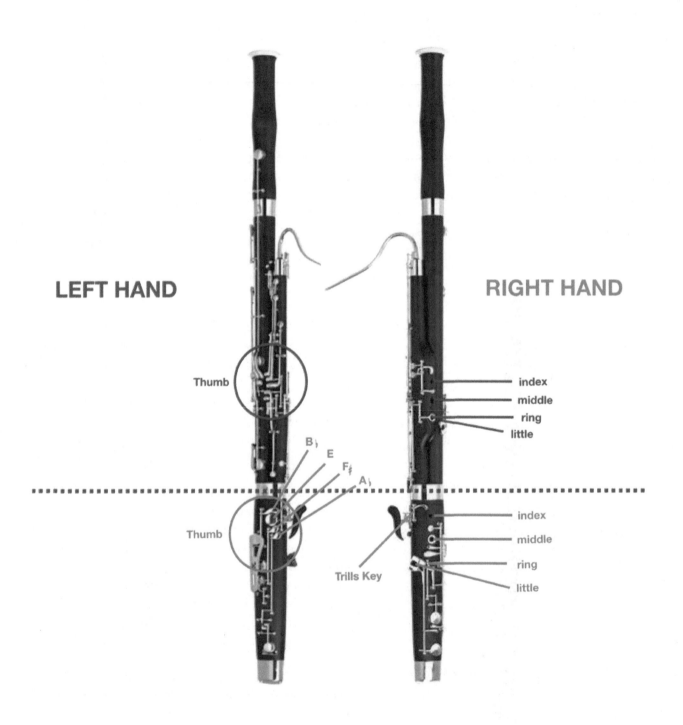

The bassoon has a considerable range:

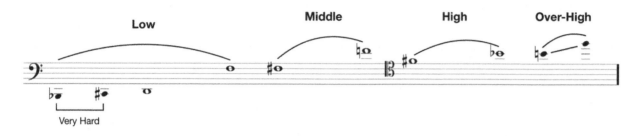

Let's analyze the register:

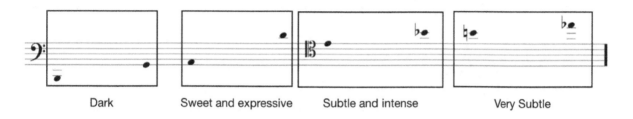

| Dark | Sweet and expressive | Subtle and intense | Very Subtle |

From a solo point of view, it is excellent in all registers, but it loses a bit in the section.

In the grave, it is excellent for doubling cellos and double basses; in fact, it is often used in the popular area precisely to give body to the low section of the strings.

In the acute, it is very subtle.

Stravinsky undoubtedly gave the most striking example of this sound at the beginning of his mammoth 'The Rite of Spring'.

Here the poor performer must take a very high C and always play in the very high register, but in the context, the effect is unique:

Example n. 66

In film music, he is very used in the Comedy genre.

But you have to be careful of the dynamics: for example, it is complicated for a bassoon to play pianissimo in the bass.

Also, when arranging, for example, a bassoon solo, you have to pay attention to the background because it is an instrument that is easily covered, so keep everything a little lower than usual concerning dynamics.

The bassoon has multiple functions in the orchestra:

The main one is to perform the bass function of the woods and often of the entire orchestra, doubling the celli, double basses, trombones, and tuba parts.

But he has absolutely a lot of space as a soloist, given his agility in all registers.

In the example below, taken from Rimsky-Korsakov's Sheherazade, the bassoon is solo accompanied simply by a light carpet of the bass strings with the mute.

N. Rimskij-Korsakov, Sheherazade

 Example n. 67

It often performs a countermelody and counterpoint function to the main melody.

A famous example is found in the last movement of Beethoven's Ninth Symphony.
Here the bassoon is in a high register and acts as a countermelody to the famous theme of 'hymn to the joy' played by violas and cellos with the bass accompaniment of double basses.

L. Van Beethoven, Symphony n.9 - V mov.

 Example n. 68

The bassoon is excellent to use as a dialogue with the other sections of the orchestra.

Look at this example taken from Mozart's "Prague" Symphony.

Here the two bassoons play together at a third distance on the high register, communicating with the strings:

W.A. Mozart, "Praga" Symphony - I mov.

 Example n. 69

From a tonal point of view, as you have noticed from the examples, the bassoon has an excellent sound in the bass and is very effective in the treble, thanks to a penetrating timbre despite being thin. It gives its best in the medium register, which is why its timbre ties nicely with the bass of the strings. The bassoon can perform practically all possible articulations and has an excellent legato, although some descending steps can be particularly complicated.

The staccato is very effective like the oboe, but the double and triple articulation is rarely used.

Indeed, perhaps the bassoon's staccato has become a common heritage since, as I mentioned earlier, it is always used in film music to describe a funny scene or comedy in general.

Trills and tremolos can be done practically all, except these too low:

Low Register

or these too acute, after the C on the third space in the treble clef:

High Register

Bell

End Pin

About the _Contrabassoon_, there is not much to add.

Indeed, the morphology changes a little.

Being a huge instrument, the performer, while seated, must keep it standing on an endpin.

Furthermore, as can be seen from the image, the bell is not placed upwards, but since the bore is longer, it goes downwards.

The contrabassoon has practically the same range as the bassoon but an octave lower.

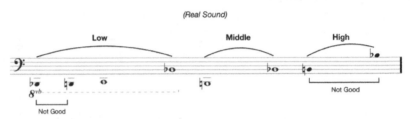

As you can see, I have brought you the real notation because the contrabassoon is a transposer, and this is its range in real sounds: note how grave it is!

The transposition of the contrabassoon, like the double bass in the strings, is an octave below and is obviously written in the bass clef:

Its primary use is that of the extreme bass of the orchestra together with Contrabasses and Tuba.

It basically has the same articulations as the bassoon; the only problem is that many of them are slow due to the size of the instrument (I have already told you about strings and brass: the bigger the instrument is, the slower it is).

An example of the depth of the contrabassoon is in the "Alla Marcia" movement of Beethoven's Ninth Symphony.

Here the contrabassoon doubles the second bassoon, giving the march great depth in the bass with a beautiful piano attack of the percussion.

THE SAXOPHONES

That of the saxophones is really a big family.
There are six types of saxophones used in various musical styles.

Sopranino   Soprano   Alto   Tenor   Baritone   Bass

In this book, I will not talk about all of them: I will exclude the Sopranino and the Bass that are less used apart from the symphonic bands.
The soprano, alto tenor, and baritone, on the other hand, can be defined as truly fundamental.
Indeed, they really wrote the history of jazz and revolutionized making music, inevitably influencing classical music: see Gershwin or Bernstein.

The saxophone has been successful because it is a hybrid instrument between brass family and wood.
Brass family because the material it is made of is brass, and woods because the way it is played derives in particular from the clarinet. Hence, it is a simple reed instrument, and the arrangement of the keys is the same as the oboe.
In addition, the saxophone is one of the most recently built instruments.
In fact, it was conceived by Adolph Sax (from which it later took its name) around the mid-19th century, although some precursors of this instrument had already existed since the beginning of the century.
At first, it evolved as a symphonic band instrument - the whole family is part of it - but they made this instrument's real revolution in the jazz area.
Let's think about the whole period of swing, the great orchestras of Duke Ellington, the bebop of Charlie Parker, the hardbop of Coltrane, the experiments of Whine Shorter. I could safely say that probably if it hadn't been for the saxophone, history would have taken another path.
Beyond the purely historical aspects, the saxophone has been used in the classical symphonic context.
There have been many classical scores with this instrument - usually the alto anyway.
As for the jazz area, the entire family of instruments is now an integral part of all big bands.

Usually, there are 2 Alto, 2 Tenors, and a Baritone in the classic big band, but the soprano is not forgotten, on the contrary!
The Sopranino and the bass, on the other hand, are used primarily on symphonic bands or in wind orchestras in general. Therefore, as I told you, I will not consider them in this book.

Here is the image of the Alto sax to show you the parts it is composed.
As you can see, it is divided into four parts:
The mouthpiece, where there is the simple reed;

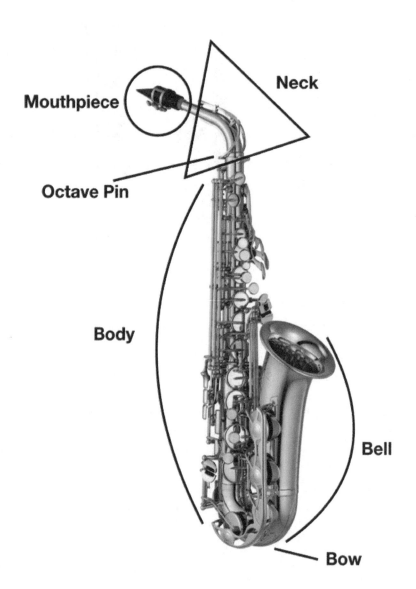

The neck, that is the curved part that merges the mouthpiece to the body;
The body, where there are all the holes and keys to be used with both hands;
and finally, the bell, from which the sound comes out.
To make you understand how it works and how to play it, I'll show you the image of a soprano so you can better see the keys mechanism:

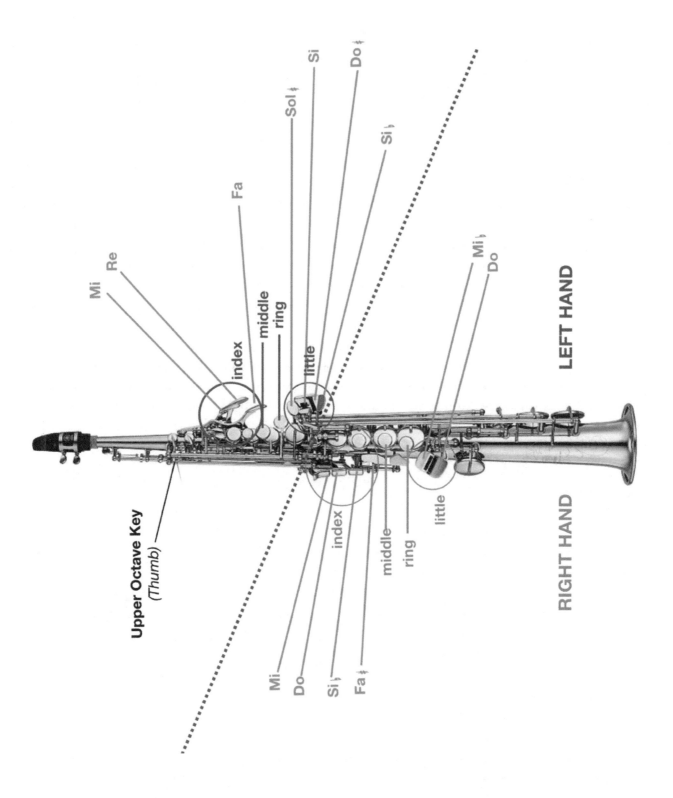

The sax family has all the same range at different pitches:

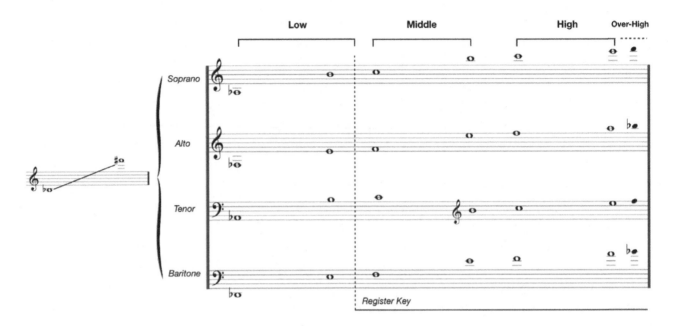

In the image, I have inserted the range of all four saxes, which I will talk about in effect notation, just to understand the height of each saxophone. The sax sound is somewhat good in all registers.

However, we must pay attention to some aspects: generally, the sax is an instrument that is not easy to intonate, especially the soprano (together with the Sopranino).

The sounds of the very high register, tending to the upper note, are hard to emit, so it is better not to use them a lot in section.

A good soloist will have no problems, although the sound in that register may still be a bit squashed and squeaky.

Saxophones are all transposing instruments.

The four I'm telling you about can be divided like this:

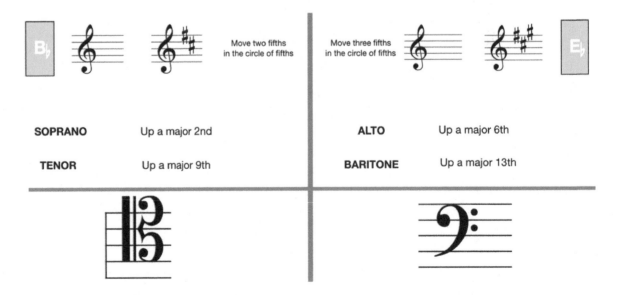

Soprano and Tenor are in B flat, but the second has the resulting sound one octave below.

So, we will write these saxes by moving two fifths in the circle of fifths (basically one tone above) plus a major second above for the soprano and a major ninth for the Tenor.

For reading, it is advisable to use the tenor clef.

Alto and Baritone are instead in E flat, and, here too, the second plays an octave below the first.

To write them, we will have to move three fifths in the circle of fifths plus a major sixth above for the alto and a thirteenth for the baritone.

Let's now discover these saxophones one by one.

Let's start with the *Soprano*. (left)

As I have already mentioned, it is a transposer in B flat, and like all saxophones, it is written in the treble clef.

It is a very shrill instrument in the high and upper notes.

Like all the family instruments, the best register is the medium.

Example n. 70

The _Alto_ (right), on the other hand, is transposer in E flat, and this too is written in the treble clef:

This saxophone is the backbone of the Big Bands: it is used a lot and often leads the entire section.

The altos are usually paired in big bands if the soprano is absent. For this reason, it is excellent as a soloist and in section.

Example n. 71

The _Tenor_ is a transposer in B flat precisely one octave below the soprano. The tenor is also written in the treble clef:

As I said, it plays a lower octave than the soprano; in fact, it is in the medium-low register of the Big Band, and, in this context, it is essential.
Tenors are often paired like Altos in Big Band.
Widely used alone and in section, with an excellent sound
in the middle register and shrill in the treble.

Example n. 72

The lowest I have told you about is the Baritone, transposer in E flat, exactly one octave below the Alto.

Obviously, to avoid countless ledger lines, the baritone is also written in the treble clef:

Without a doubt, it is the Bass par excellence of the Big Band.
This sax is not just the bass of the section but of the whole big band.
In fact, contrary to those who may think that the trombone plays the bass part, the baritone has this function.
Less agile than other saxophones, but very functional.

Example n. 73

The use of saxes has already been understood in some way;
let's do a little summary:
It was born as an integral instrument of the symphonic bands and still is;
the symphonic band is the only one in which the whole sax family is often present.
They are widely used as soloists in the popular area, especially jazz.
The classic quartet has contributed to the unmistakable sound of the Big Band for over a century.

Look at this example of a Special made by the five saxes in a block chord writing.
It is a passage by Thad Jones.
In this example, we can see how agile the saxes are and how effective their sound is for this type of music, even when they play homorhythmically:

GROOVE MERCHANT

Thad Jones

🔊 Example n. 74

They are also used in the symphonic area, especially the Alto and the Tenor; Romanticism and the early twentieth century were golden years for the saxophone in the orchestra.

Leonard Bernstein uses three types of Saxes in his 'West Side Story':
First, Alto exposes the theme of the prologue doubled by the Vibraphone.
Then the bass sax moves together with the bassoons in a sort of jazz walkin' bass with interventions by the tenor sax that doubles the clarinet at the low octave.

Maurice Ravel extensively used the saxophone in his Bolero, attributing the famous theme to the Sopranino, the Soprano, and the Tenor.

THE WOODWINDS TECHNIQUE

The woodwind is a significant section of the orchestra.

Beyond the color I mentioned earlier, the agility of all these instruments certainly gives this importance.

The concept of proportion obviously also applies to woods: a contrabassoon will never be as agile as a flute.

However, the technical possibilities of this section are endless, and the limitations are very few, even fewer than brass.

The intonation indeed dictates a limitation.

It is difficult for woods to tune each other; in fact, I often avoid unisons that are too long to avoid beats.

But good performers can quickly solve this problem.

One of the prerogatives of woodwinds, especially clarinets, is undoubtedly the dynamics.

The sound intensity varies from instrument to instrument.

For example, as you have seen, the flute and the piccolo are practically almost deaf in the very low register, unlike the clarinet, which can make wonderful pianissimo in the chalumeau register.

The oboe and the bassoon also have difficulty playing very softly in the low register (the sound might sound like a raspberry).

So, at the end of it all, we can safely say that the only wood instrument that controls all the dynamic range in all registers is definitely the clarinet.

As in strings and brasses, vibrato is also very important in the wood family: all woods can vibrate in a somewhat distinct way.

For example, saxophones and clarinets vibrate with the lips and jaw movement.

Oboes and bassoons vibrate through the movement of the muscles of the diaphragm and the flutes of the throat and diaphragm together.

Obviously, vibrato is a technical principle linked to interpretation, so as I explained to you for the strings, it should not be marked in the score, except in cases where you want a lot of it or don't want it (in practice in that case it is enough to mark 'no vibrato' or 'without vibrato')

The staccato of the woods is very agile in all dynamics and speeds.

I have already told you a little about the staccato for each instrument I listed.

However, the way to do it is by using the consonant "T" for a firm attack and "D" for a softer attack.

All the instruments can perform double and triple staccato, even if the flute is more agile in doing so.

The technique is always to alternate the famous "Ti-Ki-Ti" that I explained to you in the brass technique.

The example below is taken from the beginning of Mendelssohn's Fourth Symphony.

Here the woods, excluding the oboe and with the horns, perform a high-speed staccato that provides the rhythmic engine necessary for the very famous melody of the symphony made by the strings.

F. Mendelssohn, Symphony n.4 "Italian" - I mov.

 Example n. 75

As in all musical instruments, the staccato notation is always indicated with a dot above the note.

Sometimes there is staccato inside ligatures (like picchettato in the strings).

You can also find small lines on the notes inside the ligature, such as the portato for strings.

In that case, the performer will play the so-called "Appoggiato", a softer staccato.

As with brass, woodwinds can play all kinds of marcato and accent on notes.
Obviously, they do not have all the brass articulations that are still so many for the jazz tradition.
However, the falls and rips that trumpets make are often found in woodwinds.
Let's say they are articulations borrowed from brass in their jazz language.

The legato of the woods is fantastic!
As I have already told you, their agility is comparable to the strings, so all fast scales and runs are excellent with woods.
If you think about it, John Williams has made his fortune in orchestrating many of his film music.
Double-reed instruments can bind several notes by releasing the air a little at a time.
Flutes, clarinets, and saxophones need to take in more air, so pay attention to writing too-long ligatures.
We have already seen the glissando done by the clarinet with that splendid incipit of Gershwin's Rhapsody in Blue.
Glissandos work very well with clarinets and saxophones, but be careful. Wide glissandos can be done from the bottom up.
On the contrary, you can only make small bends.
On the other hand, the harmonic sounds are well playable only by the flute.
On an ordinary flute, all the notes above C#4 are played by hyper-insufflation and coincide with the second partial of the harmonic sounds.

The notation of harmonic sounds is like natural harmonics on strings, i.e., a small circle on the note.

Another technique of significant effect in woods is the Frullato.
It is achieved by rolling the tongue or with a long "R" throat.
The frullato is very effective in flutes and clarinets but not in double-reed instruments.
The notation of the frullato is like that of the tremolo for strings with the indication "frullato".

I close the chapter right with a repetition of the main jazz articulations for woodwinds:

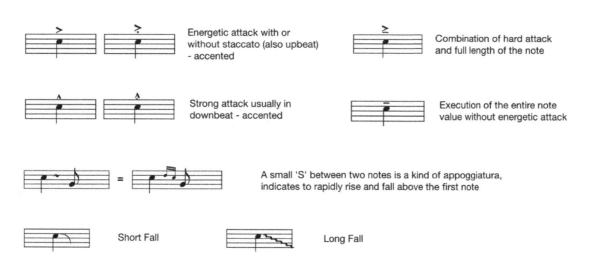

SUBDIVISION OF THE WOODWINDS

This paragraph shows how the woods are usually divided in the score.
As you have seen from the chapter, the woodwinds are represented by several instruments, so it is usual to organize them in the score by range and family, from the highest to the lowest and specifically:

Piccolo
Flute
Oboe
English Horn
Clarinet
Bass Clarinet
Saxophones
Bassoon
Contrabassoon

The woodwinds in the symphonic orchestra are paired and are usually written in a single staff.

So, you will find written, for example, Flute 1,2:

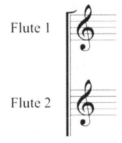

This happens unless the two parts are extremely different from a rhythmic point of view, so you might have some confusion in reading them.
In that case, the staves split (Flute 1, Flute 2):

As we have seen for the brass instruments, when there are more instruments, the staves are usually divided, trying to keep a coupling.

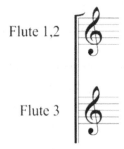

The instruments are positioned in order of range even within the family itself (E flat Clarinet, B flat Clarinet, Bass Clarinet):

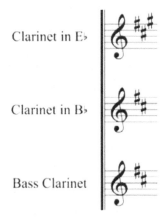

As far as the symphonic score is concerned, Saxophones are written between the clarinets and bassoons, and each sax has its staff unless the performer needs to change the instrument during the performance.
In that case, the name of the staff is specified with the first instrument present in the piece, and the instrument to be changed during the performance is indicated:

On the other hand, in the big band, the saxes are at the top of the score, before the trumpets.
Often the second flute can also play the piccolo parts if the score allows it, so just indicate it in the score.
The same thing is for the second oboe, often entrusted with the English horn part.
The problem does not exist if 2 Flutes and the Piccolo or 2 oboes and the English Horn were to play simultaneously.
In that case, there will be 3 performers.

When one of the two instruments has to perform a solo, just indicate it with "solo" in the score.

If, on the other hand, you want to specify which of the two instruments should play a particular melody, just indicate it with the number (1st or 2nd).

In fact, there is no word "Divisi" in the woods. That is only for the strings that divide a double part.

When the instruments play a unison in the same staff, it is explicitly expressed with the terminology A2 or A3.

It depends on the number of players present in that musical staff.

Keep these things in mind because they will be very useful when writing and reading the score.

THE BAGPIPES

In this paragraph, we talk about the bagpipe and the Italian bagpipe.

I want to talk to you about these instruments because they are very present in the world's popular imagination.

Both are aerophones (wind instruments) and are defined as "tank" or "bag" aerophones precisely because of their morphology.

I have included them in the woodwind family because, like woods, they use reeds to reproduce sound. These instruments are identified with certain folk cultures, think of Scotland or Ireland, and even the Italian bagpipe, in particular, is often identified as the classic Christmas instrument from the popular cultural imagination.

However, apart from that, they are instruments that have been lucky for essentially two reasons:

First, they are very loud instruments; they have a high volume, so they do not need amplification, particularly in the squares or at a popular party.

Second, the presence of Bordon, a continuous accompaniment to the melody.

However, some negative factors prevented this family of instruments from being even more present. For example, the transmission of the music of these instruments is almost always entirely oral, which somewhat prevents their diffusion. In short, this instrument, between ups and downs, is still present in popular culture, and I find it correct that an arranger/composer should know its possibilities and morphology.

When we talk about bagpipes, we are talking about a family of bagpipes (many!).

However, we can divide them into two main branches:

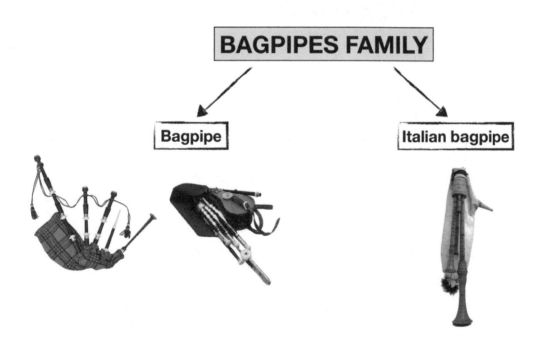

Pay attention! There are so many bagpipes: each region has different ones, the same goes for Italian bagpipes.

The ones I showed you in the image are the most common in the popular imagination, namely the Scottish, the Irish, and the classic Italian bagpipe.

Let's see the morphology of this instrument:

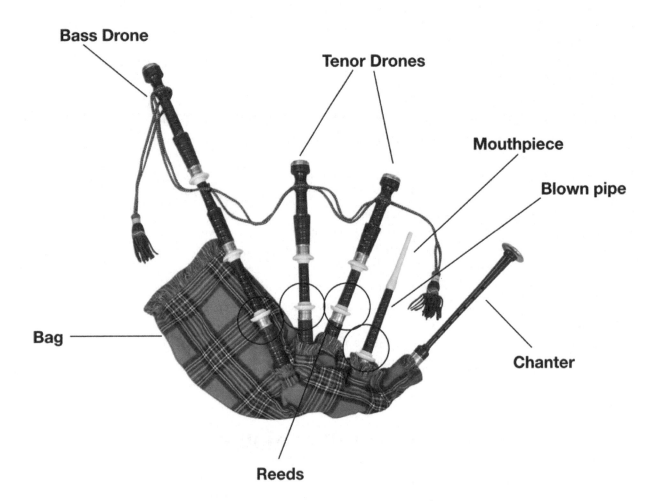

Bass Drone

Tenor Drones

Mouthpiece

Blown pipe

Bag

Chanter

Reeds

Here you see the Scottish bagpipe.
I brought this back to you because, unlike the Irish, it also has an insufflator (with the Irish, they use a bellows for the air).
The Italian bagpipe is similar to this in functioning.
As you can see from the image, all these instruments are composed of a bag containing several tubes.

- An insufflation tube through which the bag inflates.
  The performer holds this tube in the mouth or connects it to a bellows (as I explained to you for the Irish bagpipe);

- Then, all have one or more tubes with holes called Chanter to produce the melody;

- And finally, they all have one or more tubes that produce a single and continuous note, a sort of pedal that works as a harmonic accompaniment:
  I'm talking about the classic Bordon;

The bag is usually made of animal skin. Even in many models, they use the entire skin of a sheep without any cuts, inserting the tubes in place of the legs and closing the other orifices.
Although in truth, most of the bagpipes have the bag with seams.

There are two essential parts of a bagpipe:
Chanter and Bordon.

These two parts are the soul of the instrument and can be different depending on the type of reed they wear (they can be as clarinets, therefore with simple reeds, or as oboes, with double reeds):

Simple Reeds

Double Reeds

The player inflates the sack through the insufflator.
When the sack is raised, air passes through the reeds, vibrating, producing sound.
The Bordon or Bordons produce a single note (usually the tonic or dominant), while, through the use of the chanter holes or the chanters, the melody or melodies are produced.
The sack is generally held under the player's arm.
He, alternating insufflation and arm pressure, creates a continuous sound.

The bagpipe has a fairly particular notation.
This is a very important aspect for anyone who is about to write for this instrument, and I'll explain why:

The bagpipe chanter has nine notes only:

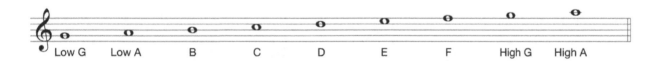

The eight holes on the chanter are covered by the thumb and first three fingers of the upper hand and the four fingers of the lower hand.
Pay Attention! The bagpipe is as if it were a transposing instrument; in fact, there is no correspondence between the written notes and the real ones:

Writing Notation	Real Note
Low G	A♭
Low A	B♭
B	C
C	D
D	E♭
E	F
F	G
High G	A♭
High A	B♭

The bagpipes have a very typical phrasing, made up of many little notes.
The so-called *Gracenotes* give this phrasing.

Let's make a priori speech:
Suppose you listen to the melody of a piece with the voice or with an instrument such as the violin or any other instrument.
In that case, you will notice that the phrasing is obtained from the variation of the dynamics within the phrase itself.
You cannot do this with the bagpipe because it cannot reproduce dynamic variations.
A practical way to make the articulations and the constructive dynamics is to use the grace notes. They are very brief notes that emphasize a note in piping (blowing technique in the bagpipes). Practically, they play a very short note between two adjacent notes to emphasize the melodic trend. They are written using a small note.

You can repeat the same note using either the same Grace note or different:

Until you get to mix grace notes and notes or play more grace notes together and thus compose the typical phrasing of the bagpipes:

Example n. 76 *Bagpipe's phrase*

CHAPTER 5

THE PERCUSSION FAMILY

When I started studying how to structure this chapter, honestly, I found myself in a bit of trouble for a straightforward reason:

the percussions are many, really many!!!

It isn't easy to structure such an immense family of musical instruments.

Certainly, one of the main causes must be attributed to their history.

Percussion has always existed. If we think that already by hitting our body, we can obtain thousands of distinct percussive sounds, we realize that in some way, these instruments were born with man and grow with man.

So, where to start?

I would say that it is good to clarify the fact that percussions are so varied that they embrace all classification groups, even chordophones and electrophones.

Most people think of percussion as something that you hit rightly, but there are so many ways to hit that you can't just think only about drum set, for example.

Since we are studying instrumentation in this book, which embraces the symphonic and jazz, I find it helpful to talk about the most used percussion in the symphonic and popular areas.

Pay Attention! Suppose we were to go even deeper into the popular area. In that case, we will discover other percussion typical of particular places in the world with a folkloric flavor that we may never have seen. Still, it is impossible to make a rundown of everything (I say this with absolute sincerity)!

The thing that is even more stunned is that percussion has really taken over in the orchestra and jazz or pop in the last century.

Can you imagine a large orchestra without the Timpani?

Or a jazz trio without the drum set?

Or wouldn't it seem strange to you to listen to Latin American music without any percussive element??? Impossible!

The most appropriate thing I would say is to divide the percussion into two large parts in the meantime:

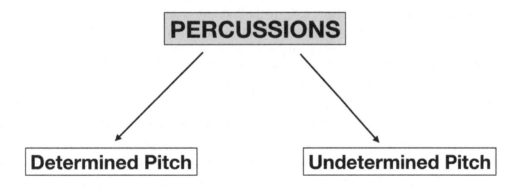

In this way, we can discern better.

However, this division is not enough since percussion instruments are very different in how they are played and their features.

We must necessarily refer to the classification I told you about in the first chapter of the book and find out what kind of percussion there are:

IDIOPHONES   They produce sound through the vibration of their entire body

MEMBRANOPHONES   They produce sound through the vibration of a membrane or skin

AEROPHONES   They produce sound through the vibration of an air column in a closed body

CORDOPHONES   They produce sound through the vibration and percussion of a string

ELECTROPHONES   They produce sound through electrical impulses

I find it extremely useful in this paragraph to divide percussion further, considering their use.
I say this because it is correct, indeed quite right, to talk about classical percussion since they are the ones most used in the symphonic area. Still, the ultimate aim of this instrumentation book is to give you knowledge and experience on the instruments used in the popular area.
Let's say we cannot separate the two things. As you can well understand, the arrangement is also a matter of colors, so it is not forbidden to use Timpani, for example, in a rock band (everything can be justified by creativity).
I will start talking to you about classical percussion and at the same time about those used in pop or jazz or rock areas.
I will investigate every percussion taken into consideration and demonstrate its use as I did with the other families of instruments in this book.
The tonal possibilities of percussion are limitless, and you have no idea how many colors you can give to your arrangements by studying them well.
You will increase your tonal vocabulary exponentially. Then, of course, it is up to you to decide what to use and above all how.
There is no limit to creativity, and with percussion, you have a smooth road.

IDIOPHONES

This percussion family is infinite: theoretically, anything ready to be hit can be an idiophone. Obviously, I will consider a good part, not all (impossible !!!!), but the most used ones.

We define Idiophones as those instruments that produce sound through the vibration of their entire body; that is, they themselves create the sound.
The ways of playing idiophones are multiple: they can be hit, rubbed, scratched, shaken, in short, in any way a body can vibrate.
Like all percussion, there are two types of idiophones:
those at a determinate pitch and those at an indeterminate pitch.
Here is the list of instruments that I will consider:

IDIOFONI

Determined

XYLOPHONE
MARIMBA
VIBRAPHONE
GLOCKENSPIEL
TUBULAR BELLS
CROTALES
STEEL DRUM
GONG

Undetermined

CYM
CYMS A 2
TRIANGLE
COWBELL
TAM-TAM
WIND CHIMES
RATTLES
WOOD BLOCK
TEMPLE BLOCKS
CLAVE
CASTANETS
MARACAS
CABASA
SHAKERS
GUIRO
CAJON
CAXIXI
AGOGO
UDU

Let's start with instruments at a *Determined Pitch*, that is, in which a note is clearly expressed.

The first instrument I will talk about is the <u>*Xylophone*</u>.
It is no coincidence: I decided to talk about this first because it was one of the first to be incorporated into the orchestra.
It is a magnificent instrument, and the vibrating bodies are wooden tablets that reproduce the keyboard of a piano.
As you can see from the photo, below there are metal or brass tubes that have the function of acting as resonators.
But the Xylophone can be WITH or WITHOUT resonators.
Being the tablets made with wood, we can make short and clear notes: you must use the tremolo to lengthen the note.

We all know that wood does not have a considerable capacity to resonate. Mallets are used to hit the tablets: I will discuss them in-depth in the paragraph dedicated to the percussion technique. These idiophones are of different types, both in register and in range. The Xylophone is a transposing instrument: it transposes an octave above

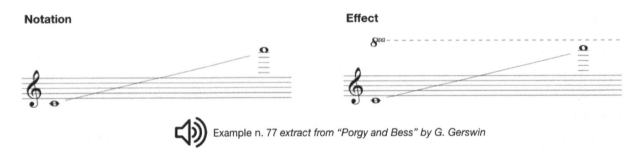

Notation	Effect

Example n. 77 *extract from "Porgy and Bess" by G. Gerswin*

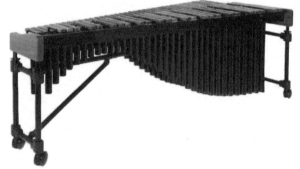

Another instrument that is part of the keyboards is the <u>*Marimba*</u>.
As you can see from the image, it is very similar to the Xylophone. Although the dimensions are larger, it has thinner, wider, and longer tablets.
Unlike the Xylophone, a more recent instrument in its use (mid-last century), which may not have resonators, the Marimba has always had resonators.

They are played with wool or soft rubber Mallets and often used 2 (or 3) per hand.
Unique tonally, it can be written on a single staff or even on two like the Piano, and it is not a transposing instrument.
The repertoire for Marimba is not so vast; in fact, often marimbists transcribe pieces from the violin repertoire rather than from the piano one.

It has a range similar to the Xylophone, but at a lower octave, so it also proceeds on the low register:

Example n. 78 *extract from Bach, Violin concerto in A minor*

Continuing to talk about 'keyboard' idiophones, let's now talk about the *Vibraphone*.

This instrument is better known because its applications are not limited only to the classical music.

A noticeable difference compared to the Xylophone and the Marimba is the material of the plates,

which here are not made of wood, but of metal.

It is widely used in jazz, thanks also to great performers who have raised its importance, first of all, Gary Burton.

The peculiarity of the Vibraphone is linked to the presence of the engine. It is a series of micro-fans placed in the resonators that allow the effect of the vibrato when turned on.

Even the Vibraphone can be played with 4 Mallets (2 for each hand), and the types of mallets used are many and of different material depending on the desired sound.

Example n. 79 *Gary Burton solo*

The plates can also be rubbed by a bow (generally from double bass), giving a mysterious sound.

The metal plates and the pedal placed under the instrument allow the notes to be longer.

In fact, the pedal below is comparable to the Piano's sustain pedal. There are several sizes of vibes, but the most common has this range (left):

It is not a transposing instrument and is written on a single staff.

The engine of the Vibraphone significantly changes the timbre of the instrument; therefore, the composer must notify when he wants you can use the engine on or off and the pedal in the score with the same indications used for the Piano.

The sharpest 'keyboard' idiophone is the *Glockenspiel*.

The name of this instrument derives from the German "Glocken," which means 'Bell'. In fact, it has a lot in common with bells since the sound it produces seems to be that of tiny bells.

As can be easily understood, it has metal plates like the Vibraphone, and its sound is very penetrating. To play it, they use different Mallets and considering the use of the instrument, brass or metal ones are also used.

The vibration of the plate is much longer than the Xylophone and the Marimba, and the performer can dampen the vibration using the same mallets. It can also have a damper pedal (in professional models) and is a transposing instrument: the effect is 2 octaves above.

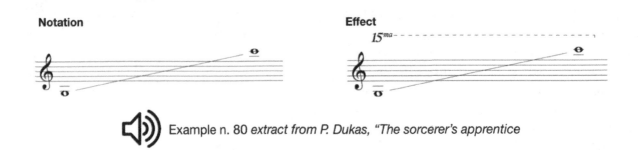

Example n. 80 *extract from P. Dukas, "The sorcerer's apprentice*

The following instrument I take into consideration is the one called *Tubular Bells*.

They call them this way because they sound exactly like a bell and are circular metal tubes (hence the name 'tubular').

Good tubular bells can do the entire chromatic scale and are played using a hammer (covered in felt if you have to play softly).
To prolong the sound, they have a damper pedal.

Example n. 80b *Tubular Bells sound*

This instrument is written on a single staff in the treble clef and transposed to the upper octave:

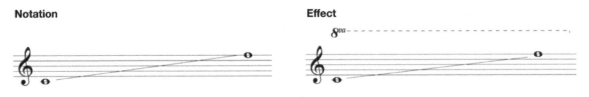

I keep talking about the most used idiophones in symphony orchestras considering the *Crotales*:
they are metal discs of different sizes mounted on a small scaffold and usually arranged like a piano keyboard.
They sound similar to the Glockenspiel and are generally played with a metal stick.
We can also play them by rubbing them with a cello or double bass bow, such as the Vibraphone.
As most of these idiophones, it is a transposing instrument (*2 octaves above*)

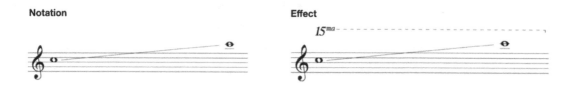

Notation   **Effect**

 Example n. 81 *Crotales sound*

I am now talking to you about two instruments that are very similar to each other:
the *Gong* (right) and the *Tam-Tam* (left).
At first glance, they look like the same instrument, but actually, they have quite substantial differences.
First, they are a large brass circle played with a large padded beater.
The substantial difference between the two is that the Gong is a tuned instrument: it is slightly rounded; the Tam-Tam, on the other hand, has no defined pitch and is smooth.

These musical instruments are widely used in symphony orchestras with huge ensembles and have a deep, particularly long sound.
They exist in different sizes, even huge ones.

 Example n. 82 *Gong sound*   Example n. 83 *Tam-tam sound & effects*

bow
bell
edge

An instrument widely used in the orchestra but also very common in the popular area is the *Cymbal*.

In this case, I consider the classic cymbal; I want to clarify it because the cymbals are of different types.

It is a convex metal disc made up of three parts (which I indicate in the image). They can be of different sizes (they are measured in inches).

The drum set can be provided with different numbers and quality (splash, crash, ride, hi-hat ...) and can be played with wooden sticks, brushes, or mallets, depending on the desired effect.

 Example n. 84 *Cymbal sounds*

Of the cymbals present, *Orchestral Cymbals* are probably the most common in orchestras. In practice, they are two cymbals held in the two hands of the performer who are beaten against each other. They can have a vast dynamic range and excellent articulation. In the forte, they are beaten against each other and then raised above the percussionist's head to make the vibrations resonate even more, but they are also very effective in the Piano. The sound is muffled by placing them, after beating, on the performer's chest.

 Example n. 85 *P.I. Tschaikowsky, Romeo and Juliet ouverture*

 Example n. 85b *Orchestral Cymbals sound*

Another very common instrument in the orchestra is the *Triangle*.

It is a steel rod bent in the shape of a triangle that is hit with a small steel rod, and there are different sizes. It can play both long notes (letting it vibrate) and staccato (stopping the vibration with the hand), but also tremolo (obtained by moving the knocker on the Triangle from one side to the other). You must always specify the length of the note in the score and add a slur when you want to let the instrument vibrate.

It is not only used in the classical music. On the contrary, it is omnipresent in many South American music. When there is an alternation of open and closed sounds, they use a circle for open sounds and a + for closed sounds:

 Example n. 86 *Triangle sound & effects*

Another metal instrument widely used in the popular and folkloristic (but also classical) music is the *Cowbell*.
Its name derives from its morphology and its sound.
It is widely used in Latin American music and is hit with a wooden stick.
Nowadays, it is often also mounted on the drums just to play Latin.
The Cowbell can be of different sizes, and in the symphonic context, there are often several mounted all together in order of relative pitch. It can be written on a single staff or the five-line staff if several cowbells are together by distributing the notes according to their relative pitch.

 Example n. 87 *Cowbell sound & effects*

Some idiophones have totally embraced a particular culture.
One of these is the *Steel Drum* (left), typical of Caribbean music.
Despite the translation of its name ('Steel drum'), it is not a drum.
In practice, it is the upper part of a hot-worked oil barrel with engraved sections and hammer-beaten and tuned sections that are usually played with wooden beaters.

 Example n. 88b *Steel Drum sound*

An instrument similar to this with a lovely and relaxing sound is the *Hand Pan* (right).
It has the same mechanism as the steel drum but is convex, positioned between the legs, and played by the hands.

 Example n. 88 *Hand-pan rhythm*

Some idiophones have now become very important in the popular area. One of these is the *Wind Chimes*.
It is an instrument made up of small metal pipes hanging from a wooden bracket.
These tubes are of different sizes and cause a kind of glissando.
They are widely used in the symphonic area to color and in the popular area also as intermittence or launch of a particular part of the piece.
They can also be made of wood, bamboo, or even glass. The notation is similar to an open Triangle.

 Example n. 89 *Wind Chimes sound*

There are many small idiophones and are commonly called 'little instruments'.
One of these instruments is represented by the *Rattles*.
They are small bells hung on a piece of wood or held in hand.
They can be held in both hands and have a typically Christmas sound (think of
the sound of Santa's carriage).

Very similar to the Cowbell as a way of playing it, but made of wood, is
the *Wood Block*.
As the name suggests, it is a rectangular piece of wood with a
longitudinal cut. They can be of different sizes and are often mounted
together placed on a pedestal. It is played with wooden, plastic, or
rubber sticks and can also be held in hand.

Example n. 90 *Wood block sound*

Similar to the woodblock are the *Temple Blocks*.
They are much more used in the symphonic area and are always
made of wood but have a shell shape.
They are usually found in groups of 5 of different sizes
mounted on a pedestal.
Unlike woodblocks, temple blocks have a noticeably softer
sound.

Example n. 91 *Temple blocks sound*

Moving on with the wooden idiophones, let's consider the *Claves*.
They are simply two sticks that collide with each other using the hand
that holds one of the two still as a sounding board.
Despite its simplicity, it is perhaps one of the basic percussions of all
South American music; it represents the fundamental obstinate of
rumba and samba.

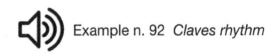
Example n. 92 *Claves rhythm*

Speaking of folk instruments, we have to talk about the *Castanets* as it is the typical instrument of Spanish Flamenco.
They are a pair of spoon-shaped pieces of wood, and there are three types:

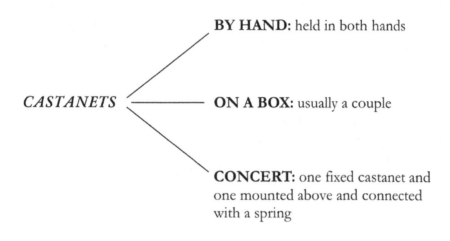

BY HAND: held in both hands

CASTANETS

ON A BOX: usually a couple

CONCERT: one fixed castanet and one mounted above and connected with a spring

Example n. 93 *Castanets sound*

Maracas (left) also play a key role in Latin American music.
They are containers made of pumpkin, wood, or plastic, placed on a handle with pebbles or sand inside.
They are usually played by shaking, but they can also be struck or turned on themselves (like a tremolo).

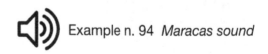
Example n. 94 *Maracas sound*

Cabasa (right) is also the basis of South American culture. It is a metal cylinder on which a chain of small steel marbles is rolled.
It is of African origin but is widely used in Latin American rhythms, especially in bossa nova, and is played by shaking or rotating it.

Example n. 95 *Cabasa sound*

The *Shakers* are similar to maracas but with a sharper and more delicate sound. They are played by shaking them in time or with tremolo, and you can also hold more than one in each hand and play them by shaking.
They are widely used in Pop.
The 'eggs' are also smaller, with a more acute and less present tone.

 Example n. 96 *Shakers sound*

Another instrument with a typically folkloristic taste is the *Guiro*. It is so-called because it was built initially by emptying the fruits of the Guira. Today these instruments are made of wood, plastic, or metal and are played by holding it in hand and rubbing the serrated surface with a wooden stick.

Example n. 97 *Guiro sound*

A very particular idiophone with various timbres is the *Cajon*. As can be seen from the image, it is a plywood box on which the performer sits.
It is of Peruvian origin but is also used in Spanish flamenco and can be played with the hands and brushes or other types of sticks.
There are three types of cajòn: traditional, Spanish (with a rattle tailpiece), and another with a snare-style tailpiece.

 Example n. 98 *Cajon sound*

Another very fascinating shaking instrument is the *Caxixi* (right).
It is nothing more than a small wicker basket with seeds or shells inside. It is of African origin but is used a lot in Brazilian music.

 Example n. 99 *Caxixi sound*

Another instrument of African origin but widely used in Brazilian music is the *Agogo*.

It comprises two iron bells held in hand and played by a wooden knocker.

It has the primary purpose of bringing time into Brazilian music. In fact, in Brazilian, the term "agogo" really means 'meter of time.'

 Example n. 100 *Agogo sound*

I close this long roundup of musical instruments with an instrument that I really like: the *Udu*.

It is an instrument of African origin represented by a kind of ceramic or clay amphora.

It is played by holding it and hitting the side hole for a low sound and the amphora's fingers for a more acute sound.

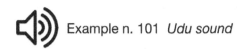 Example n. 101 *Udu sound*

MEMBRANOPHONES

Membranophones are also very numerous so that I will tell you about those most in use in the symphonic and popular area.

Let's start by specifying that membranophones are those instruments that produce sound through the vibration of one or more membranes.

The ways of playing them, like all percussion, vary according to the instrument: they can be hit, rubbed, scratched, shaken, and played with hands, sticks, or different types of beaters.

I will discuss the following list, dividing them into instruments at a determinate and indeterminate pitch.

MEMBRANOPHONES

Determined

TIMPANI
ROTO-TOMS

Undetermined

DARBUKA
DJEMBE
CONGAS
BONGOS
SNARE
BASS DRUM
TOM-TOMS
DRUMS
TAMBOURINE
CUICA
TABLA
TAIKO
TIMBALES

The first and most important instrument of the family of membranophones is certainly the Timpano, or rather the Timpani since there are almost always more than one playing together. In the image, I show you a modern Timpano with its parts, the one used in all symphony orchestras, to be clear:

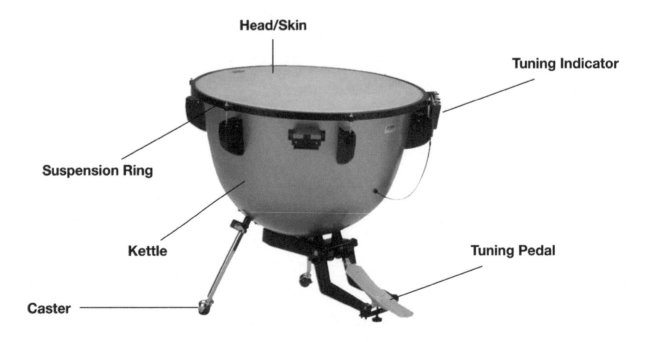

The Timpani are widely used and are the oldest in use in the orchestra.
They are of different sizes depending on the pitch of the sound they must produce and are measured in inches - usually, they are 4 or 5 for a complete orchestral set (32 ", 28", 25 ", 23", 21 ")
The part of the Timpani is written in the bass clef.
They have a considerable range if we use all five:

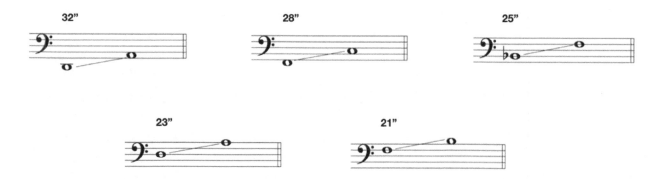

The role of Timpani in the orchestra has changed a lot since the beginning; they have evolved a lot. In fact, before Beethoven, the Timpani were often paired with trumpets, then they acquired a more solo role. Now they are also used alone in the orchestra. The example in the next page is from Sibelius' 3rd Symphony: here, the timpani sound very forte, practically expressing the theme that the strings will later make.

III.
Scherzo.

J. Sibelius, Symphony n.1 - III mov.

 Example n. 102

Technology influenced their solo role.

The old Timpani could not tune, so they emitted pre-established notes, so they made few interventions.

Technology has made them more versatile both from the point of view of dynamics and intonation, thanks to the invention of the Pedal, which changes the intonation in a very short time.

They are played with different mallets depending on the required sound (wood, felt ... hard, soft, medium sticks ...)

For example, in this famous score, the Timpani are completely alone: I refer to the beginning of 'Also Sprach Zarathustra' by Strauss, made iconic by the renowned film '2001 A Space Odyssey' by Stanley Kubrik. Here the Timpani emit only two notes, the tonic and the dominant. Still, it is interesting to see how they are practically left alone as an instrument that acts as an intermittence between the exposition of a theme and its second part.

Example n. 103

By now, the Timpani are very versatile, and the notes have a fairly precise duration; you can only roll when the notes are very long.

For this reason, you must specify the articulation and duration of the note in the notation.

As I told you before, very long notes must be trilled or rolled, and you must always specify when it ends.

On the left, you can see the roll and its end with the final stroke in the image below. In the image on the right, instead, a tremolo made on two different Timpani.

Another fantastic instrument with a determined pitch is the *Rototom*.

In this case, we are talking about rototoms because there are always at least three or more membranes.

Rototoms have also undergone significant development over the years.

In practice, they are drums that you can tune thanks to the rotation of the frame. There are seven sizes of roto-toms, from 18 "to 6", so they have a considerable range and are played with wooden sticks. Now they are seven, but they were only three previously, and they could not vary the pitch. Now the new Remo rototoms do this too.

 Example n. 104 *Rototoms sound*

Here is their range from largest to smallest:

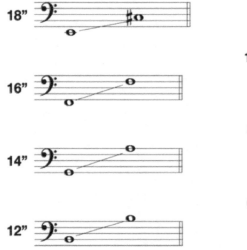 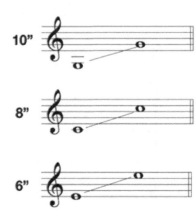

We are talking about membranophones of indeterminate pitch.

The father of all is undoubtedly the <u>*Bass Drum*</u>.

This instrument is nothing more than a big two-skin drum with a powerful and dark sound, and it is used a lot in the orchestra thanks to its low frequencies.

Another reason for its frequent use is that it has a very high dynamic range and is usually played with felt beaters. It also has a remarkable technical ability, useful for marking time and accompanying or strengthening orchestral cymbals. It can also be written on a single staff, being a single instrument.

 Example n. 105 *Bass Drum sound*

Now I begin to talk about the membranophones used mostly in the popular area and little in the symphonic one. The first one I will tell you about is the <u>*Darabuka*</u>.

Many of you will know it; it has an unmistakable sound:

it is a small chalice-shaped drum built first in terracotta and now

mostly in aluminum. It is well known because it is typical of Middle Eastern and North African music, so anyone who has listened to that

type of music at least once will surely recognize the Darabuka. Unlike most membranophones, the Darabuka membrane is not animal but synthetic. It is played with the hands and fingers by placing it on the leg and holding it under one arm.

 Example n. 106 *Darabuka sound*

Another membranophone very similar in shape to the Darabuka and well known is undoubtedly the <u>*Djembè*</u>.

It is an instrument of Arabian-Egyptian origin. It is very popular! Who, among us, has never seen some African man in a square or on the beach playing this instrument?

It is played by holding it between the legs while seated using the hands and fingers. The sound changes and becomes lighter or darker depending on where you play the skin.

Usually, the skin is made up of animal membrane (usually goatskin), but they also do it with synthetic membrane.

It is interesting to see the context in which it is played.

Africans are very good at polyrhythm, and often these polyrhythmic games are played with the Djembè.

 Example n. 107 *Djembè sound*

A well-known instrument in the popular area is the *Conga*. They are usually coupled and are two high barrel-shaped drums with the skin at one end. They are played mainly with the hands, but you can also use wooden sticks. They are not widely used in the symphonic area; they are instead of cult in Afro-Cuban and Latin American music.

They can have different sounds depending on where they are played and how they are played.

They are usually written on a staff at two distinct pitches:

Tonally they are very agile, and for this reason, they use different techniques to obtain distinct sounds.

Here are the essential sounds of the congas:

Bass: dropping the hand to the center of the skin

Open tone: with the hand with closed fingers parallel to the skin

Slap: in which the middle part of the hand rests on the edge

Palm-fingers: alternation of the two parts of the hand for different effects

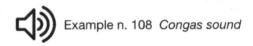 Example n. 108 *Congas sound*

A similar but much smaller instrument is the *Bongos*.

Also well known, usually coupled, are two small drums with the skin at one end.

They can be in tune (usually at a distance of a fourth or fifth). They are played with the hands by holding them between the legs or on a pedestal, but you can also use wooden sticks.

About the notation, they are usually written on a staff at two distinct pitches like the Congas, but writing on only two staves is also acceptable.

They are widely used in the setups of Latin American and pop percussionists, but they have also been used in the symphonic area: think of Gershwin's Cuban Overture.

Leonard Bernstein also used them extensively in his 'Mambo' from 'West Side Story'. In this context, bongos play a fundamental role in percussion ensemble.

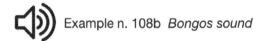 Example n. 108b *Bongos sound*

One of the most widely used membranophones of all is undoubtedly the Drum or the *Snare Drum* defined in the jargon.

There are different types of drums: the body's height often varies, for example, the marching ones are much higher, but here we are talking about the classic drum used in orchestras and drums.

As I told you, together with the Timpani, it is the instrument that has been part of the orchestra for the longest time.

It can be made of metal or wood, with two skins: an upper one called 'beating skin' and a lower one called 'timbre skin'.

Its peculiarity is that of having pulled strings on the skin of the timbre, usually of metal or nylon, which give its characteristic sound.

A lever on the side of the drum loosens the strings inside, preventing them from vibrating on the skin, thus obtaining a different tone.

It is widely used in orchestras, especially since the twentieth century, also an integral part of the drum set and is usually written on a one-only staff.

Everyone imagines the role of the drum in a drum set, but I'll talk about it later anyway. An emblematic example of the use of the drum is in Ravel's Bolero.

 Example n. 109 *extracts from "Bolero" by M. Ravel*

Now let's see the other part that will compose the drum set: the *Tom Toms*.

They are drums of different sizes with two skins that can be approximately in tune and are usually written in the four spaces of the staff.

They have a very clear sound and are played with wooden drumsticks.

Together with the snare drum, they are an integral part of the drum set.

And now let's talk about the *Drum Set*, an instrument that we all surely know:
it is a set of drums and cymbals of different kinds and sizes.

Basically, it consists of a snare drum, a pedal-operated bass drum, several toms, a hi-hat, one or more cymbals.

It is one of the most widely used instruments in the popular area and is played with both feet and hands: the right foot controls the kick pedal, the left foot the Hi-Hat, and both hands the drums and cymbals.

The technical possibilities of the drums are innumerable, and its way of being played changes according to the musical style considered.

It has a polyphonic notation, basic with three voices, and four if you want to indicate both feet.
As a rule, it is advisable to specify in a legend which sound is assigned to each drum:

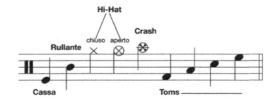

And here's an example of drum notation:

It is generally played with wooden sticks, but you can also use different brushes to obtain distinct sounds and techniques (the different sticks or brushes to be used must be specified in the score).

Another widely used instrument is the *Tambourine*.
It is a small tambourine, which can be of different sizes, with a skin stretched over a wooden frame and, at the edges, some slits with small cymbals inside. There are also Tambourines without little cymbals, even if the real basque Tambourine still has them. The others are derivations of this instrument.

It is played in different ways: with the fingers, hitting it with the knuckles, shaking it (tremolo), even using the thumb in the piano tremolo, using mallets, or resting it on other drums (a snare drum, for example).

 Example n. 110 *Tambourine sound*

224

The instrument I am showing you is part of the family of ethnic instruments, such as the Djembè or the Darabuka.

Let's talk about the *Tablas*.
Surely you will have heard its sound once in your life, also because it is truly unique and by now it distinguishes a sound of a particular area of the globe as far as folk music is concerned.

It is an instrument of Indian origins; it consists of two drums, one in wood and the other in clay metal, with a skin pulled by leather ties. You play it with your hands, resting the instrument on your legs or sitting on the floor. It has a circle of black paste at the center of each membrane composed of manganese powder and iron filings. It is precisely this that gives the Tablas that typical sound that distinguishes all Indian music.

 Example n. 111 *Tablas sound*

We continue with the membranophones that belong to the Latin American tradition. Let's talk about the *Cuica*.
It is a drum with only one skin, but it has the particularity of having a shaft in the center that makes the skin vibrate.
In place of the shaft, there may be a thick rope.
It is used very little in the orchestra but a lot in the folkloric tradition.
It is very much used in Brazilian music.

 Example n. 112 *Cuica sounds*

We still go on with membranophones of folkloristic tradition. One of these is *Taiko*.
It is a barrel-shaped drum of Japanese origin with two skins at the ends. It can also be huge, and its sound is impressive and low.
It is widely used in applied music and in general in Japan and is played using wooden sticks.
Taiko orchestras are often formed in Japan, creating typically oriental and massive grooves and often accompanied by outstanding ensemble choreography.

 Example n. 113 *Taiko sounds*

I conclude this series dedicated to membranophones with *Timbales*.

These instruments, too, well known and widely seen worldwide, are fundamental in many world regions. It is very similar in appearance to snare drums: they do not have resonance skin and are of Cuban origin.

They are two metal shells just as often in drums and are played by usually thinner wooden sticks than standard drum sticks.

They are widely used for Latin American music, especially mambo, reggae, cha-cha-cha, and salsa.

Often, they are played in kits with instruments such as wood blocks, small cymbals, and cowbells.

 Example n. 114 *Timbales sounds*

OTHER PERCUSSIONS

Most percussion is part of the family of idiophones and membranophones.
However, as I told you at the beginning of our journey on these instruments, they embrace all classifications.
The other types are less frequent, but many of them are catching on thanks also to new technological discoveries, especially those related to electronics.
This paragraph will discuss Aerophones, Cordophones, and Electrophones for other percussion.
I start with the aerophones, which, I remind you, produce sound through the vibration of a column of air in a closed body.
I'll tell you about two instruments that have entered the popular imagination: the Whistle and the Taxi Horn.

The _Whistle_ is a standard whistle with a very high-pitched sound. It is widely used in Latin American music, especially Brazilian (think of the great parades of the Rio de Janeiro carnival).
It has two side holes that allow the whistle to alternate between a closed and an open sound, typical of Brazilian samba.

The _Taxi-Horn,_ on the other hand, is a trumpet that is played by the hand.
They used it at the beginning of the twentieth century to evoke urban life and are often found mounted in Set, in groups of 3 or 4, depending on the needs and are tuned according to use (Gershwin also used them inside the symphony orchestra).

 Example n. 115 *Taxi Horn from "An American in Paris" by G. Gershwin*

The percussion chordophone par excellence is the *Cimbalon*.

It is a large instrument derived from the ancient Dulcimer and is
of Hungarian origin (used a lot by Bartòk, Kodàly). In practice, it is like a piano without the keyboard: in fact, it has more strings for the same note, like the Piano, and they are hit using leather or wooden sticks.
The notation is also similar to the Piano: it can be read in bass and violin key and has an extensive range:

In addition to the Dulcimer, from which it derives, there are instruments very similar to the Cimbalon in many Eastern and Middle Eastern cultures, but smaller in size, which are played in the same way, one of them is the Chang.

 Example n. 116 *Cimbalom sound*

There are also percussion electrophones.

I remind you that electrophones produce sound through electrical impulses.

In this context, I will list two in particular: the Electronic Pad and the Electronic Drum Set.

The _Electronic Pad_ is a rubber or plastic surface on which the performer strikes. The sounds are sampled and taken either from a module built into the pad or external modules.

The pads can be of different shapes and sizes and can be played with your hands or drumsticks.

Today, many drummers include electronic pads in their acoustic sets to broaden their tonal possibilities, especially in the pop world.

If an acoustic drum set results from different drums and cymbals, the _Electronic Drum Set_ is the union of different pads controlled by sticks and pedals, like a real drum.

The sounds that the pads can reproduce are infinite. We are not limited only to the imitation of the sound of each percussion, but the Electronics play their part 100% in this organological context.

PERCUSSION TECHNIQUE

Although percussion is so different, the techniques will also be very different. I will try to enclose the most important techniques for the arranger/composer to interface with the performer.

I will not limit myself to just talking about the playing technique; I decided to include the discourse relating to the various types of beaters in this lesson since the type of mallet affects the instrument's sonority, execution, and timbre. Therefore, inevitably, on the definitive work of the arranger/composer.

I will also try to enclose the types of notations a little. For percussion, it is not universal as for other instruments; it varies according to the type of instrument, whether it is at a determinate or indeterminate pitch.

I start right from the notation.

The distinction between percussion at a determined and indeterminate pitch is fundamental in this context.

We all know that the purpose of the musical keys is precisely to define the pitch of the note within the staff.

For this reason, in percussion at an indeterminate pitch, we use a unique key which, of course, only has the function of defining the pitch minimally.

I'm talking about this:

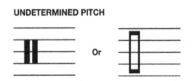

As you can see, there are two ways to make it explicit; the most used, however, is the first.

Instead, for percussion at a determinate pitch, the classic treble and bass clefs are used:

It can be read on a single staff in the treble clef (Glockenspiel, Vibraphone, Xylophone...) or on a single staff in the bass clef (Timpani) or on both as in a piano (Marimba).

Precisely for this reason, I bring you the instruments I told you about by pairing them with the various keys in which they read:

Cymbal
Orchestral Cymbals
Triangle
Cowbell
Tam-Tam
Wind Chimes
Rattles
Wood Block
Temple Block (relative pitch)
Claves
Castanets
Maracas
Cabasa
Shakers
Guiro
Cajòn (relative pitch)
Agogo
Caxixi
Udu

Bass Drum
Darbuka
Djembe
Congas (relative pitch)
Bongos (relative pitch)
Snare Drum
Tom-Toms (relative pitch)
Drum Set (relative pitch)
Tambourine
Tablas (relative pitch)
Cuica (relative pitch)
Taiko
Timbales (relative pitch)
Horn (relative pitch)
Whistle (relative pitch)

Xylophone
Vibraphone
Glockenspiel
Tubular Bells
Crotales
Steel Drum - Hand pan
Gong

Timpani

Marimba
Rototoms

It is useful now to consider the percussion technique.

For almost all percussion, the basic technique is based on alternating the right and left hand.

As you can see in the image below, the grace note, the double and triple appoggiatura have exact names. As I already did when I told you about the Timpani, the trill can be notated either with the classic trill or with the tremolo.

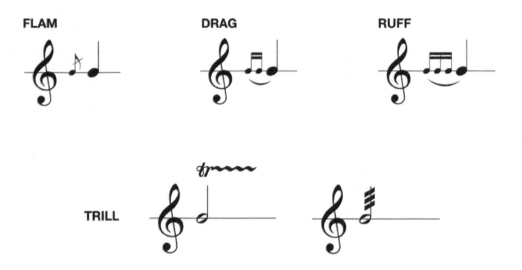

It is essential to know the means used to strike musical instruments.

Basically, they are four:

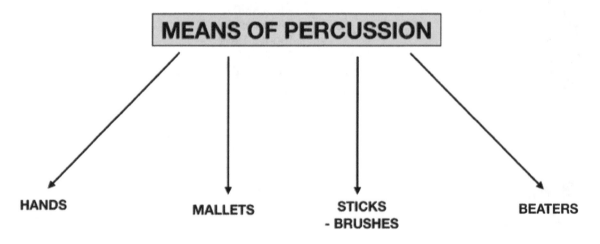

The hands are the most used means; mallets are those beaters mainly used for 'keyboards'; sticks and brushes are used for drums or other instruments; and finally, with 'beaters', I mean other different sticks used for different percussion instruments.

It is very useful for an arranger/composer to learn about mallets. I say this because they are different and, although they are used more by keyboards, they can have completely different sounds from each other. In percussion teaching, there are also four different types of mallets' grips: Traditional, Burton Grip, Musser Grip, Stevens Grip. For the most part, they are all handles given by the name of the person who invented them.

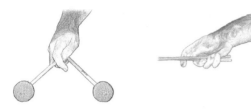

The *Traditional Grip* (left) is the oldest of the handles and has the crossed grip of the mallets, and the thumb is placed over the internal mallet.

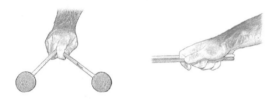

The *Burton Grip* takes its name from the great jazz vibraphonist Gary Burton and is a grip crossed with the external mallet over the internal mallet, contrary to the traditional one.

The inner mallet is held between the index and thumb, and the outer between the index and middle fingers.

The *Musser Grip* takes its name from Omar Musser, it is the second oldest grip after the Traditional one, and it is the first of uncrossed (parallel) grips the mallets never touch. This grip has an internal mallet between the thumb and index, with the tip of the middle finger anchoring the end of the ring finger to the palm at the base of the thumb. The outer mallet is held between the middle and ring fingers and is wrapped by the ring and little fingers. The end of the mallet may protrude from the palm or be held at the end of the palm.

The *Stevens grip* takes its name from the famous Howard Stevens and resembles the Musser grip.

Differs in vertical hand position and inner mallet handling, where the mallet does not go under the thumb when playing larger intervals but is instead held between the outer phalanges of the thumb and index finger, and the other end it is moved from the base of the thumb towards the base of the middle finger.

I go even deeper with the Mallets because I think they are very important.
When you have to interface with a percussionist, it is good to know what kind of mallets you want to choose for a particular passage.
Mallets are usually distinguished by construction material and hardness:

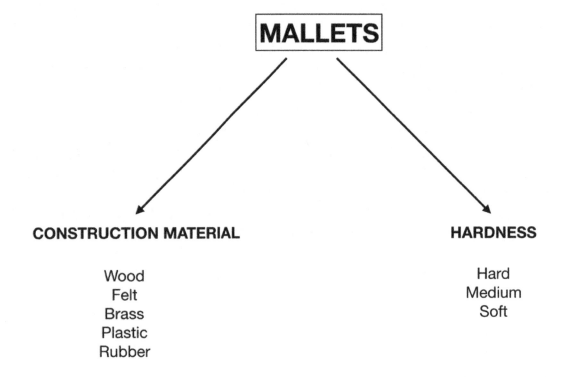

MALLETS

CONSTRUCTION MATERIAL

Wood
Felt
Brass
Plastic
Rubber

HARDNESS

Hard
Medium
Soft

These two aspects are fundamental because they considerably affect the sound of the musical instrument that is struck.
In the following images, I show you the types of mallets used for the different instruments:

TIMPANI

FELT

FLANNEL

LEATHER

BAROQUE MUSIC

MARIMBA

Wool

Birch

VIBRAPHONE

flexible rush

GLOCKENSPIEL

PLASTIC

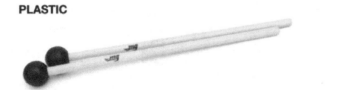

BRASS

XYLOPHONE

PLASTIC

RUBBER

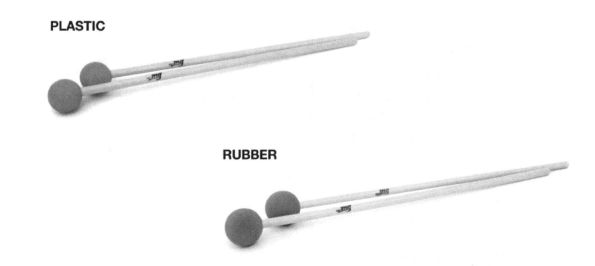

The drum set usually uses three types of sticks: the classic wooden ones and two different types of brushes:

Wooden Sticks   **Brushes**

In the image below, I report the other most common beaters:

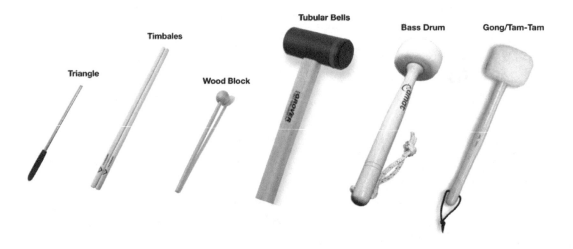

Triangle   Timbales   Wood Block   Tubular Bells   Bass Drum   Gong/Tam-Tam

CHAPTER 6

KEYBOARDS AND HARP

We all know a little that the evolution of keyboard instruments has been enormous.

Suppose I think of the Baroque period, for example. In that case, the harpsichord or the big organs of the great churches immediately come to mind, often with keyboards not related to equal temperament.

If I think of the classical period, on the other hand, the fortepiano or the harpsichord comes to mind.

If we go on to the romantic period, we inevitably think of the piano.

Going further, in the twentieth century, we think of the first Hammond organs, the evolutions of the electric piano, the fender piano, the clavinet, up to the synthesizers.

In this chapter, I will not talk about the ancient instruments (the pipe organ or the harpsichord, the clavichord, or the fortepiano). Still, as I have done throughout the course, I will deepen the discourse on the instruments most in use, both in the symphonic area that popular. When we talk about baroque music, it is natural to talk about the harpsichord and the continuo: this is a practice explicitly linked to that historical period (the baroque).

Today, we can find a certain similarity in the jazz field with the chord signing (a bit like a harpsichord player reads the chords following a bass line and numbers).

Over the past 50 years, keyboard instruments have undergone a crazy evolution.

Of course, everything has been influenced by the advent of electronics in the musical area: from the invention of the MIDI interface, samplers up to the plug-ins and consequently the use of mute keyboards that reproduce the sounds loaded inside of a computer.

Then, what about the synthesizer? If it hadn't been there, we probably wouldn't have the music we have today, that's for sure!

Even the harp, an instrument I will talk about in this chapter, has had a huge revolution, especially with the advent of the pedals.

Also, in this case, I will limit myself to talking to you about the modern harp, the one you commonly see in an orchestra, also because it is an apparently simple instrument but very complex.

In short, we will see the keyboards used in the symphonic area and modern popular music.

We will move from acoustic instruments to strictly electric ones, so the breadth of the speech will be considerable, but it will undoubtedly increase the tonal spectrum for your arrangements and compositions in some way.

THE HARP

The harp is perhaps, after percussion, one of the most ancient instruments ever, as evidenced by countless iconographic sources; even Dante talks about it in his Divine Comedy.
The great treatises on organology of the Renaissance and Baroque such as Virdung or Praetorius, already speak of it.

But be careful! The harp we see now is the modern one with only the shape in common with the ancient harps.
The harp has always been considered the English and Irish national instrument (again, thanks to the iconographic findings).
In ancient times, first of all, they did not have pedals (we'll talk about them in a while), they differed in size (some were small enough to be hung on a strap and worn, while others were too large to be portable.

Towards the end of the Middle Ages, the harp then had two main phases: the first corresponds to the *Roman Harp* and the second to the *Gothic Harp*, which we all know as the Irish harp.

This paragraph will talk about the modern European harp, which stands out within the orchestras with its classic triangular shape.

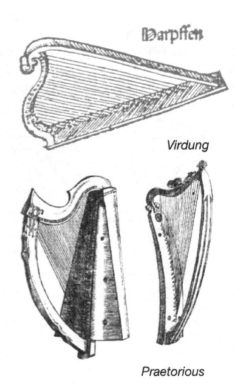

Virdung

Praetorious

Gothic Harp

At the beginning of the 1700s, the harp differed from medieval instruments only in the number of strings, but its tuning was still diatonic, without semitones.

They made many interventions on the instrument to get to the modern harp.
I'm not here to explain the whole story step-by-step, even if it's still an interesting topic, but I'd like to focus more on the modern instrument.
Of all the solutions found to improve the harp, the first important was the pedal harp, towards the first two decades of the 1700s.
The hooks that were placed before, and operated manually, were now employed by pedals. This system, however, made it impossible to play keys with flats.
The turning point was in 1820 when Sebastian Èrard built the harp that is in use today after a first attempt at a double pedal harp towards the end of the 1700s. The modern instrument is diatonically tuned in C flat, each of its seven pedals has a double movement, and rotating discs replace the hooks with two protruding buttons.
They also tried to build a chromatic harp, that is, a harp with 12 strings for each octave.

It was, however, complicated as an instrument as the strings would have been too close and would not have been able to vibrate without touching each other. As I told you, the harp today is diatonic, tuned in C flat. The rest is done by using the pedals with their double movement.

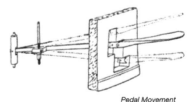

Pedal Movement

First of all, let's see the morphology of the harp:

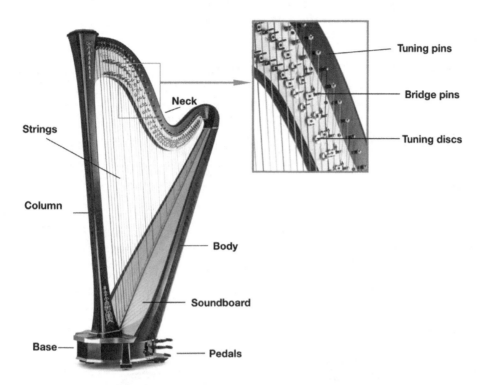

Looking at the image, its grandeur and its remarkable number of strings already stand out.

The pedal mechanism is operated by some rods hidden inside the column.

The harp has a triangular shape and, being 1.80m high, can be played seated by placing the instrument's body on the right shoulder.

As you can see from the image, I have enlarged the part relating to the mechanism that allows the instrument to change the string's pitch.

Beyond the tuning pins, which are the ones that the instrumentalist uses to tune the instrument before playing, it is interesting to see the tuning discs, which instead are those mechanisms controlled by the pedals that pull and loosen the string according to of use.

The range of the harp is extensive and is not a transposing instrument:

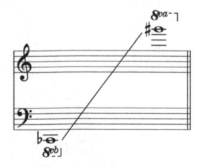

It is written like the piano, therefore on two staves, but we must make a note:

Although piano music is often distributed in the staves according to the hand playing, the harp does not work like this.

We must always write harp music in the staff to which the pitches of the notes belong.

The harp has a silent sound compared to most orchestral instruments, but on the other hand, it can perform many special and very useful effects.

Its sound changes a lot depending on the register in which it plays:

LOW REGISTER	**MIDDLE REGISTER**	**HIGH REGISTER**
Notes have great resonance that works great with arpeggios. Pay attention to the damping of notes. This register is also excellent for doubling the bass instruments of the orchestra	It is the most used for solos, glissatos, arpeggios and chords. The sound is very clear, gentle and is much brighter and less metallic than the low register	The sound is not very resonant, very clear and sparkling

The modern harp has 47 strings: 7 per octave (excluding the last, which has only five strings); The first 12 strings are made of metal (steel wrapped with copper or silver plated), the other 35 are gut or nylon.

Each string is attached between the tuning pins on the neck and the holes on the soundboard.

Strings attached to the tuning pins and soundboard

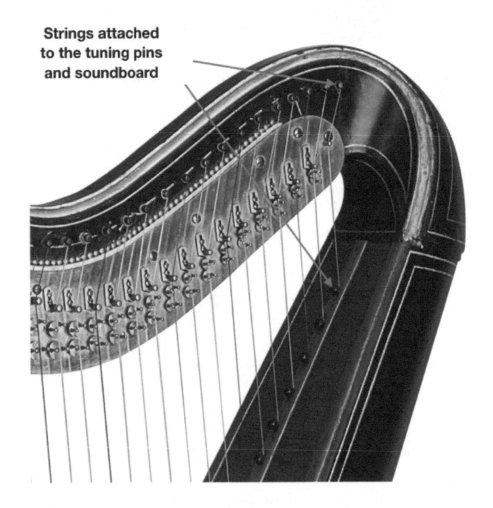

The strings have different colors to be recognized:

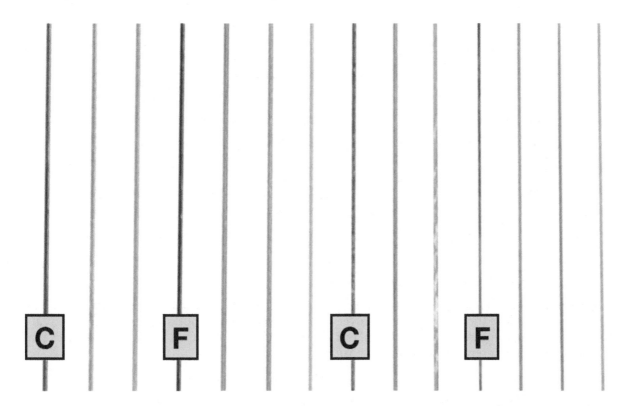

The C in red, the F in Black / Blue, and the others in the construction material color.

The harp is played with all fingers except the little finger, which is too short of taking the strings well.

The position is with the thumb up and the other fingers placed horizontally.

The thumb pinches the string forward and the other fingers towards the performer's body.

The extension of the two hands is not the same:

While the left hand can play the instrument's entire range, the right is limited in the low register because the harpist must hold the instrument on the right shoulder.

The maximum interval that we can take with one hand is a tenth.

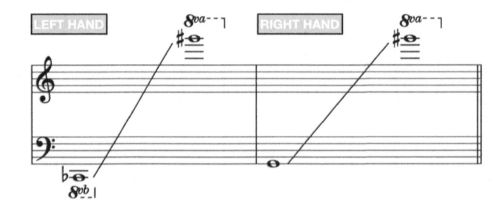

It is a diatonic instrument: it has seven strings per octave with the interval relationship of a diatonic scale. The pedals allow the instrument to cover all twelve chromatic notes of an octave: they are 7, positioned at the instrument's base on the player's side. They are connected to the tuning discs placed on the neck thanks to a series of rods found inside the column.

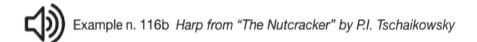 Example n. 116b *Harp from "The Nutcracker" by P.I. Tschaikowsky*

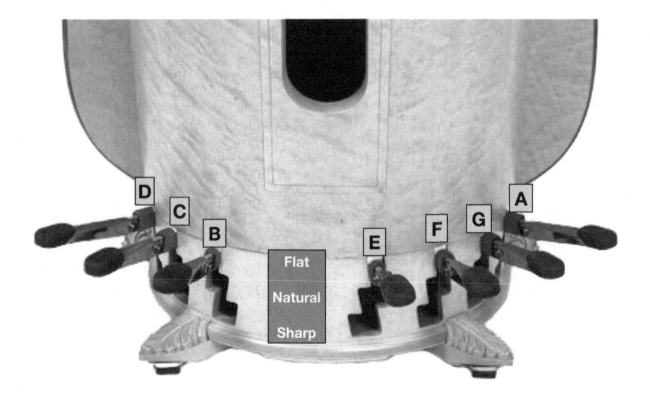

The pedals are positioned like this: three on the left and four on the right.
Each of the pedals has *three positions*

♭ **FLAT**   Pedal all over. No discs are used and the strings have their full length

♮ **NATURAL**   Pedal one step below. Only one disc is used. The strings are 'shortened' by a semitone

♯ **SHARP**   Pedal two steps below. Two discs are used. The strings are 'shortened' by two semitones

The pedal system is so complex that a notation is made just for them.
It should be indicated at the beginning of the piece, or after a long pause, a new movement, or any other point where you need to change the pedal.

Letters   Letters   Diagram

D♮ C♮ B♮ / E♮ F♮ G♮ A♮

D♮ C♮ B♮
E♮ F♮ G♮ A♮

Given the scale in the image above, we have three notation possibilities:
two using letters and one using a specific diagram.
In the letter notation on the far left, the bar divides the right foot from the left, as well as in the diagram. In the central letter notation, the feet are indicated one under the other.
The accidentals (flat, natural, sharp) correspond to the pedal's position, as you saw in the image of the pedals a little while ago.
The diagram, on the other hand, needs to be explained better.
I start from the principle that it is a perfect system because it remembers the exact position of the pedals, so there is no risk of having two pedals change in the same part.

In the image below, you can see exactly how to use the diagram notation:

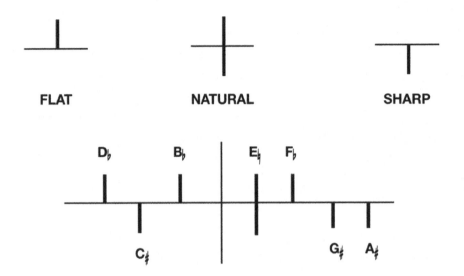

A problem that the pedals can cause in the composition of a harp piece is the chords' writing.
As you can imagine, since the harp is a polyphonic instrument, chords are daily bread. Still, you have to be very careful when writing the notes as we know that when a pedal is lowered, the entire length of the string taken into consideration changes.
The solution to this problem is simply to work enharmonically;

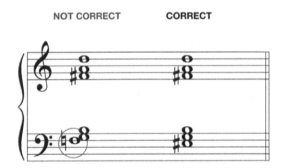

Then, we must remember that the harpist uses only four fingers on each hand so that you can play chords of up to 8 sounds.
However, the opening of the hand also allows you to take the tenth interval well, and in a chord, you can play all the notes together or arpeggiated using this sign (right):

The harp is a widely used instrument and in different ways: as a soloist, to add color to the orchestra with glissandi and arpeggios, especially in the medium register and in the orchestral crescendo, to double other instruments, especially strings, woods, timpani, and keyboards (Glockenspiel, Xylophone).
For example, the harp contributes to the attack of instruments with a slower attack (clarinet, horn) and is excellent for accompanying a voice, like a piano, and filling the background accompaniment, in other words filling the orchestral texture.

With the advent of pedals, the leap in quality from a technical point of view has been enormous. You can make an excellent legato, and it is very common: the harpist lets the strings vibrate until the end of the slur.

One of the characteristic effects of the harp is undoubtedly the glissando, which is obtained simply by sliding the finger along the strings.
We can play this effect can in several ways:

Still talking about technique, the Arpeggio is very common, in which the harpist plays the notes of the chord one at a time in quick succession;

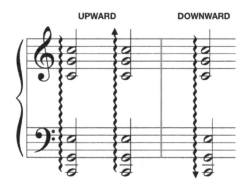

The Resonance, in which the harpist lets the strings vibrate without dampening them;

The Tremolo: the repetition of the same note or the same chord, possible thanks to the pedals since it is not possible to do it on a single string:

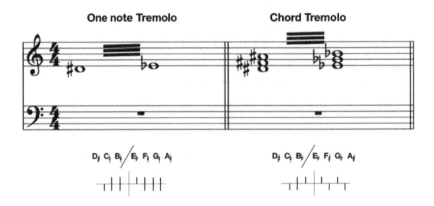

The Bisbigliando, very similar to tremolo but very quiet.
We can do this effect using both hands for a single chord or different chords in both hands:
or ¼ grand

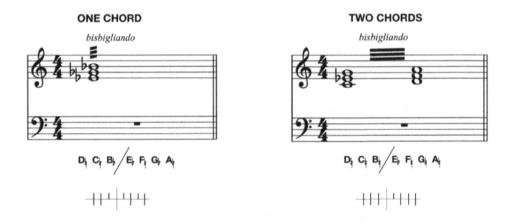

And finally, the Harmonic Sounds.
The octave ones are widely used and obtained by touching the string at the center of its length after plugging it. They can be seen with the classic circle above the note:
I report below a part taken from Tzigane by Maurice Ravel:

THE PIANO AND THE CELESTA

Who doesn't know the piano?

It is practically the best-known instrument in any musical area, but its history has been somewhat shaky.

In the beginning, when in 1709 Bartolomeo Cristofori conceived his gravicembalo with the piano and forte, it was not very successful.

The piano had certain notoriety only when Mozart began writing and playing for the instrument.

It is almost evident that the direct descendants of the piano were the harpsichord and the clavichord, although the first used the pick to pluck the string and not hammers like the piano.

However, the mechanics invented by Cristofori certainly made a difference even if, at first, it presented some problems since its structure was not strong enough to support a sufficiently heavy string. In fact, they fully exploited these mechanics only with the metal reinforcement system.

We now basically have two widely used types of acoustic piano: grand, half or ¼ grand, and so-called upright pianos.

The piano was, however, a musical miracle if you think that it was born precisely to be able to express musical colors that the harpsichord, for example, could not express.

As I already told you at the beginning of this book, the piano is of Italian invention, but the Germans perfected it.

The first registers, still used today, derive from the harpsichord.

We think of the forte register or the mute (which inserts a strip of felt between the hammers and the strings, muffling the sound).

The pedals, for example, are now an integral part of the instrument, and the first pedal patent was in 1783.

In the modern piano, the strings are thicker and, consequently, the soundboard more robust.

Even the upright or wall-mounted piano was born more or less like the normal piano, but they were sporadic until the end of the 1700s.

Today the piano is a wonderful solo instrument, an excellent instrument for chamber music, widely used in orchestra and many jazz and pop productions.

On the other hand, the Celesta has recently gained momentum thanks to film music.

Many compositions related to fantasy scenes, for example, are told with the Celesta.

We can say that this instrument is the most used keyboard in the orchestra today since the piano has now taken on more of a role as accompanist and soloist.

On the other hand, there are many compositions with the Celesta, even in the classical area, even dedicated to her: I am thinking of Bartòk's Music for strings, percussion, and Celesta.

However, both the piano and the Celesta are now fully part of today's musical scenario and are easily recognizable.

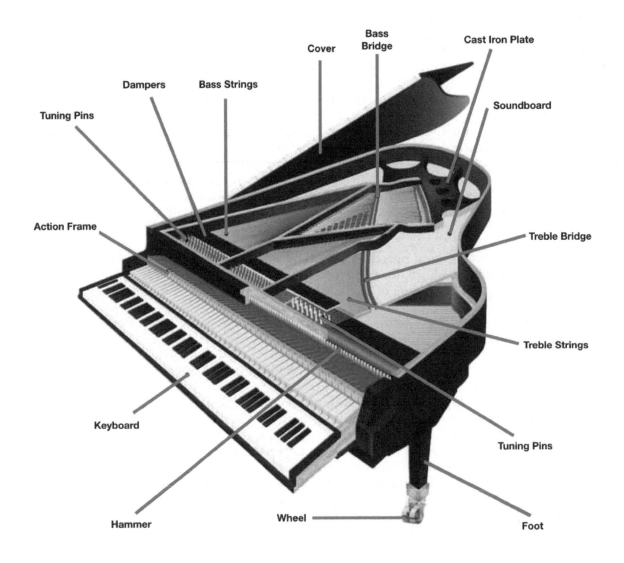

As you can see from the image above, the piano, apart from its size, is an instrument with very complex mechanics.
The parts that make up this instrument are many and also quite complex, but I think it's worth it.
The piano strings are mounted on a large cast-iron plate, helpful in supporting their tension.

The image on the previous page represents a Grand Piano, but even in the Upright piano, things do not change: it is the exact mechanism, reduced and set up:

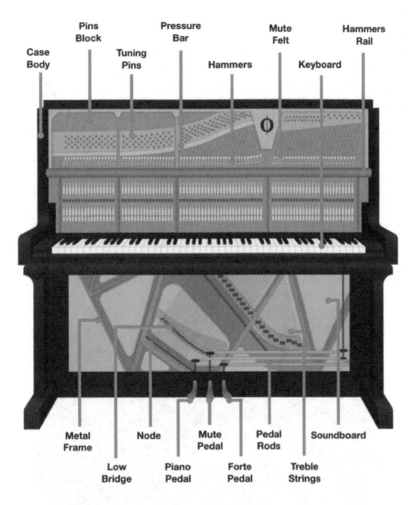

All this gives life to what produces the sound, namely the hammers.
The hammer mechanism is easy to understand, but its implementation is complicated:

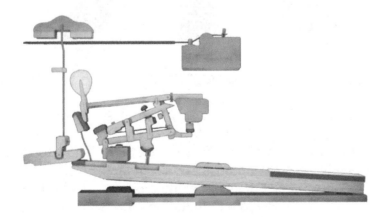

Everything starts by pressing the button.
This pressure will give rise to a movement of levers that will cause the hammer to strike the string.
Not only that, the mechanism allows the hammer to move away from the string once struck to allow maximum vibration.

The piano has had so much luck, perhaps due to its range.

It has 88 keys and the widest range of all instruments (excluding the organ, which covers a greater range with the pedals).

Precisely for this reason, the pianist uses the double staff, the bass clef for the low notes, and the treble clef for the high ones:

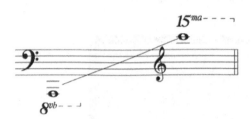 

The modern piano has three pedals that have specific functions.

Look at the image below:

"ONE STRING" PEDAL	TONAL PEDAL	DAMPER PEDAL
Move the hammers so that they can hit only one string or two at the most. The aim is to decrease the dynamics	It lets vibrate only the notes that are played when pressed. It is used a lot for making bass pedals, in fact it does not work above middle C. In the upright piano it is the soft pedal	By pressing it moves the dampers or shock absorbers away from the strings. This way the string vibrates even when the fret is released

Let's start by saying that piano literature is vast.
In the Romantic period, the piano had a crazy 'boom'.
This surge has undoubtedly been helped by many composers and excellent pianists who have elevated the piano both technically and tonally.
I think of Liszt, Rachmaninov, for example.
The evolution it has had from a compositional point of view, from Mozart's concerts to Beethoven's 5s to the great romantic concerts by Chopin, Rachmaninov, Tschaikowsky, and many others, has been exponential.

The first role of today's piano is that of the soloist.
The piano pieces written only starting from romanticism are innumerable:
just think that Mozart had already written 18 Sonatas for solo piano, Beethoven 32.

Then with the passage of time and the advent of instrumental virtuosity typical of the 19th century, the piano repertoire also had the purpose not exclusively of music but also to highlight the virtuosity of the performer.
The transcriptions made by Listz of famous pieces of the period, for example, are clear proof of this.

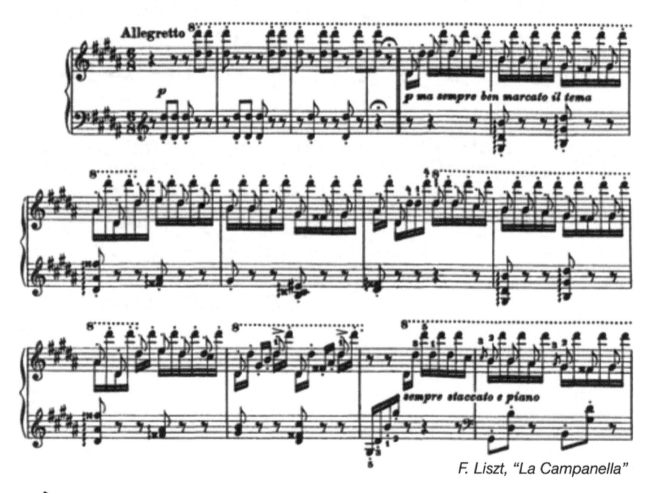

F. Liszt, "La Campanella"

Example n. 117

The virtuosity was also linked as a timbre of the instrument, think of Chopin's famous nocturnes.

F. Chopin, Notturno op.9 n.2

 Example n. 118

Since the piano is a very versatile instrument, it could perform the most varied articulations and timbres. It was the main accompanying instrument (it still is if we think about it).
We think of the great compositions for solo melodic instruments and piano.

L. Van Beethoven, Violin and Piano Sonata "Spring"

 Example n. 119

Not only that, let's think of the operatic reductions written for singers, the reductions for two pianos written for conducting courses.
It is useless to specify it, also because it is very evident. It is still the most widely used instrument in all areas, from classic to popular.
We think of the great jazz trios of history or the great jazz pianists (Bill Evans, Monk, McCoy Tyner, Chick Corea, Jarrett...). These characters have certainly influenced the piano's use and its further dissemination.
The piano is now an integral part of symphony orchestras and big bands and the rhythms of pop bands. As a member of the team, the piano takes on different roles in the orchestra, from the doubling of some parts to the rhythmic accompaniment.

In the example below, taken from Stravinsky's 'Petrushka', the piano rhythmically and harmonically doubles the whole orchestra in the first part and accompanies it in the second part, creating a very effective rhythmic background.

I. Stravinsky, Petrushka

 Example n. 120

The other keyboard instrument widely used in the orchestra is the _Celesta_.
As you can see by sight alone, the Celesta is a miniature piano not with strings but with metal bars.
These bars give the instrument a sound similar to a softer Glockenspiel.

Keyboard **Cover**

Damper

About that, it is interesting to look at the inside of the instrument:

Interior of the Celesta

As you can see from the photo, it has felt hammers hitting the metal bars.
The celesta also has a damper pedal to let the notes vibrate further.
It is a transposing instrument: the effect is one octave above the written note.

Here is its range and its effect:

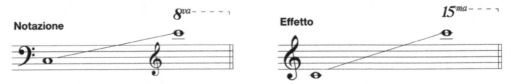

The Celesta is widely used in the orchestra, even as a solo instrument.
Tschaikowsky, for example, used it as a solo instrument in his 'Nutcracker':

Example n. 121

The last example that I bring you is from the soundtrack of the Harry Potter film written by John Williams. By now, the theme you will see is very famous and is the cornerstone of the whole Harry Potter saga.

I. Hedwig's Theme

JOHN WILLIAMS

Example n. 122

ELECTROMECHANICAL KEYBOARDS

We have seen how lucky the piano has been.

With the advent of electricity, this fortune has increased exponentially.

I must point out from the outset that there is often confusion between an electric instrument and an electronic instrument.

A synthesizer could be an electronic piano.

The electric piano is not theoretically an electronic instrument. Instead, it is an electro-mechanical instrument.

This means that, unlike the synthesizer, the mechanical component is at the basis of the instrument's operation.

The electronic part undoubtedly comes after the mechanical one.

Certainly, these instruments have revolutionized popular music, especially the mainstream area, dance music in the 70s, jazz, giving rise to further sub-genres of popular music, first of all, fusion.

Let's go step by step: in this paragraph, I will talk about electro-mechanical instruments, and I find it essential to know their morphology and sounds, not only to enrich your vocabulary but also to understand where you started from, where you arrived and where you are going.

In short, we now have an infinite timbral texture for our arrangements. It is up to us to manage these timbres as we please and in the best way.

We start from the assumption that being an electric piano, we will speak of instruments that have a keyboard like the piano.

I want to clarify the difference between electronic and electro-mechanical instruments, and here are the ones I will talk about:

KEYBOARDS

ELECTROMECHANICAL

Yamaha CP70
Piano Fender Rhodes
Piano Wurlitzer
Clavinet
Mellotron

ELECTRONIC

Hammond Organ
Synthesizer

Obviously, I will consider the most important ones, those who built the newly popular genre.

These instruments can somehow be classified by considering their morphology and the mechanical means they use to emit sound.

I will divide them into strings, reed, and diapason instruments:

TYPES

STRINGS: Yamaha CP70, Clavinet   **REEDS:** Wurlitzer   **DIAPASON:** Rhodes

The first prototype of an electric piano was built in the early 1930s by the Bechstein factory, later called Neo-Bechstein.
It was a simple grand piano with electromagnetic pickups.
However, he revolutionized the concept of the piano.
If you think that great Beatles recordings have been made with this piano, it almost shivers ('Hey Jude' for example)
It has also been used a lot by great pianists (Oscar Peterson, for example) or big names in popular music, from Queen to Supertramp, from David Bowie to Elton John, in short, it was a fantastic instrument.

Piano Neo-Bechstein

Example n. 123 *C. Debussy, 'Clair de Lune' with Neo-Bechstein*

One of the most famous electric pianos was the *Yamaha CP70*.

The electromechanical instrument produced at the turn of the 70s and 80s has 72 keys instead of 88, and the hammers are covered in deerskin instead of felt.

The strings are equipped with pickups, so the operation is similar to an electric guitar. Under each string set, a contact piezoelectric brings the sound produced by the string's vibration to specific controls such as tremolo or equalization.

Look at its interior in the image below:

 Example n. 124 *Yamaha CP70*

One of the most famous was undoubtedly the *Fender Rhodes Piano*.

Still widely used, it was born almost by chance in 1942, in the middle of the world war, by an American aviator, Harold Rhodes. Following the need to play an instrument similar to the piano but lighter and more portable, he used pieces of recovery from an American bomber to build an instrument of reduced size and weight by hand.

Let's say that the sound is derived in some way from both the celesta and the electric guitar; in fact, it is generated by the mechanical action of hammers, like the acoustic piano. However, it is not the strings that are struck, but the metal bars (in aluminum in the acoustic prototype and steel in the standard electrophone versions).

Pick-ups similar to those used on electric guitars, placed on axis on the bars, pick up the magnetic field variation and generate an electro-acoustic signal to be amplified.

Thus, was born, in 1942, the prototype of the Rhodes electric piano: a new concept instrument, with a tone very similar to the sound of a vibraphone, which is baptized "Army Air Corps Piano".

The father of the new instrument immediately understood the advantages of the particular sonority and versatility compared to the acoustic progenitor, so, in the mid-40s, he founded the "Rhodes Piano Corporation" and produced the first model: the 'Rhodes Pre-piano'.

The evolution of the Rhodes is manifested through models produced in the 50s and 60s. The peak of popularity is still reached in the 70s with the 'Stage Piano Mk I and Mk II' versions, particularly appreciated in live situations and music. jazz, in which it is widely used, especially in the fusion field.

In the 1950s, Fender bought the Rhodes company.

There are 73 and 88 keys versions.

 Example n. 125 *Fender Rhodes*

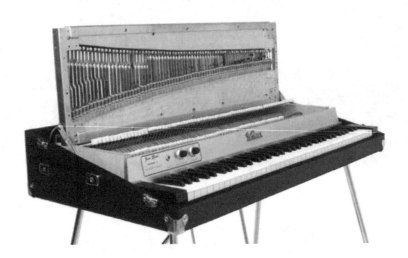

Another very important electro-mechanical piano is the _Wurlitzer_.

It has an unmistakable sound and has been heavily used.

Invented by Benjamin Miessner, it has been in production since the 1950s.

It is similar to the Rhodes, but it changes the mechanics.

A metal reed generates the sound with a felt hammer that induces an electric current in a pick-up.

The sound is more transparent than the Rhodes and changes with the dynamics.

In fact, in the piano dynamic, the sound of the Wurlitzer is very similar to that of a vibraphone like the Rhodes, but in the

loud, the sound becomes much more aggressive, as if it had an overdrive (think about Supertramp songs)

Already seeing it open, you realize how it works:

Widely used in schools, they were built especially for students and teachers.

They produced many Wurlitzer models until 1984, then supplanted by the digital synthesizer.

However, the most popular is the Wurlitzer 200, widely used in many successful tracks.

Example n. 126 *Piano Wurlitzer*

Another instrument that has made Funk history in a particular way is the *Clavinet*. Invented by Ernst Zacharias and built by the Hohner company, it is a clavichord with pick-ups.

It usually has 60 frets and the same mechanism as the clavichord: each fret ends with a rubber "tangent" pushed against the string.

The tangent interrupts the length of the string, establishing its pitch, and the pick-ups electrically convert the vibration.

It symbolizes funk, dance, reggae, jazz-funk, rock, soul, and lots of music from the 70s.

It is often paired with the wha-wha effect or phaser, and its sound is very similar to that of an electric guitar, very dry and short.

They built seven models in all, but the most famous is the 1971 D6.

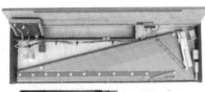

Opened Clavinet

Four other switches activate many filters (two high-pass and two low-pass, named Brilliant, Treble, Medium, and Soft), modifying the harmonic content at the output. There is also a special Damper controlled by a slider on the side of the fingerboard, which gradually reduces the decay of the strings' vibration; in this way, the instrument presents a remarkable tonal variety.

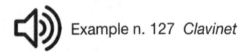 Example n. 127 *Clavinet*

The *Mellotron* is an electromechanical keyboard that has had a lot of luck despite not being a chordophone.

This instrument generates sound from recorded tapes, so it is as if it were an ancestor of the sampler.

As long as you press the key, the tape runs over the head,

and the sound comes out.

A spring pulls the tape back to its rest position when the key is released. It is small, with only 35 keys, and can play different sounds depending on the tape you are using. It was very popular in the late 1960s and early 1970s.

 Example n. 128 *Mellotron*

ELECTRONIC KEYBOARDS

Electronic keyboards do not have a mechanical component that affects the sound, but the sounds are produced electronically.

The first of these instruments I discuss is the *Hammond Organ*.

Its sound is immediately recognizable and has truly made the history of twentieth-century music, first in the ecclesiastical sphere and then in the jazz area.

Born from an idea of Laurens Hammond in 1934, the first was the A model, but the one that had great relevance and that unmistakable sound was built 20 years later: the B3 model.

Although the Hammond is now practically a transistor instrument, it was born as a mixture of electric and electromechanical since the sound generator is Tonewheel.

As you can see from the image, next to the organ, there is a wooden cabinet: it is an essential part of the instrument, the so-called Leslie, that is a particular speaker, in practice "Rotating".

This rotation allows the organ to express that typical sound.

Most Hammond instruments have two 61-key (5 octaves) keyboards, called *Manuals*, and Hammond console organs also have a 25-key bass pedal.

 Example n. 129 *Hammond organ*

I will show you the Leslie seen more closely in the following image.
It will be helpful for you to understand how it works:

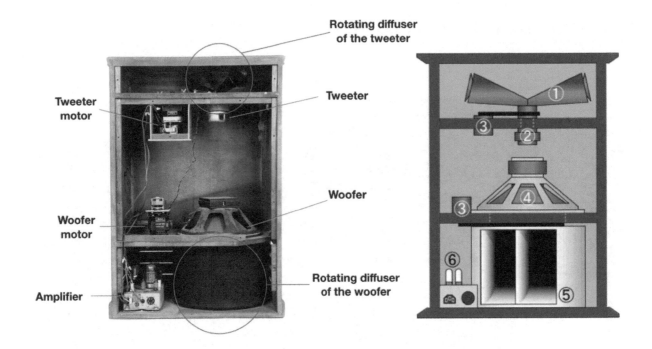

As you can see from the image, these two cones stand out, one for the low sounds (woofer) and one for the treble (tweeter).
However, what distinguishes Leslie are the rotors that give the characteristic effect.
As you can see from the drawn image, the two rotors are free from each other and rotate at different speeds.
The resulting effect is a wave effect.
In fact, the two speeds of the Leslie are the Chorus and the Tremolo (the slower Chorus and the faster Tremolo), and they are both oscillation effects.
There have been many models of Leslie, but the most famous and used is Leslie 122.
Let's see how the sound of this instrument is born:

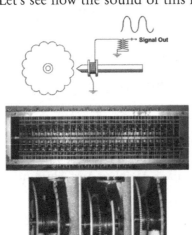

As I told you before, the mechanical element that allows the sound of the instrument is the so-called *Tonewheel*.
The Tonewheel is a simple electromechanical device for generating electric musical notes in the Hammond.
In the image on the left, you can see the drawing of the wheel and below a specific photo of the whole device.
This system is not very recent; it dates back to 1910.
The Tonewheel consists of an e motor that drives a series of rotating discs. Each disc has a given number of smooth bumps on the rim; these generate a specific frequency as the record rotates near a pick-up assembly consisting of a magnet and an electromagnetic coil.
We can combine a single fundamental frequency with one or more harmonics to produce complex sounds with this system.

Who decides which tonewheels need to be driven to produce a particular tone are the so-called *Drawbars* or ToneBars:

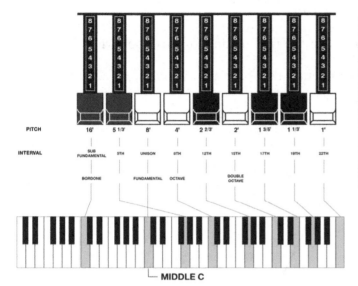

As you can see, each drawbar is marked by a number (pitch) which indicates the feet of the organ 'pipe', and by an interval which is the result of the sound and harmonics that come out.
The numbers from 1 to 8 of each drawbar represent the degrees of volume: 1 is the softest and 8 the loudest.
As you can see from the image, the drawbars are divided into three groups of sounds and three groups of colors: the first two reddish ones that indicate the sounds below the fundamental .... the next four the fundamental and the last three somehow the brilliance.
The combination of these drawbars positions produces a specific and distinct sound, bringing them closer to a clarinet or a flute, for example.
In addition, the concept of "Harmonic Percussion" was also introduced in the Hammond B3 and C3 organs, designed to emulate the percussive sounds of the xylophone or harp, for example. The selected percussive harmonic goes away immediately after you press the key, leaving the notes sustained by the player with the drawbar selections. The volume of this percussion effect is selectable as normal or soft.

The instrument that, in my opinion, really revolutionized all music after the 1950s was undoubtedly the *Synthesizer*.

You could spend days talking on the Synthesizer.

I will just limit myself to making you understand what types of synthesizers exist, which are the most used in the popular field, and above all, what types exist.

I'll just give you a few historical hints to make you understand the operating mechanism of the instrument, also because I already talked about it in the first module of this book when I explained the evolution of electrophones.

As the term itself says, the Synthesizer is an instrument linked to sound synthesis.

There are four types of synthesis on synthesizers (see graph below).

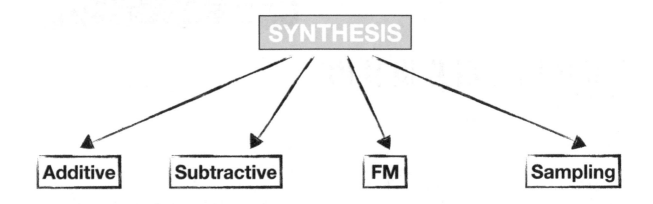

Additive Synthesizers are the least used. They haven't had much luck.

You create a sound with additive synthesis by adding different fundamental frequencies and distributing them in the sound spectrum.

This is a very complex mechanism, which is why, as I said, it was not very successful, also because, although theoretically being able to recreate any sound, the fact of adding different frequencies and organizing them without starting from a sound with already a harmonic spectrum, was left out.

Another type of Synthesizer, this time widely used, is the *Subtractive Synthesis* one: the Minimoog, for example.

It was the most popular type because it started from a pre-established waveform and changed its structure through filters and envelopes of different kinds. The most used envelopes are those that affect volume (attack, release, sustain ...) [VCA], oscillation or tremolo [LFO], or pitch [PITCH].

One of the hugely successful synthesis modes was *Frequency Modulation* synthesis, commonly called FM. Famous Yamaha's DX7 was one of those synthesizers. This synthesis had a lot of luck in the 1980s because the resulting sounds from these synthesizers were very authentic.

How does FM synthesis work?

In practice, we can modify the timbre of a simple waveform by modulating its frequency with a modulation frequency, obtaining a more complex waveform and a tone with a different sound.

It starts with an oscillator that generates a carrier audio signal with a particular frequency. An audio signal modulating with another frequency is applied that "modulates" the carrier wave frequency generated by the oscillator.

The 90s were fundamental for the dissemination of *Sampling*.
This is now the present: think of all the plug-ins or virtual libraries present today; they are all based on pre-recorded sounds. Very famous in the 90s is the so-called PCM sampling (pulse-code modulation), coded pulse modulation. It is a type of Sampling of which the JD800 is part, the one you see in the picture. In short words, we start with a sound recorded either analogically (tape) or digitally (encoded in numbers).
We then intervene on the recorded tone to modify its variables.
PCM synthesizers provide a very authentic sound and allow multiple tones to be layered together to make the sound even more complex.

About that, I bring you the image (next page) of my personal Roland JD800.
This synth helped me understand how envelopes and sound synthesis work in general.

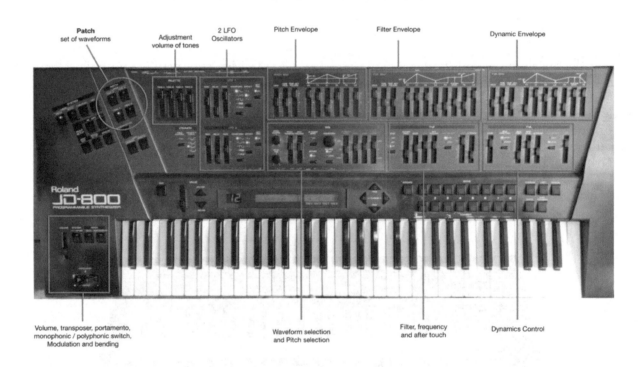

The useful thing about this synthesizer is that it looks like an analog model digital machine.
All the envelopes are available to the performer in real-time.
As you can see, it has 2 LFO oscillators (I'll explain what it is later in this book), a pitch envelope, the filters (equalization), the ADSR (I will also talk about this later), a section for managing the waveforms and the various tones of each patch.

Synth Keyboards have become so important that they have been shrunk and carried away.
Today it has reached a level that was unthinkable until some time ago.
Finally, let's see two very important instruments in recent years.

The instrument you see in the image on the left has revolutionized the role of the keyboard player, always seated and in a non-central position on a stage.
Finally, a keyboard player can stand up and play in the center of the stage like a lead guitarist.
For this reason, the instrument in question was called *Keytar*, born from the synthesis between the word 'Keyboard' and 'Guitar'.
The invention of this instrument is attributed to a guitarist, Steve Masakowski, and was marketed by Moog in 1980.
In most cases, they are Master Keyboards, so without any sounds inside.
They, therefore, make use of external modules and develop MIDI technology to communicate with other instruments.
It is worn over the shoulder like a guitar and retains the bending and modulation lever in the left-hand grip, typical of electronic keyboards.
As it has to be transported, it is not very big.
It usually has 49 keys (4 octaves), but its range is practically infinite with specific octave commands.
This instrument is used in all popular areas: from pop to rock, from metal to jazz.
Chick Corea, the great jazz pianist, used the Keytar extensively in his Electric Band.

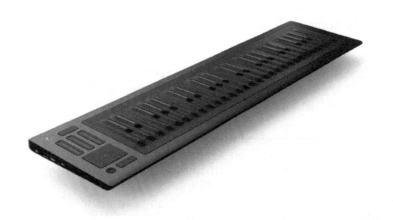

Technology has become more important and, in recent years, has produced a new type of synthesizer, the *Seaboard*.

The name explicitly derives from its shape so thin that it looks like a surfboard.

The instrument produced by Roli stands out precisely for its keyboard, completely different from standard keyboards: it is smooth, continuous, and sensitive to the touch.

It is almost flat allows the musician to intervene on many tonal aspects of the sound: bending, modulation, aftertouch, glissando.

Let's think about the glissando: no keyboard can do a glissando without the help of the bending lever. With this instrument, just move your finger from one key to another, or move it by swinging it to vibrate.

Like all electronic keyboards today, it has a USB interface and is an excellent MIDI controller.

There are Seaboards of different sizes: from the 25-key laptop to the 49-key.

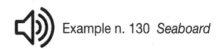 Example n. 130 *Seaboard*

The musical instruments we have seen in this lesson certainly make us understand how much technology affects the growth and evolution of music itself.

The 1900s was a century of fundamental importance precisely for the aspects linked to technology, and the steps forward that have been made are truly giants.

Obviously, there is a bit of melancholy if you think that 50 years ago, these instruments were avant-garde, and now they are practically vintage.

In the historical period we live in now, synthesizer and sampling have reached incredible levels.

Now, with a simple master keyboard, you can practically faithfully reproduce an entire symphony orchestra with all its dynamics, articulations, and all its most important effects.

A little sorry that today, for example, musicals are practically performed without the orchestra, using backing tracks, being so true.

Indeed, the instrumental ensembles have considerably decreased because, if you think about it, three keyboard players are enough to do practically everything, from the rhythm section to the whole orchestra.

Not to mention the sequencers that have further enriched the tonal possibilities of the arrangements.

I am thinking, for example, of the productions in which we use pre-recorded sequences to increase the timbres, also using the electronic ones, of a musical formation.

HOW A SYNTHESIZER WORKS

In this paragraph, I will explain the operating principle of a synthesizer.

Since synthesizers took over, the whole modern music system has changed.

Certainly, their invasion was most evident in the pop-rock and psychedelic areas (think of the Pink Floyd studio sessions).

However, many believe that playing a synthesizer is like playing the piano.

Nothing falser!

They are two completely different instruments.

This rumor has only come about because many synthesizers often have a piano keyboard incorporated, a bit like the accordion.

The synthesizer instrument has a particular function. Knowing its basic functioning is important for the arranger since the tonal possibilities that such an instrument can give you are practically endless!

As we have seen throughout the book, each musical instrument has an element that allows the reproduction of sound (a reed, a mouthpiece, a bow, free reeds, electricity...... in short, they are various).

The synthesizer also has its tone generator.

I must say that it is an electric instrument and that the same sound is generated electronically.

I want to clarify this thing because, as I will show you, everything starts from an electronic circuit that generates the sound source.

This paragraph will obviously be theoretical, not being able to play in a book, and I will explain to you the main components that make a synthesizer so fascinating.

There are four fundamental components that a synthesizer uses to produce sound:

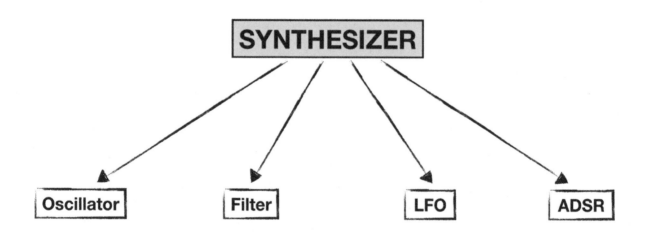

What makes it possible for the synthesizer to reproduce sound is the *Oscillator*.

Since the Oscillator is an electronic circuit, this instrument will be part of the electronic instruments, as I have already explained to you in other paragraphs.

So, the Oscillator is nothing more than an electronic circuit, of which we can have control, which generates a sound wave in constant repetition.

We could compare it to a reed for a clarinet or strings for a violin. So, it is our sound source.

The nice thing about the synthesizer is that it allows the sound generated by the oscillator to be filtered, modulated, and transformed up to a particular final sound different from the source one.

For this reason, we speak of *Sound Synthesis*: a source sound is synthesized in another in practice.

Then the oscillator creates our basic *Waveform*.

It is, therefore, necessary to specify what a waveform is and what types of waveforms an oscillator creates.

A waveform is an electrical signal generated by the oscillator, represented on a Cartesian axis.

The following image shows you the three most common waveforms that you can find today in both real and virtual synthesizers.

Obviously, they are not the only ones; they are just the most common:

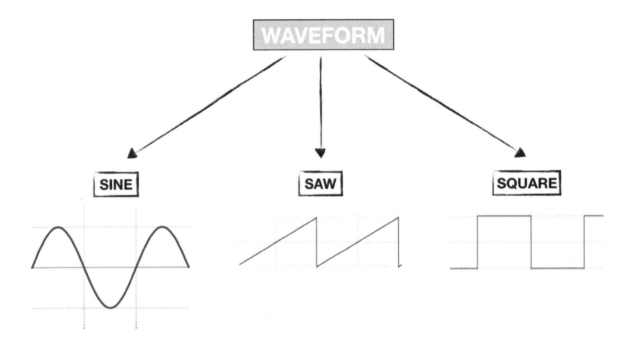

Often, in addition to the sawtooth, the triangular shape is also very similar but has a different decay.

However, beyond the diffusion of the various waveforms generated, the important thing is to listen to the sound of each waveform that an oscillator produces.

Today, most synths have more oscillators; therefore, we can combine more sound generators, generating the various waveforms.

The *Filters* are another essential element in a synthesizer.

In particular, the filter acts on the equalization of the sound. They are used to filter parts of the frequency spectrum, so they pass only specific frequencies of the audible spectrum.

The three types of filters most used in synths are three:

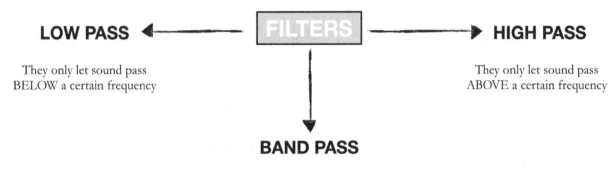

LOW PASS ◄——————— **FILTERS** ———————► **HIGH PASS**

They only let sound pass
BELOW a certain frequency

BAND PASS

Mixture of the two filters

They only let sound pass
ABOVE a certain frequency

To make the filters work, on each machine, you will find two basic controls:

Cutoff: that is the cutoff frequency, which determines the frequency on which the filter intervenes;

Resonance: determines the volume of the frequency on which the filter acts.

The third fundamental element in a synthesizer is the *LFO*.
LFO stands for Low-Frequency Oscillator and is an additional oscillator that affects certain specific sound parameters.
What will you find in an LFO?
Meanwhile, a series of waveforms, such as those I told you about at the beginning (square, sawtooth, triangular, sinusoidal ... etc.);
A rate command, i.e., oscillation speed based on the waveform chosen. In today's virtual synths, for example, you can also synchronize the oscillation tempo with the metronome of the DAW.
And finally, an intensity control, which you will find as Depth or Amplitude or Intensity, regulates the intensity of the LFO intervention, which can act on the volume or pitch (intonation).
The exciting thing is that it can be combined with filters, thus increasing the tonal possibilities.
As I showed you earlier in the Roland JD800, there can be multiple LFOs in one machine, and you can combine them, so think about how many combinations you can make!

The last element, which I believe is the most important, is the *ADSR*.
The acronym ADSR is for Attack - Decay - Sustain - Release.

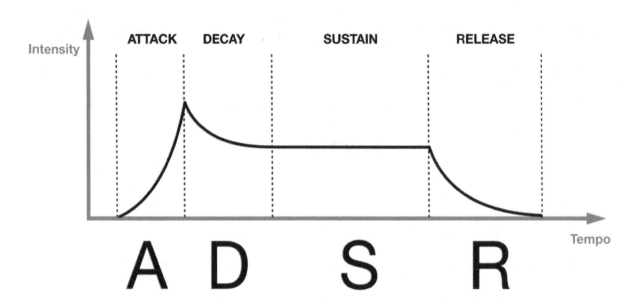

As you can see in the image above, there is precisely the representation of sound on a Cartesian axis in which we have time on the abscissa axis and intensity on the ordinates.
The graphic representation is evident.
Every sound in nature is composed of an attack, decay, sustain, and release.
However, ADSR expresses 100% the physical properties of a sound, and you can understand the type of sound simply by moving these parameters on your synth.

I'll quickly explain what the four parameters are for:

Attack: How long it takes for the sound to reach peak volume

Decay: How long it takes for the sound to decay at the second volume

Sustain: How loud is the volume of the decay per the second volume

Release: How long does it take for the sound to disappear (the classic fade out)

So, in summary, here are the four fundamental elements of the synthesizer:

Oscillator: Sound generator   **Filter:** To cut out harmonics you don't need

LFO: To create movement   **ADSR:** Affects time

CHAPTER 7

PLUCKED STRING INSTRUMENTS

In this chapter, I will talk about plucked string instruments.

As you can imagine, these instruments are very numerous. I will limit myself to illustrating the instruments most used today.

I will not talk about the ancient plucked instruments, but I will limit my field of investigation to those that today have a fundamental role, both in the symphonic and popular areas.

By plucked instruments, I mean all those instruments that require the fingers to vibrate the strings.

I will not limit myself to talking about guitars but also about new instruments, increasingly present today. They are increasingly entering the collective organological imagination.

THE GUITAR

Beyond its centuries-old history, the guitar is perhaps one of the instruments that have most influenced popular music of the last century.

In this context, as I have always done in this book, I will tell you about the guitars in use today in symphonic and popular areas. There are many guitars that we use today; rather, I would say that a specific musical sub-genre is often almost represented by a different guitar.

The twentieth century was the golden century for the diversification of popular music, and indeed, the guitar accompanied this diversification hand in hand. We all know the guitar, but it is good to deepen the discussion to learn how this instrument can be useful for our arrangements. Today, the guitars used are different, depending on their application in a piece. Since the guitar has become, over the decades, a very versatile instrument, its functions start from the simple rhythmic accompaniment to the wildest soloism. This versatility has also given rise to the solo guitarist figures, who, in the meantime, have become an integral part of the evolution of a particular language. If we think of the ancient renaissance and baroque guitars, lutes, chitarrones, tiorbas of centuries ago, it also makes us a little strange to see how far we have arrived. I will not tell you the evolutionary history of the guitar because it is very long, and we do not need it for an instrumentation course; instead, we must try to understand the morphology of the different guitars in use now. The key element of the development of the guitar was undoubtedly the pick-up. The substantial problem of the guitar has always been its low volume, and this has affected its use in various contexts up to the invention of the pick-up.

It is useless to assert it again because it is all too evident: electricity has upset everything in a positive sense. With the invention of the microphone, the guitar finally emerged from that glass bell that limited it to small or even chamber ensembles. If I think that listening to a Vivaldi guitar concert now would be very reductive from an orchestration point of view, I am amazed. Imagine a classical guitar in a symphony orchestra. It would not be heard even if the orchestra played pianissimo; these guitar concerts are almost always orchestrated with a small string section. Today an electric guitar could easily override the sound of an entire orchestra that sounds even loud. So certainly, a huge step forward in terms of dynamics has been taken.

In this paragraph, just to make a quick classification, I divide the guitars into three large groups:

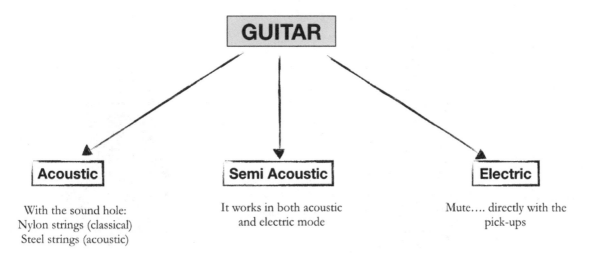

GUITAR

Acoustic

With the sound hole:
Nylon strings (classical)
Steel strings (acoustic)

Semi Acoustic

It works in both acoustic
and electric mode

Electric

Mute…. directly with the
pick-ups

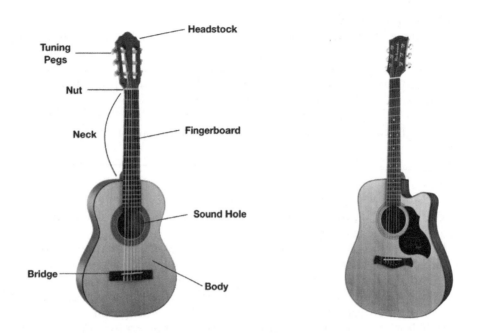

The morphology of the guitar is similar for all models. Obviously the classical and acoustic one (pictured above) differs somewhat from the sound hole and the lack of pick-ups, potentiometers, levers or any other piece of an electric guitar.

 Example n. 131 *Classical Guitar: J. Bach, Gavotte and Rondeau from Partite n. 3*

 Example n. 132 *Acoustic Guitar: Extreme, 'More than words'*

Below we have an electric guitar on the left and a semi-acoustic guitar on the right:

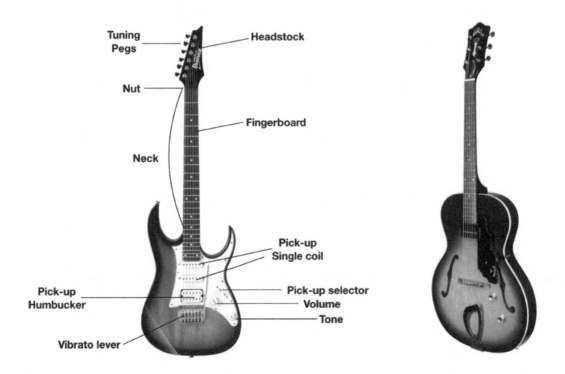

The guitar is tuned entirely by fourths except the third and second strings, which are tuned together by third:

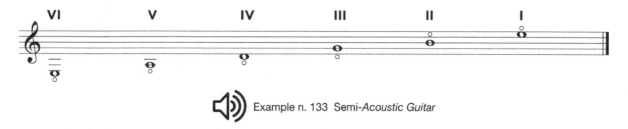

Example n. 133 Semi-*Acoustic Guitar*

It is interesting to see what the inside of a soundboard appears.
Note the arrangement of the 'braces', which help transmit vibrations throughout the case.

Today particular guitars are now part of the organological scenario.
One is the *7-String Guitar*.
This Guitar has extensive use in rock or metal, and one of the first to use it was the amazing guitarist, Steve Vai.
A lower string is added, a B, being 7-stringed.

Here is its tuning:

1

Another guitar very used, especially for rhythms, is the *12-String Guitar*.
The peculiarity of this Guitar lies in the fact that the twelve strings are not positioned in the usual way, but it is as if they were six coupled strings.

Here is its tuning:

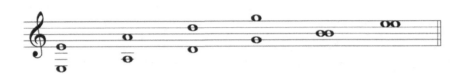

As you can see from the image, the first two strings are tuned in unison, while the remaining four are in octaves.
The resulting sound is very rich in harmonics, ideal for particular passages and rich accompaniments (think Pink Floyd's "Wish You Were Here").

The guitar is a transposing instrument. The effect is one octave lower than written and has a considerable extension, especially if with a 24-fret neck.

NORMAL GUITAR

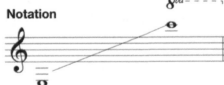

7 STRINGS GUITAR

Example n. 134   *12-Strings Acoustic Guitar: Pink Floyd, 'Wish you were here'*

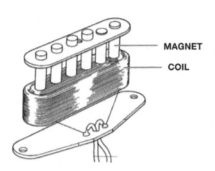

MAGNET

COIL

You will surely have understood how vital the electric guitar is today.

Therefore, I cannot fail to mention the *Pick-up* in this paragraph since it is the only instrument that allowed this remarkable dynamic transition to the guitar.

The pick-up has revolutionized the history of musical instruments, not just guitars, of course. Basically, they introduce it in the 1930s, beginning with a single coil.

It is a device that allows you to transform the string's vibrations into electrical impulses.

The most common is the magnetic pick-up, in which a skinny wire, usually made of nickel, copper, and other metals surrounds a magnet.

In practice, it is he who allows the amplification of the instrument.

Its position is also very important for capturing the different harmonics generated by the string's vibration.

The pick-up had its origin - no doubt.

A famous pick-up was that of Rickenbacker (left), a so-called 'horse shoe' and was mounted in what was probably the first electric guitar, the renowned Frying Pan (below).

The frying pan, dating back to 1931, can be the first electric guitar, despite being a steel guitar.

 Example n. 135 *Frying Pan*

Since I mentioned the Frying Pan speech to you, it is fitting to explain what a *Steel Guitar* is.

You can define it as a guitar because it has the same tuning.

The substantial and obvious difference is that it is placed horizontally.

It is played seated using the so-called 'bottleneck', which has the purpose of being swiped on the strings to obtain a glissando effect.

 Example n. 136 *Steel Guitar: Pink Floyd, 'High Hopes'*

The bottleneck is also used on guitars in different musical styles.

The steel guitar has a very recognizable sound and is widely used, for example, in Hawaiian music, even if David Gilmour, the guitarist, and frontman of Pink Floyd, has made great use of it.

Bottleneck

It is helpful to know which are the most used pick-ups now.

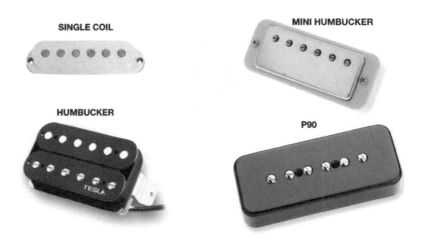

From a chronological point of view, the Single Coil (top left) is the first.

In fact, the first pick-ups were single-coil.

In 1946 Gibson introduced the P90, also single coil.

The P90s are larger than the standard single coil.

However, single-coils have always had a particular problem: they pick up the hum of the electrical network. To solve this problem, they created the double coil pick-up, the Humbucker, whose name means "hum suppressor".

The Humbucker is nothing more than a pair of single coils coupled to be magnetically and electrically opposite each other. This creates constructive and destructive interference, which cancels the hum and produces a darker sound.

The modern form of the Humbucker was, however, market in '55.

An essential element for expressing the sound of the pick-ups is certainly the selector that electric guitars have.

Usually, the selectors can have 3 or 5 positions: it depends on the number of pick-ups present and their combination.

Below I report, for example, a Fender Stratocaster.

I chose this guitar because it has five selector positions.

The selector is nothing more than the activator of a particular pick-up concerning another.

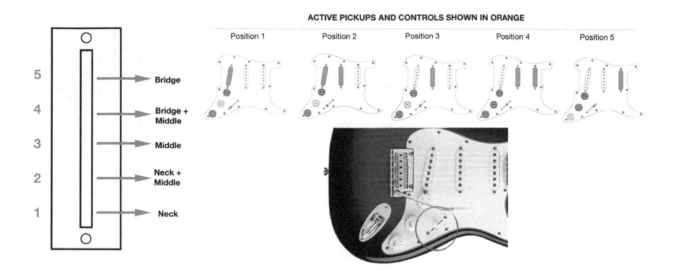

The sound that distinguishes each pick-up and the combination of multiple pick-ups is different first of all, for the type of pick-up and the proximity of a particular pick-up to the neck rather than to the bridge.

It is assumed that a bridge pick-up amplifying a much longer portion of the string will have a sharper sound, also because it is close to one of the string anchors.

By the same principle, the neck one will have a softer sound and the middle one a mixture of the two. Initially, the Stratocaster had only three positions: the bridge, center, and neck. So, no intermediate combinations.

Although Leo Fender did not like the sound of the pick-up combination, musicians preferred it, and in '77, Fender was forced to produce its guitars with a 5-position switch as standard.

Another element that appeared with the advent of the electric guitar is the *Vibrato-Tremolo lever*.
In practice, it is a type of mobile bridge operated by a lever, which acts on the tension of the strings.
There are several, and it is called 'vibrato' because it is also used to vibrate.
They are of different types and vary according to the action of the rear springs on the strings.

Below are the three most used:

SYNCHRONIZED TREMOLO   **FLOYD ROSE**   **TREMOLO SPRINGS**

The first is very present on Fender guitars; the central is called Floyd Rose and usually has a much wider action.
On the far right of the image, you can see the part behind the guitar: note how the springs allow the action of the vibrato lever.

As for the notation, the guitar always reads in the treble clef.
They used tablature in ancient times: today, this type of notation is mainly used for educational purposes as it indicates the precise fret where a note is placed.

The notation also changes according to the musical genre.
Here is an image showing you two examples related to this discourse.
With the alternative notation, you can:

Define the musical sub-genre   *Indicate a specific rhythmic sequence*

I think the use of the guitar is quite clear nowadays: it is a skilled rhythmic accompaniment instrument; it can be incredible from a solo point of view and can easily double other musical instruments.

In my opinion, one aspect on which we must dwell is that of timbre.
The reason is evident: with the advent of electronics, the tonal possibilities of this instrument have increased dramatically.
So, technology certainly plays an essential role in this discourse.
If I think that you could only hear the natural sound of a guitar until a short century ago, I shudder.
If we were to compare that sound to the infinite possibilities that exist today, a whole book would not be enough just to list the different options.
Today, for example, effects are like real science, studied and practiced very carefully.
Each guitarist manages, in some way, with the help of technology, to build their sound, which then, with a little, can become unmistakable.

Pedal Effects   Wha-Wha Pedal   E-Bow

In the image above, I show only a few examples of the possibility of timbral change.
Pedal effects (called 'little pedals' or 'pedalboards' in jargon, if they involve multiple switches) have literally invaded electric and acoustic guitar.
There is everything: Reverbs, Delays, Compressors, Phasers, Spectrum, Limiter, EQs of all kinds, Overdrives, and distortions of hundreds of types, Chorus ... etc.).
For example, there is a very famous Cry Baby at the center of the image: a pedal that creates the unmistakable Wha-Wha effect also used by Jimi Hendrix.
Finally, you can see a relatively recent "device" on the far right: the E-Bow, or Electronic Bow.
In practice, it is a magnet that approaches the string, continuously vibrating it and creating an incredible sound that resembles that of the bow of a violin or cello.
In short, there is truly an embarrassment of choice.

As for the techniques, it is good to remember the most used ones.
However, I must specify that there are many, and many of them were born evolving based on the evolution of the musical instrument itself.
I'll give you a quick list hoping that you go to deepen the sounds of each technique:

Rasgueado: A typical flamenco technique that consists of a fast tremolo (usually on the classical guitar) given by the alternation of the movement of the fingers of the right hand.

Tambora: Technique in which the strings are struck with the fingers stretched towards the bridge, giving the sound an unmistakable percussive flavor.

Hybrid Picking: Playing the strings with both the pick and the fingers. It is used in the country.

Finger Picking: Playing the strings with your fingers. Classical guitarist setting.

Legato: The guitar can have a wonderful legato, especially electric.

This technique is divided by guitarists into 'Hammer-on,' meaning ascending legato, and 'Pull off,' meaning descending legato.

Mute: It consists of stopping the strings with the palm while playing. Think of the beautiful dance rhythms of the 70s.

Bending: it is a slight ascending glide performed with the fingers of the left hand. The string is raised during the execution of a note, and, consequently, the frequency increases. You can also perform a bend up to three tones (it goes without saying that the slide is only ascending).

Alternate: that is the alternation of the plectrum down and up. It is noted as in stringed instruments.

Sweep Picking: it would be the string-tied picking, excellent for arpeggios. Literally "brushed picking". A great performer of this technique is the guitarist Frank Gambale.

Tapping: One finger of the rhythmic hand is used directly on the keyboard. Great for large ranges.
This technique can have different applications: it can add additional fingers to the four available fingers of the left hand, thus making long and faster legato and arpeggios (think Eddie Van Halen). It can be used using all eight fingers to make the guitar almost a piano-style instrument (as does the great guitarist Stanley Jordan).
An arranger/composer must keep in mind that this instrument has become really important today, especially in pop, rock, or all its derivatives.
In these areas, the sounds are truly infinite, unlike in the jazz world where, for example, with a semi-acoustic guitar, the timbre is preserved in some way original or at most with a bit of distortion.
Having said that, try to imagine Pink Floyd without the experiments made with the effects on guitars .... they would be quite another thing.
I could extend this discourse a little to the whole scope.
Knowing the timbres of an electric guitar is very important, even understanding which pick-up is best to use in specific contexts or even which guitar: a Fender Stratocaster, or a Telecaster, will always sound differently than a Gibson or an Ibanez, but of these, I could give you many examples.
The only way to understand and explore the timbres of this instrument is to listen to a lot of music, watch dedicated videos, study guitarists of all kinds (from John Scofield to Steve Vai, from Frank Gambale to John Petrucci ... etc.).
No matter the popular sub-genre they embrace, it is essential to understand how they use the instrument technically and from a tonal point of view.
So, I leave you with this advice:
"Listen to a lot of music, transcribe it and analyze the timbres. I can assure you that they can really make a difference in the timbre drafting of your arrangement!".

THE BASS

The Bass is one of the cornerstones of popular rhythm music today.

I am therefore talking about a bass "guitar" specifically. It is born like this, and it also develops in its use in this way.

As the name itself implies, this instrument has the characteristic of being part of those instruments with a low texture, practically similar to the Double Bass. Still, virtually I can say that, despite its proximity to this instrument of the strings, it has developed a lot since its invention.

Its invention dates back to the 1930s, and the first Bass marketed was a 4-string Fender about 20 years later.

In the beginning, there were hardly any examples of electric Double Bass amplified through the small amplifiers of the time, which in any case were insufficient to reproduce such low frequencies.

Leo Fender then made a real revolution; the curious thing is that the trade of this instrument came almost together with that of the Telecaster, another mainstay guitar from Fender.

So, we finally talk about a bass guitar, something that is no longer played like a double bass, vertically, but like a guitar, horizontally.

The instrument's scale also changes: the length of the strings is shorter than that of the Double Bass to allow guitarists to switch from one instrument to another easily.

The fretboard has the frets like the guitar: although this instrument derives a little from the Double Bass, the fretless version will come out later.

Suitable amplifiers are also essential; in fact, they introduced a specific amplifier with a 15-inch speaker able to render the low frequencies best.

The Fender Precision Bass will be sold starting in 1951 and will change, together with the BassMan amplifier, the modern rhythm section.

As we have seen with other instruments, the evolutions never end.

For example, from the 1950s to today, the Bass changed its strings from smooth (whose sound was almost similar to the double Bass) to rough, also excellent for the slap technique.

Now the Bass, especially the electric one, has evolved a lot, even morphologically.

5 or 6 string basses are very common, and there are even 8 or 12 string models.

In the 1970s, some bass players took a step back, giving life to fretless electric Bass, brought to the fore by a great Jaco Pastorious, bassist of Weather Report.

Then in 1974, bassist Anthony Jackson's desire to explore new horizons led to the creation of a six-string bass.

However, now the Bass, created to fill the void of sound power of the acoustic instruments used in the styles of country music, rock n 'roll, jazz, and blues, is the backbone instrument of a rhythm section, be it acoustic, electric, 4, 5 or 6 strings.

In this paragraph, we will consider three substantial types of Bass:

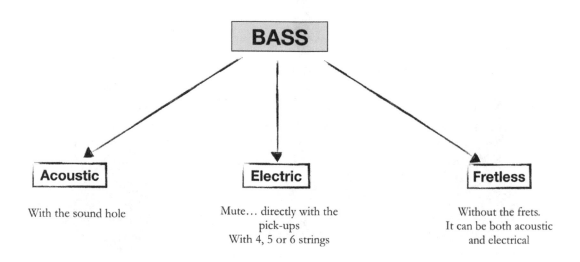

Acoustic	Electric	Fretless
With the sound hole	Mute… directly with the pick-ups With 4, 5 or 6 strings	Without the frets. It can be both acoustic and electrical

Let's examine its morphology:

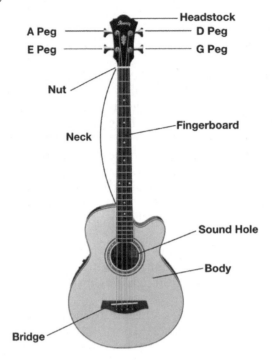

Example n. 137 *Acoustic Bass*

Above is an Acoustic Bass and, as you can see, it is a 4-string guitar with a different range, which I will show you later. The acoustic bass can be with or without frets and is used in unplugged formations to preserve that typical sound of a resonance chamber.
After the invention of Leo Fender, let's say that the instrument that has caught on most is the *Electric Bass*:

These you see are the three types of electric Bass most used today in all popular music genres: 4, 5, and 6 strings.
Since they have different numbers of strings, it is important to know their tuning.

Let's start with the *4-string Bass*.
This is its tuning:

The *5-string Bass*, on the other hand, has a lower string than the 4-string.
This low sound will be the B (here, we can also notice the difference with the 5-string double basses, which instead have C as the fifth string)

The *6-string Bass* instead, born from the explorations of Anthony Jackson, is a 5-string bass with an additional string, in this case acute, and being it tuned for fourths like all these types of instruments, the acute string will be a C:

The ones you see on the sides are fretless basses.

As I have already mentioned, the Fretless Bass is nothing more than a bass without frets, so as if it had the fingerboard of double bass, for example.

Fretless instruments have always existed somehow; just think of the strings family (they are all fretless). Besides, there are fretless guitars, too; however, I have not talked about them in the paragraph dedicated to the guitar because they are very rare.

The fretless bass, on the other hand, is very common.

Legend wants Jaco Pastorius, the legendary bassist of the Weather Report, wanted to remove the frets from his Fender Bass.

The problem and the beautiful thing at the same time of this type of bass lies precisely in the fact that, as in stringed instruments, there is no specific reference for intoning the note, since, already moving the hand a little, the sound pitch changes. On the other hand, if you think about it, Fender called his first bass with the name of "Precision" precisely because, in antagonism with the double bass, it provided, thanks to the use of the keys, to perfectly intone the note.

 Example n. 138 *Acoustic Fretless Bass*

 Example n. 139 *Electric Fretless Bass*

Over the years, some somewhat unusual basses have also been created. For example, one of these is the 8-string bass, which is nothing more than a four-string bass with coupled and octave strings (a bit like a 12-string guitar).

 Example n. 140 *8-Strings Bass*

Here are the most used bass ranges:

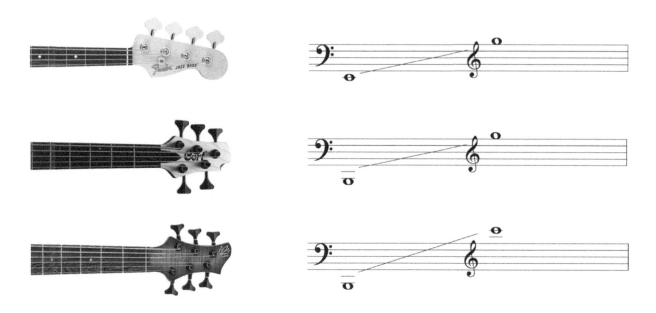

Given its range, they often use the 6-string bass polyphonically, a bit like a guitar.

Example n. 141 *Polyphonic 6-strings bass: "What a wonderful world"*

The electric bass, like the electric guitar, is amplified by the pick-ups (I told you about it in the chapter on the guitar, so I don't go into much detail).
I'm just referring to you that the two types of pick-ups used most are these two:

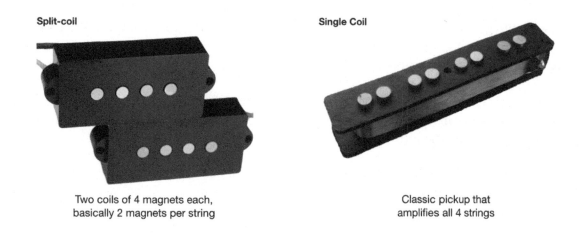

Split-coil

Two coils of 4 magnets each,
basically 2 magnets per string

Single Coil

Classic pickup that
amplifies all 4 strings

Let's explore the bass notation now.
As you can imagine, this instrument reads in the bass clef and like
the double bass is a transposing instrument: the real sounds are transposed one octave below:

Each technique that must be used must be specified in the score (slap, mute ....)

Also, in the writing of the bass parts, there are different ways of abbreviation, like the guitar:

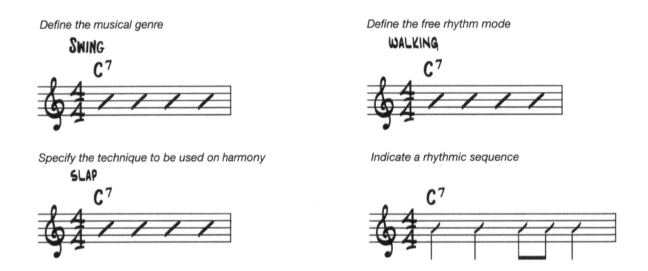

As I did with the guitar, I will show you some of the most important and most used techniques with this instrument. Knowing them is also fundamental because, paradoxically, each technique could give the piece a completely different tonal aspect.

Finger Picking: Typical bass technique in which the strings are plucked mainly using the index and middle fingers of the right hand, but if you use the guitar posture (especially with the 6-string Bass), also the others (excluding the little finger).

Legato: As in the guitar, it is divided into 'Hammer-on', which is ascending legato, and 'Pull off', which is descending legato

Bending is a slight ascending glide performed with the fingers of the left hand (exactly like in the guitar. On the Bass, it is less effective due to the greater thickness of the strings, but it is done quietly).

Alternating: The Bass is also played with the plectrum, so this technique represents the alternation of the picking down and up.

Mute: Very practical with the Bass, it consists in stopping the strings with the palm while playing, but some musicians also use the left hand to make this technique effective.

Tapping: As in the guitar, tapping is also a technique used in the Bass.
One finger of the rhythmic hand is used directly on the keyboard.
Excellent for wide intervals, several bassists extensively use it in different popular sub-genres, and some elevate it to the maximum as Stanley Jordan did with the guitar.

Harmonics: as in the double Bass, they are very effective, both natural and artificial. Jaco Pastorius was a great performer of harmonic sounds.

The last technique I want to tell you about is the **Slap**.

I keep it last not because it is less important. Indeed, it is a symbolic bass technique. It is used a lot and practically consists of striking the string with the use of the right hand with the thumb (Thumb) and pulling the strings (Slap); it is a technique widely used in specific musical genres (especially in a funk, for example).
Then, the techniques also evolve:

Marcus Miller often uses the so-called Double Thumb (It would be double thumb), in which the thumb works by stroking both down and up; Victor Wooten has made slap a cult.

I conclude this paragraph with a mention of the timbres on the Bass.
Beyond the single simple techniques that change the instrument's timbre, it is interesting to update with technologies.
As for the guitar, for the Bass, too, the dynamic ranges and effects created by different devices are many.
As you can see with the Bass, you can change the sound in real-time as you do with the electric guitar and all electronic devices.
The use of effects on the Bass has been gaining momentum lately. Still, from the origins of the effects, they are also used on the Bass (think of the delay of 'One of these days' by Pink Floyd, or the distortions of Billy Sheenan or the envelopes of pitch used by Henrik Linder, Dirty Loops bassist).

The Bass is a fantastic instrument, in all its facets, from acoustic to electric, from 4 to 6 strings and how many different techniques and timbres! from mute to slap, from effects to tapping. In short, the Bass is an instrument that every arranger must know very well, from the morphological point of view and linked to writing and notation. On the other hand, if you think about it, today, the Bass is the backbone of all popular music and, together with drums, they form the essential foundations for every sub-genre of popular music.
The advice is always to transcribe a lot of music for this instrument and, why not, be daring in the timbres .... it is always good.

OTHER PLUCKED STRING INSTRUMENTS

There are many stringed instruments, and it isn't easy to consider them all by investing in so many cultures.
However, in the collective musical imagination, I believe that four plucked strings instruments, in particular, have now become part of it: the mandolin, the banjo, sitar, and the ukulele.

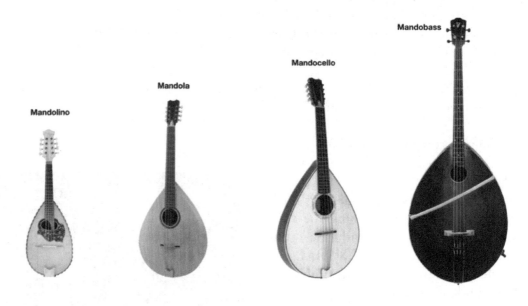

The famous Neapolitan mandolin, the one we all know a little bit, is the soprano of an entire family. In the image below, there is the classic soprano mandolin on the far left. We have the mandola, which is nothing more than a mandolin tuned precisely one octave down. The mandocello, the baritone of the family, is tuned like a cello (hence A, D, G, C). Finally, on the far right, the Mandobass, the double bass of the family, differs because it has 4 single and unmated strings. The peculiarity of these instruments lies in the soundboard, with a classic shell shape. In this paragraph, I will not tell you about the whole family, but only about the traditional soprano mandolin, the most used.

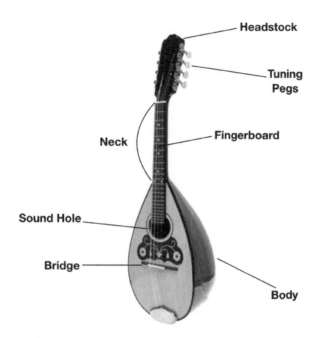

The mandolin has 8 strings (4 coupled). Here is its tuning.

In practice, it is very similar to a violin; in fact, often, many violinists delight in playing the mandolin since the fingerings are practically the same;
it is widely used in Italian folk music and has become the emblem of Neapolitan iconography.

Despite its small size, the mandolin has a considerable range:

 Example n. 142 *Mandolins Ensemble: "O Sole mio"*

This instrument is very ancient, even used by Mozart, Respighi, Stravinsky, and many other famous composers:

A. Vivaldi, Concert for 2 Mandolin RV 558

Example n. 143

Unfortunately, its volume is very low, leading it to be used exclusively alone or with small instrumental ensembles.

It is played using a pick and, since the string's vibration is too short, the tremolo is used to play particularly long notes.

The mandolin is undoubtedly a versatile instrument; however, despite being present in the classical repertoire, it has always been seen as an instrument of folkloristic tradition.
This is not a negative side; on the contrary, it somehow identifies a specific area and characterizes its sound.
If you think about it, having a tuning like that of the violin, the composers could have indulged more ... yet it wasn't like that.
Of course, Vivaldi composed concertos for mandolin and orchestra; Mozart used it in his "Don Giovanni", even Mahler in some of his symphonies.
Today the mandolin occupies a fundamental place in folk music all over the world, from Japan to Europe, to America, and often transcribed music is also performed for the whole family of this beautiful instrument.

Another essential instrument in some popular subgenres is the _Banjo_.
An Instrument of African origin is very important in North American folklore; let's think of country music.
The peculiarity of the Banjo lies in its resonance box, which is made up of a drum with skin stretched on a round case.
24 brackets stretch this skin.
It can have 4 or 5 strings, even if the 5 string is more used thanks to the short fifth string that gives it its characteristic sound.
Widely used in Dixieland, especially the 4-string one, it is played using the so-called Fingerpicks, i.e., rings with a pick at the end that are usually worn on the first three fingers of the right hand.
However, I must say that even classical composers have used the Banjo.

Below I bring you this magnificent part of the love theme of George Gershwin's Porgy and Bess:

G. Gershwin, Rhapsody in Blue

Already looking at it, the shape of the case and the composition with a skin immediately stand out. Today, the leather is synthetic, but goat or calf leather was used in ancient times.
The resonator is immediately evident, a kind of pan placed behind the box that has purely timbral and dynamic purposes (the volume is greater with the resonator).

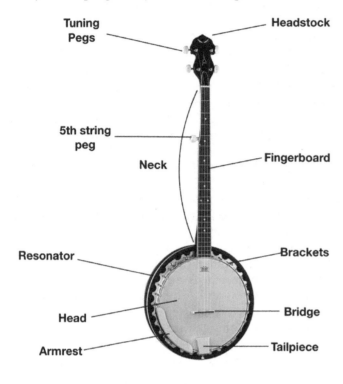

 Example n. 144   *Banjo in Dixieland*

The tuning of the banjo is very particular:

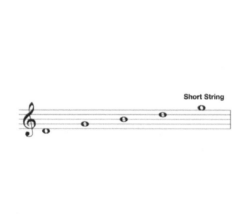

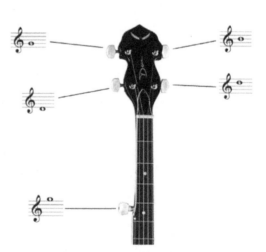

As you can see from the image, the short string, despite being positioned above, at one-third of the length of the neck, has the highest pitch of the tuning.
It allows the performance of the beautiful arpeggios that are also typical of country music.
As I have already anticipated, the 4-string banjo is widely used for Dixieland music, typical of the ancient New Orleans orchestras. In contrast, the 5-string banjo reigns in the Bluegrass genre, the most famous Country music, a folkloric genre typical of North America.

 Example n. 145   *Banjo in Bluegrass genre*

One of the 'foreign' instruments that perhaps most of all has entered the popular imagination is undoubtedly the *Sitar*.

Originally from India, it started as the favorite musical instrument of Indian classical music. The presence of great performers has somehow exported the classic use of this instrument to other musical genres of clear popular derivations. I am thinking of Ravi Shankar, for example (how can we forget the famous Shankar recording with the great American violinist Yehudi Menuhin?)

The charm of this instrument is that not all strings are plucked; some, in fact, have a sympathy vibration, giving the instrument that characteristic timbre that has distinguished Indian music for decades.

It was born as an instrument consisting of only three strings (in Indian terminology, the term 'SI' indicates the number three, and the word 'TAR' stands for 'strings').

Of course, it doesn't look like that now. Modern Sitar is composed of 7 fretted strings and 13 that vibrate by "resonance" (this can also be seen from the number of pegs in the image on the left). Seeing it at first sight, it seems all made of wood, but actually, only the handle is made of wood: the soundboard is obtained from a pumpkin.

The way of playing the Sitar is similar to the classical guitar: a particular pick of bone or wood is worn on the index finger of the right hand.

Unlike our guitar (which has a shorter neck and a larger soundboard), the Sitar has a small soundboard and a very long neck (in fact, it measures about 1.2m) made up of 20 movable bowed frets.

These convex metal keys are tied along the instrument's neck and can be moved according to the needs that a particular 'raga' requires.

It is an instrument played while seated, holding it at an angle of about 45°.

 Example n. 146 *Sitar sound*

In the following image, I will show you a tuning of the Sitar.

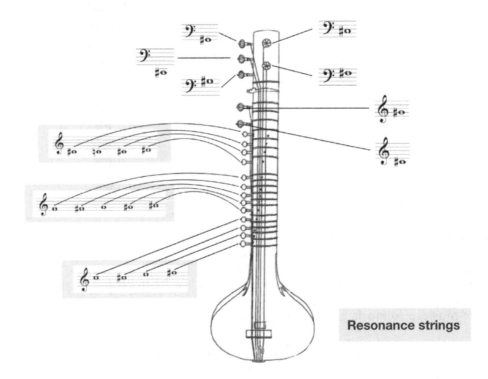

Resonance strings

I transferred the sounds by naming and marking them in Western slang (Indians call notes differently).
Note that it is a kind of C sharp tuning.
They are found in this tuning or one semitone above.
The Sitar became very famous in the 60s: the Beatles guitarist, George Harrison, studied it and used it in some songs of the famous British group.

Another very popular instrument is the _Ukulele_.
It is very important in Hawaiian music. It is an instrument dating back to the end of the 19th century and is of Portuguese origin, or instead brought to Hawaii by the Portuguese; it is still totally identified with Hawaiian folk music.
This instrument is also part of an entire family; there are different sizes. The soprano is, however, the most common one (the one you see in the image);
over the years, it has become a widely used instrument for rearranging famous songs. It has been widely used in many famous scenes of American cinema, from Marylin Monroe to Ollio of the couple Laurel and Hardy and, you can already see it by sight, it results in practice, from the morphological point of view, a small guitar with nylon strings even if the tuning has nothing to do with the guitar. It is almost always played using the fingerpicking technique, even if sometimes a pick is used, particularly for the upbeat rhythms typical of Hawaiian music.

Here is its tuning, also in this particular case because the fourth string is not the lowest of all as usually happens in guitars:

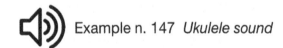 Example n. 147 *Ukulele sound*

I want to conclude this chapter with a recent musical instrument: the *Harpejji*.

Although it is not a classic 'plucked string instrument', I decided to include it in this paragraph because it is a chordophone.

Its particularity is that of being a hybrid instrument. The same name derives from the union of "Harp" and "Arpeggio".

Lately, it has had great fortune thanks to influential musicians' use on the international popular scene (Jacob Collier, Stevie Wonder ...).

It was only invented in 2007 by an American audio engineer, Tim Meeks.

It could be a hybrid between a piano and a guitar, to be more precise. It is evident since you play using the guitar technique of tapping using both hands (as the guitarist Stanley Jordan did) but holding it on a piano or the legs as if it were a keyboard.

There are 24 and 16 string models, and the largest has a considerable extension:

The operation is not very simple (on the right is an example of correspondence of the notes to the keys), and there is no consolidated technique. In fact, the great performers on this instrument have developed their own technique and fingering of the ten fingers

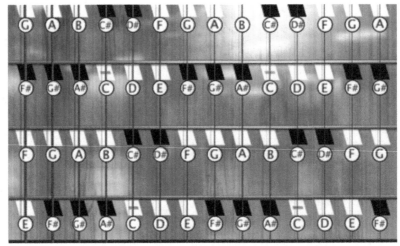

Example n. 148 *Harpejii sound*

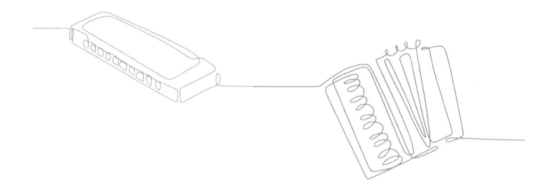

CHAPTER 8

FREE REED INSTRUMENTS

In this chapter, I will talk about free-reed instruments.

You already hear about reeds. You will have understood that they are "wind" instruments or better aerophones.

I have quoted the term wind instruments because I will talk about instruments that use air, but they are not the classic and conventional wind instruments that we all know.

Free-reed instruments are those instruments in which the air is basically not enclosed in a tube or something similar, but it is the instrument itself that generates the sound, so the air is not contained in the instrument; it is around the instrument, surrounds it.

Free aerophones are different, but in the popular area, only some are widespread: the harmonica, the accordion, and the bandoneon will be the ones I will talk about, even if I could also mention the diamonica or melodica that today prevails in all school averages for the study of music education.

THE HARMONICA

The harmonica is a widely used free-reed instrument surrounded by a long history.

The sound is produced by air over the reeds, usually made of brass.

I think we all know the harmonica; it is a very important musical instrument in blues, folk, country, and even in film music.

I have already told you about wind instruments in this book, but this has a peculiarity that no other wind instrument has: it is the only wind instrument in which notes are produced both by blowing and sucking from the same hole.

When we see it, we think it can't do much given its smallness, but, despite its size, it has an extension that starts from two and a half octaves up to over 4 octaves.

Here below is the section of a harmonica:

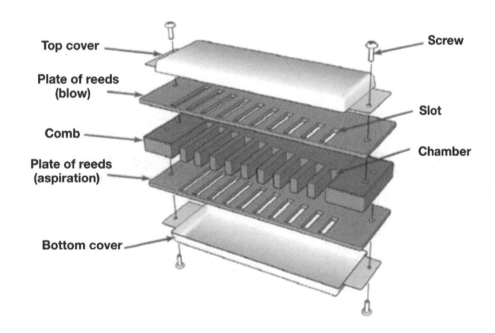

There are several types of harmonicas.

Perhaps, seeing it like this, inside one hand, one does not even notice, but there are two types of harmonicas in use: Diatonic and Chromatic.

DIATONIC

The diatonic harmonica is the most limited because you can only play the notes for which it is tuned, and it has only 10 holes.

- Blow notes: C – E – G – C – E – G – C – E – G – C
- Draw Notes: D – G – B – D – F – A – B – D – F – A (Dominant)

Due to their diatonic nature, these instruments have different tunings.

In the image below, an example of a C Major diatonic harmonica

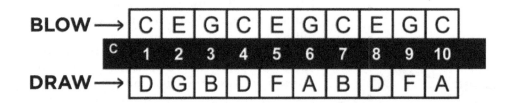

An essential technique for getting all the sounds of the scale is 'bending'.

However, there are some considerations to make:

Not all holes on the harmonica can be bent, and not all holes that you can bend allow for the same degree of bending.

Harmonica players learn to control the bending to stop at the notes within our tempered chromatic system. Often, the "bluesmen" used to exaggerate the bending. Looking at the image above, if the musician blows into hole 1, he will get a C, draw a D. When he bends, he lowers the tone of the draw 1 reed very close, but not equal to the whole reed.

In the image below the notes that are obtained blowing and drawing with bend.

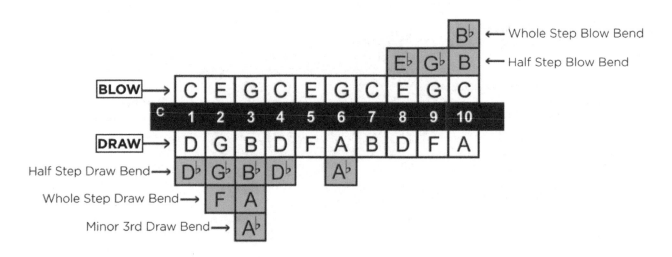

308

CHROMATIC

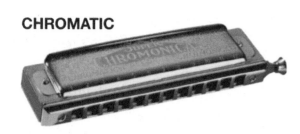

Chromatic harmonicas have four notes per hole, and a side button. When the button is not pressed, each hole sounds one diatonic note when blowing and one when drawing. When the button is pressed, the notes become sharp.

The chromatic harmonica is, inevitably, more complete since it allows to play all 12 chromatic notes.

This is allowed by the key on the right, called register, which increases the pitch by a semitone.

In both, bending can be used.

This instrument is important in popular music.

It is often identified with the blues as early bluesmen only used this instrument to accompany their lyrics.

Then, let's not talk about how much it has been used in cinema. Let's think of all Sergio Leone's westerns set to music by Ennio Morricone, or, if you do more careful research, you realize that it is also used a lot in pop.

I am thinking of many Sting songs, of the use that Stevie Wonder makes of them.

 Example n. 149 *Harmonica: Sonny Boy blues solo*

THE ACCORDION

As you may have noticed, I have not spoken in the book, and in any case, I will not speak of the classical organ (which is a free-reed instrument).
The motivation is linked to the fact that the organ is an instrument that is not really used in the popular area; it is certainly more so in the symphonic world (Strauss himself inserts it already at the beginning of "Also Sprach Zarathustra").
As we can easily imagine, it is more of an 'ecclesiastical' instrument.
The only type of organ I have considered in the book is the Hammond, whose use in many popular subgenres is abundant; indeed, I would even say characteristic.
I am mentioning a speech on the organ because the accordion, like the bandoneon, is a 'bellows' instrument and functions very similarly to the organ.
I also want to talk about this instrument for another fundamental reason:
over the decades, it has become a true icon of some musical genres.
This instrument's technical knowledge is undoubtedly of great help for the arranger/composer.
In the last 50 years, even great composers of the "cultured" repertoire have used the accordion (Sciarrino or Berio).
The charm of these instruments - accordion and bandoneon - comes mainly from their ability to create many different sounds, with rapid variations in timbre, pitch (including bending), registers, note repetitions, dynamics, chords, and more.
In my experience, in this work, it has happened many times to write both for one and the other and, as you can well imagine, in many contexts, they are very popular musical instruments both for their typically folkloric spirit and because of the often timbre it also ties well with the orchestra and in specific typically popular contexts.

There are two types of accordions, and they differ in practice from the keyboard:

PIANO KEYBOARD

BUTTON KEYBOARD

One with the keyboard equal to that of a piano and the other with a button keyboard.
The accordion with Piano keyboard is used a lot, for example, in the amateur or folkloristic area.
The classical accordionist, most of the time, uses button one.
This is because using the button keyboard imposes a similar behavior on the instrumentalist for both hands, while this does not happen with the Piano keyboard.

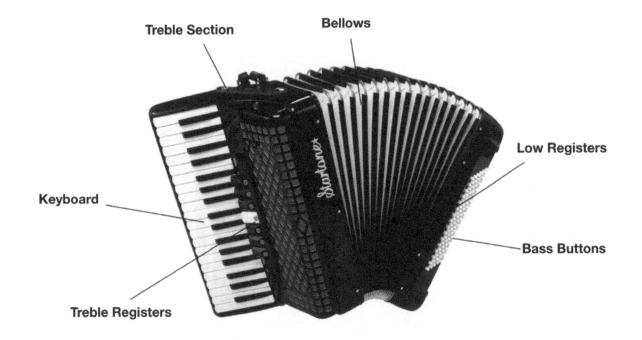

Treble Section

Bellows

Keyboard

Low Registers

Bass Buttons

Treble Registers

The sound of the accordion is produced by the air being pushed and pulled through free metal reeds.

There are two reeds per note in each register, one for the opening bellows and one for the closing bellows.

Everything is controlled by the keyboards and fingers that play the part of the tongue in wind instruments.

So, you can control in great detail every parameter of the sound, what commonly in synthesizers is called ASDR (attack, sustain, decay and release).

In practice, the accordion is a stereophonic instrument: the sound comes from two distinct sources, but having no resonance chamber, it has a very dry sound.

 Example n. 150 *Accordion: extract from "Summer" by A. Vivaldi*

In the image below the inside of the instrument:

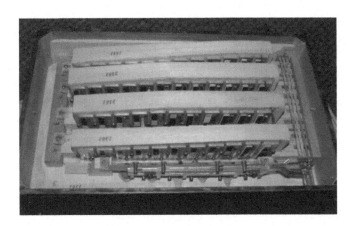

Let's analyze the button accordion better:

Right Hand   Left Hand

Here's what the right-hand button keyboard looks like:

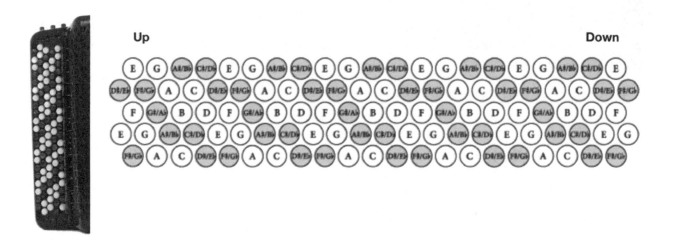

In practice, there are 105 buttons placed in 5 rows, and this is its range:

The first three rows are the fundamental ones... the last two are repeated and are used to make fingering easier.

Two main systems regulate the order of the accordion button keyboards:

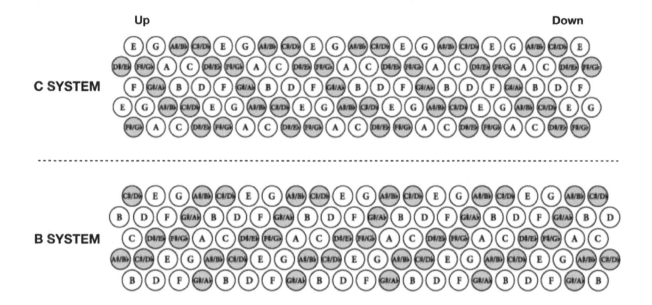

The button accordion is widely used for both the cultured and jazz repertoire (think of the great accordionist Richard Galliano).

One of the peculiarities of the accordion is precisely given by the different timbres, obtained using different registers, a bit like the organ.
Like the organ, it has the possibility of different sounds and combinations of registers.
The registers of the right hand are in all 15 and are obtained from their combination.
They are indicated with a circle with two horizontal lines and written above the staff.

All 15 registers are combinations of these 4 registers:

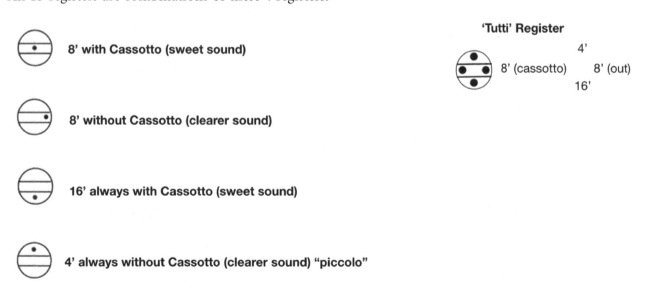

The lowest register is 16 feet, which sounds an octave below the note pressed and requires the Cassotto.
The word 'Cassotto' indicates that the reeds under consideration are in a wooden or metal box that makes the sound softer.

The left hand is the one that controls the button keyboard of the bass; it is the one tied to a strap and pulls the bellows.
The left button panel has 120 buttons distributed in 6 rows, and this is its extension:

Example n. 151 *Richard Galliano (accordion) - Ron Carter (Double Bass)*

The left-hand bass systems are two:

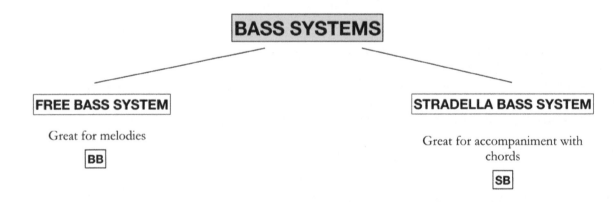

The first system is the so-called Free Bass System.

This system is the only one that allows you to play the classical repertoire on the accordion since you can play low and high melodies almost as you do with your right hand.
It has a pattern exactly like the right-hand buttons on the chromatic accordion.
Here too, there are two main systems:

C SYSTEM

The low notes are at the top of
the keyboard

B SYSTEM

Contrary to the C System: the
low notes are in the lower part
of the keyboard

The other bass system is the so-called *Stradella System*.

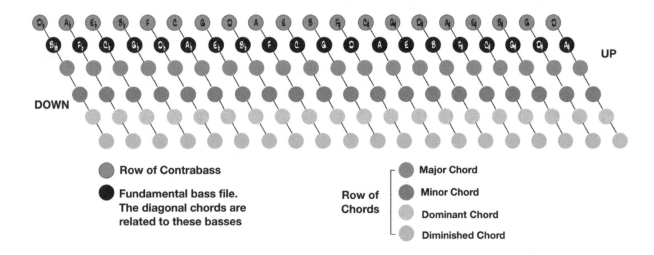

In the first two rows above, we find the double bass row (in gray), i.e., basses whose resulting sound is one octave lower than those written, then the row of fundamental basses (in black).
Starting from the third row from the top, in order, by pressing a key, you get a chord concerning the root on the black line.
This system is widely used in folk music; let's consider the classic "Zum-pà-pà."
One of the main elements, and the instrument's heart, is the Bellow.
The Bellow is an extensible element in cardboard and silk that joins the right and left body of the accordion. In practice, the lung of the instrument pulls and pushes the air through the reeds to produce sound.
There is only one Bellow for both hands, so the airflow is the same for both the right and left hands.
The accordion has a wide dynamic range from nothing to fortissimo, but it is essential to keep in mind that the air pressure produced by the bellows affects both manuals with the same power.

As you can imagine, you can pull the bellows in two directions indicated in this way (left image).
We have therefore seen that the bellows are the instrument's beating heart. The amount of air needed can vary based on:
- Volume
- Number of notes to play
- Register

The bellows allow specific techniques that are widely used:

Shake: given by the re-articulation of the bellows: a sort of tremolo

Ricochet: Similar to the ricochet in strings, it is obtained by bouncing the left part of the instrument by opening and closing the bellows very little;

Vibrato: It can be obtained by moving the knee or the left hand on the bass side;

Glissando: Slowly and partially raising the key and increasing the pressure of the bellows;

As for the notation, the Accordion is written as the Piano: 2 staves, where the upper staff indicates the right hand and the lower one the left hand:

Pay attention to the bass notation:

BB For free basses

SB For Stradella Basses (Chords):
M —->Major
m —-> minor
7 —-> dominant
d —-> diminished

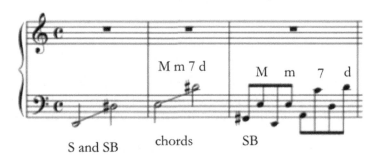

THE BANDONEON

The bandoneon, like the accordion, is a characteristic instrument of some musical genres. In recent decades it has taken hold in particular thanks to the Tango and the impressive figure of Astor Piazzolla.

The bandoneon is an instrument similar to the accordion in many respects, smaller in size, but with differences that make it one of a kind.

I believe that the technical knowledge of all these free reed instruments is a great help for the arranger/composer because, often, the Tango reigns in many concert programs and is an essential element of popular music not only in Argentina but by now worldwide.

Although this instrument is of German origin (it derives from the German concertina), it found its fortune thanks to German and Italian immigrants in South America.

Its incredible resemblance to the accordion can be seen by first sight:

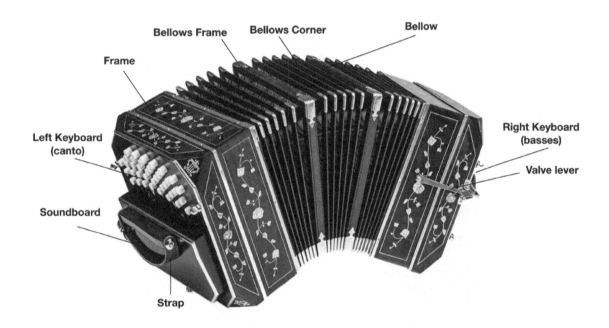

The reeds give the secret of the bandoneon's voice:

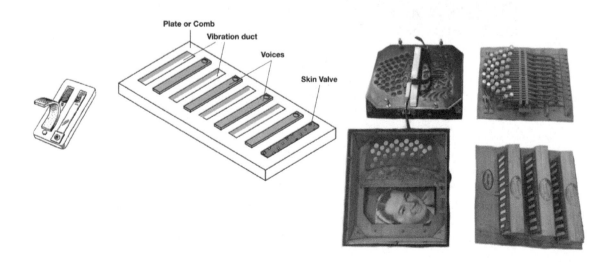

The beating heart of the instrument is the Bellow, the fulcrum of sound production.
The bandoneon's Bellow is much longer than the accordion; it can even reach a meter in length.

Each button is connected to a lever that activates a small lever. Thanks to the opening and closing of the bellows, it allows the passage of air by pressing the button.
The bellow's compression and distension movements are controlled by a lever located on the right side of the instrument: the narrower and smaller the reeds, the sharper the sound.

Although bandoneon and accordion are very similar, they have several differences:

-   With the bandoneon, you cannot play chords by pressing a single button;

-   The bandoneon can also be played standing up;

-   He embraces trying to leave the thumb of his right hand free to operate the opening and closing lever of the bellows;

-   The bandoneon has buttons on both ends;

-   The accordion is unisonoric (same note by pressing and widening the bellows), the bandoneon is bisonoric (different notes by opening and closing the bellows)

-   I repeat that the accordion bellows are shorter than that of the bandoneon, and there are no registers in the bandoneon.

Let's see how the two-button panels of the bandoneon look like (next page):

33 buttons
for the low register

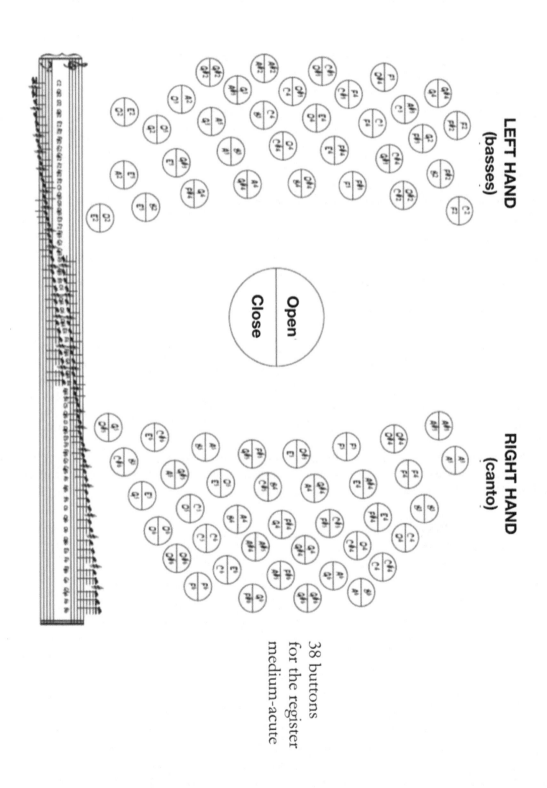

LEFT HAND
(basses)

Open

Close

RIGHT HAND
(canto)

38 buttons
for the register
medium-acute

In the image, in the center, you see this large circle divided in two that indicates which sounds are taken with the bellows open and with the bellows closed (being a bisonoric instrument).
As you can see from the image, all buttons have two distinct notes.
In the staff under the buttons, the range of the instrument is highlighted, which is very wide (up to 5 octaves).
The image shows that the two buttons are very different; on the right, we have 38 buttons for the medium-high register, and on the left, 33 for the low register.
The two-button panels differ not only in their shape but also in their stamp.
In fact, the right button panel is more ringing than the left, muffled and velvety.
This is a good thing because it gives the instrument a great dynamic and tonal variety.

In the image below, you can see the correct extension of the bandoneon divided by hands:

Even the writing of the bandoneon is practically similar to the piano, using two staves: the upper one for the right hand and the lower one for the left.

However, I still want to clarify that the sound of the two parts of the bandoneon is different:
The left hand produces a warm, cello-like sound, while the right hand has a more natural tone, almost like a trumpet. As a whole, a bandoneon is basically like a combination of two different instruments.
It is interesting to note one thing from the range: in the left hand, the range is almost identical to the combination of the human male vocal extensions (from bass to tenor), while the right part starts from the lowest part of the range of a female alto, and it gets to the highest notes of a soprano, so it's like having all four voices together.
During the golden era of Tango, in the 30s and 50s of the last century, there were real orchestras full of bandoneons, usually with piano, double bass, and a small section of strings and, in this context, the instrument a free-reed practically ruled over everyone.

Example n. 152 *Adios Nonino - Astor Piazzolla (Bandoneon)*

CHAPTER 9

THE VOICE

The voice is by its very nature the oldest instrument ever: it was born and evolved with man.

In all its timbral facets (from percussion to vocal emission), the human body is absolutely the oldest instrument.

Contrary to what many may think, the voice is a very complex musical instrument, perhaps one of the most difficult, and requires considerable study to control it.

Of course, the anatomy and propensity of each singer make a bit of a difference, but this does not mean that you cannot use this instrument as if it were a violin or any other musical instrument.

The voice has accompanied the entire history of music.

Now, I don't want to go back in time and take a lesson in the history of music, it's not the right place, but I want to make you reflect on how much, for example, the sacred and profane monody accompanied the entire medieval period.

Let's consider the etymology of the term itself. Monody, Mònos - Ode, that is, single song, we realize that singing has always been a fundamental element for all human culture.

We think of religious songs, medieval troubadours, troubadours and minnesänger, up to polyphony, Monteverdi's madrigals, Orlando di Lasso's compositions, the great sacred works of classicism (think of Mozart's beautiful Requiem), or, by way of Requiem, to that of Giuseppe Verdi ... or all the melodrama ... a period in which the role of the singer had now become primary and indispensable.

Up to the present day, the Spirituals, the first nostalgic blues, the gospel... etc.

In short, the voices are fundamental in the musical experience of each of us.

I speak in the plural because there are different types of items, and they are categorized according to gender:

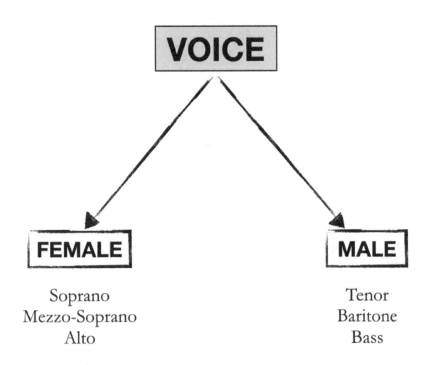

This type of classification is convenient.

It happens because it is impossible to enclose all the paradigms that an entry has in a summary list, so we limit ourselves to considering only the extension, which, of course, changes according to the gender of the singer.

Given that different extensions are highlighted within each gender sphere, the items have been categorized into three groups for each gender.

Starting from the high to the low, the female voices are represented by the Soprano, Mezzo-Soprano, and Alto, and the male voices by the Tenor, Baritone, and Bass.

As I told you, these items are divided based on acute or severe extension.

Referring to this concept, each voice was formerly indicated using a different musical key to indicate the right pitch and avoid the numerous additional cuts.

We all know that there are seven musical keys.

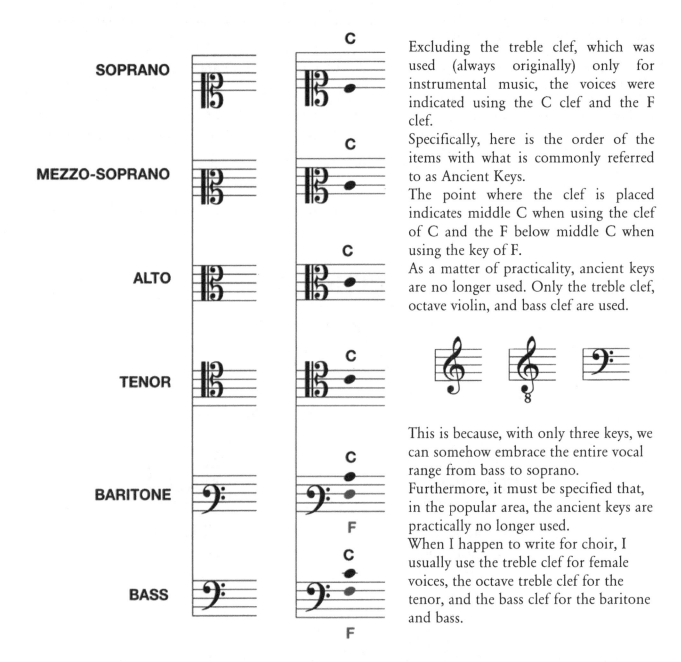

Excluding the treble clef, which was used (always originally) only for instrumental music, the voices were indicated using the C clef and the F clef.

Specifically, here is the order of the items with what is commonly referred to as Ancient Keys.

The point where the clef is placed indicates middle C when using the clef of C and the F below middle C when using the key of F.

As a matter of practicality, ancient keys are no longer used. Only the treble clef, octave violin, and bass clef are used.

This is because, with only three keys, we can somehow embrace the entire vocal range from bass to soprano.

Furthermore, it must be specified that, in the popular area, the ancient keys are practically no longer used.

When I happen to write for choir, I usually use the treble clef for female voices, the octave treble clef for the tenor, and the bass clef for the baritone and bass.

Before seeing how the various voices are used, it is helpful to understand their true extent. This helps us to understand how to write and how to handle them.

Let's start with the female voices:

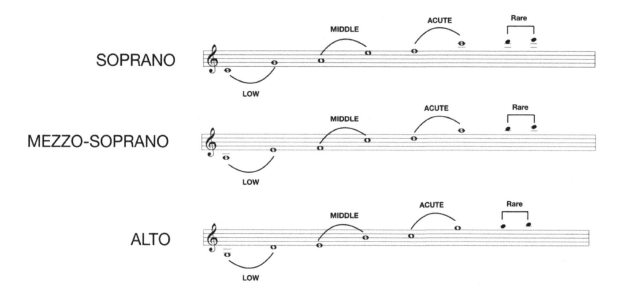

Instead, the male ones have this range:

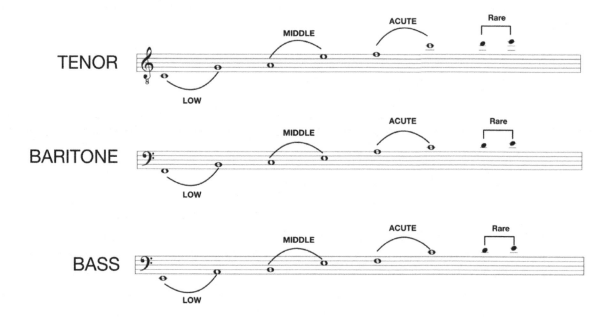

The ranges shown here are those that generally cover every single item. However, I can say that they are indicative since singers go beyond this range, both in the low and high registers.

To simplify, I usually use this range when writing for a choir, be it pop, gospel, or classical.

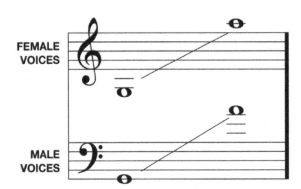

I also try to keep myself quite comfortable, especially in the male voices: a bass descends beyond the G indicated above.
However, if you are dealing with voices, for example, in a choir, following this range, you are not mistaken.

Knowing the timbres of the voice is very important
Each voice can output different tones depending on the used register.
It is because the organs and parts of the body used to sing are not tied exclusively to the vocal cords or diaphragm (if we place a microphone close to the vocal cords, we amplify a sound similar to that of a mosquito).
When we sing, there are so many parts that vibrate and allow the incredible sound of our voice to come out that way.

Voice production is a process consisting of three main stages:

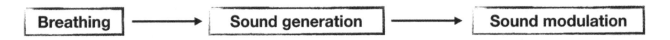

Now, it is obvious that these three elements have to coexist somehow.
This book is not technical about singing, also because I would not be able to give you precise indications: singing is a serious matter and must be studied in depth in all its facets.
So, here, when I speak of vocal emission, I am not referring to how a sound is emitted. Still, I would like to list some useful terminologies for the arranger to understand the types of sound that we can obtain - this also for a correct dialogue with the singers.

First of all, as I showed you a little while ago, the vocal range (of any type, female or male) is about one-tenth.
As I have already explained to you, there is a clear difference related to sex in the adult voice. The female voice sounds one octave higher than the male one.
There is a continuous variability in the range and timbre within each voice.

Precisely about the timbre, we could open an infinite chapter.

Paradoxically, the subdivision of the voices into the six that I listed above is not enough to define all the parameters also related to the timbre; composers, including melodrama, can only highlight certain aspects that determine the three main textures for each gender.

Consequently, different subclasses are created and developed for each voice: The Deep Bass, Basso Nobile, Bass-Baritone, Verdian Baritone, Cantabile Baritone, Dramatic Tenor, Lyric Tenor, Light Tenor, Mezzo-alto, Low Mezzo-soprano, Dramatic Soprano, Lyric, and light ...... in short, a flood of different types of singing.

These things are right to know because, although in the popular area, in most cases, the voice is not set in the 'lyrical' way, they are used to understand the timbres of the voices.

In this regard, we can introduce the discussion on vocal registers.

A vocal register is nothing more than a specific area within the range of a voice .... a sort of "sub-range."

Making a similarity with a computer, we could define the range as the main folder and the registry as a subfolder.

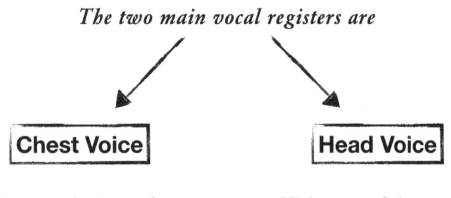

Attention! I want to clarify that the registers are commonly called this way.

Today in the study of vocality, we talk more about Laryngeal Mechanisms used based on their timbre.

In short, we all have a different tone, which is a very important factor.

However, these two registers are the ones that are best recognized from the beginning.

The chest voice covers the low and central notes of the range up to a point where the so-called passage takes place, that is, a point where the chest voice is no longer able to rise.

The chest register is immediately recognizable because it represents the voice with which we speak in practice.

On the other hand, the head voice covers the high notes of the range beyond the passage I told you a little while ago.

While the head vocal is handy for picking up high notes, it is very different.

This diversity is a problem for singers.

The problem is that considering the two fundamental registers, one can still hear the gap between one register and the other. Consequently, it is impossible to have fluidity in the entire register.

In this regard, another register comes into play that summarily solves this problem: the so-called Mixed Register or Mixed Voice, which helps to solve this break given by the passage.

The vocal break is still widely used today in the popular area (deliberately): Cristina Aguilera, Mariah Carey use it a lot - let's say it is also a bit fashionable to create these contrasting effects.

The mixed voice masks the passage quite well, giving uniformity to the voice. Think of the voices of Beyoncè, Ariana Grande, Celine Dion, or Stevie Wonder, Micheal Bolton.

This register is quite difficult to obtain because it must be developed. It is not natural; therefore, it requires a good knowledge of the two main registers and breathing and vocal emission techniques.

Two other registers are poles apart (considering frequency):

Vocal Fry	**Whistle**
In the extremely low part, under the chest voice	In the extremely high part, above the head voice

These two registers are used little, and not everyone can perform them.

For example, the vocal fry is often found in a cappella groups, think of Pentatonix or Voctave, very famous groups of voices only, or it is widely used in Metal. When I think of Whistle, Mariah Carey immediately comes to mind, who uses it a lot.

One last register that I mention you will surely have already heard of it. I'm talking about the Falsetto, which falls into the head register.

I want to specify the discourse on Laryngeal Mechanisms to be aware of how vocal technique and didactics are developing.

Let's say that in vocal practice, we speak of 4 mechanisms:

MO - M1 → M2 - M3

PASSAGE
Belting (M1)
Mixed Voice (M2)

Low Vocal Fry — Full Voice Chest Voice — Head Voice Falsetto — Whistle Scream Hiss

These are the four mechanisms as technically they are used today.

The M0 mechanism is the one that embraces the Vocal Fry, the lowest part.
The M1 mechanism is what concerns the full voice and the chest voice.
Then, as I explained to you before, we have the register passage, which includes the Belting, when a singer brings his voice from the chest beyond the break and consequently the Mixed Voice which, as I have already explained to you, somehow avoids the break.
The M2 mechanism concerns the falsetto and the lead voice, while the M3 the Whistle, the Scream, and the Hiss.

Knowing how to use the voice for an arranger is very important.
The reason is that each of its articulations produces a different sound.

For example, let's think of vowels: there are only 5, but what they render within an arrangement (a choir, for example) is so diversified that it somehow changes the timbre.

Harmonizing a choir using an "uhh" is different from using an "ahh".

Not to mention the consonants: the sound they produce is very different.

A nasal consonant will sound completely different from an occlusive one: in practice, using a 'P' changes a lot compared to an 'N'.

The voice is a fantastic instrument and should be treated as such.

The popular sub-genre that you arrange is very important for writing well for vocals.

Understanding its timbral functioning is essential for the arranger because it leads him to work more homogeneous and orderly.

For example, the Gospel has specific timbres, and often the tenors rise a lot in the range to allow a more transparent sound of particular notes.

A pop choir, which is usually composed of a maximum of 4 or 5 people, should generally be treated following the progress of the voices of the chord itself.

So be careful when writing for a choir and remember that establishing the correct key of a piece you have to arrange depends exclusively on who has to sing it, so your work with singers must be very close.

Only in this way will you be able to obtain satisfactory results.

CHAPTER 10

ETHNIC INSTRUMENTS

It is impossible to list all the ethnic instruments.

A book of thousands and thousands of pages would not be enough.

I have decided to consider some ethnic instruments that are now an integral part of world culture.

Even the definition of ethnic might seem unsuitable. Still, it is the most correct in the musical area since the instruments I will talk about are precise indicators of a specific ethnicity or a particular group of ethnic groups.

I have played many of these instruments that I will talk about in this chapter, and I have also had a good fortune, often working in the Middle East, to write songs and arrangements using them.

I will not make a classification of these instruments. I will try to adapt to the standard classification of musical instruments. Furthermore, the various ethnic groups around the world have embraced all types of possible classification of each musical instrument so that the work would be practically useless.

So, let's stick to the classification I made in the book's first chapter.

In this chapter, I will not discuss European instruments since I have kept in previous chapters to explain the instruments in use today in Europe. Still, I will embrace all the most important instruments in the world by dividing them by geographical area:

o   Ethnic instruments from the Americas
o   Ethnic instruments from Africa
o   Ethnic instruments from the Middle East
o   Ethnic instruments from the Far East

I have deliberately divided all these musical instruments because the cultures I will talk about in this chapter are very ancient. So, each of them has had a development in its own right and developed different types of musical instruments that still exist today.

Classifying them by separating the cultures from which they come would be, in my opinion, a mistake since every musical instrument I will tell you about in this chapter is firmly rooted in the culture in which it was born and developed.

ETHNIC INSTRUMENTS FROM THE AMERICAS

American culture, as we know, is very varied, not only for the size of the continent but also for a reason expressly linked to colonization.

North America and Canada have particularly young traditions; in fact, most of the instruments I will tell you about in this paragraph come from the central and southern areas of the American continent.

The first instrument I speak of is the *Rainstick*.

It is also called the Rain Pole and was born in Chile, more precisely in the big Atacama Desert, in South America.

It is a shaking idiophone, although I must specify that its shaking is not rhythmic but effective.

It is a long wooden tube, usually a trunk of a typical cactus of the area dried and closed at both ends, which has the thorns of the cactus itself and small stones inside that, bumping together, produce the classic sound of Rain.

It was born as a propitiatory instrument for rain. It is also used in Africa and Australia and can be of different sizes, even very large.

 Example n. 153 *RainStick*

The *Vibraslap* is another idiophone I didn't tell you about in the percussion chapter.

It is not an ethnic instrument, and they don't widely use it. Still, it is limited to the South American area, and we find it in practically all the banks of percussion sounds of today's synthesizers, so in my opinion, it should be mentioned.

It is an instrument that has indirect percussion.

It is formed by a kind of metal U with two wooden parts at the ends, a ball and a kind of woodblock with a metal tooth mechanism. It is played by holding it in hand and hitting the wooden ball, or a stick can also hit it; in fact, some drummers use it for effects by mounting it on their instrument.

With the hit, the wooden box vibrates, and the mechanism starts working.

Think, it was born from an ancient African instrument obtained from the jaw of a donkey. (To the right)

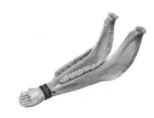

 Example n. 154 *Vibraslap*

In South America, many wind instruments are used.

In this paragraph, I will tell you about two fundamental and widespread wind instruments: the Quena and the Pan Flute.

The *Quena* is a typical instrument of the Andes, made of bamboo cane.
It has a lovely sound and different sizes: they vary both in length and diameter.
The length of the Quena is usually around half a meter, although it varies depending on the model. Its tube is hollow, with a diameter of about two centimeters, which blows through a mouthpiece that can have a V or U shape. Depending on the length and other characteristics, different types of Quena can offer different sounds.
The most used are the Quenilla, the Quena en Sol, the Quena en La, the Quenacho en Re, the Quenacho en Do, the Mamaquena en Sol and has an extension of about three octaves.
It is generally a seven-hole instrument plus a rear thumb hole.

 Example n. 155 *Quena*

 The *Pan Flute* is also of Andean origin.
Despite its practically prehistoric origins, it is a well-known instrument today and is also used in the popular field, especially in applied music.
It is formed by a set of reeds of different sizes placed in a row in which the musician blows. Pan flutes vary in size: those with a small number of pipes and others with more pipes and a bigger range.
Often the rows of reeds are more than one placed on top of the other.
Therefore, its extent varies accordingly. Leaving a small slit open on his lips while holding the instrument, the player blows into each reed to produce the sound.
It is a widely used instrument in the Andes area.

 Example n. 156 *Pan Flute*

Stringed instruments are also very popular in the Americas.
The first that I will illustrate to you is the *Charango*.
The Charango is a very common guitar in South America of obvious Spanish origin (remember that the Spaniards colonized much of South America).
Its South American origins are still Bolivian, but it is widespread throughout the Andean region (Perù, Chile, Ecuador, and Argentina).
It is a coupled 5-string instrument (like a 12-string guitar), therefore 10-stringed, and is used with the rasqueado technique.
It has a very clear sound, also given by its tuning.
In fact, like the Ukulele, it does not have a tuning that starts from the highest note to the lowest one.
Here is its tuning:

 Example n. 157 *Charango*

Another very famous type of guitar from Mexico on down is the *Guitarròn*.

As you can see from the image, which does not perform much, it is a guitar of enormous dimensions.
There are many different types of guitarròn in South America.
It is widespread in Mexico, but the Bolivian, Uruguayan, and Colombian versions are also there.
However, all are similar except the Chilean guitarròn, which is different.

It has a very low sound; some think that the bass guitar also derives a little from this instrument.
The Mexican version is the bass of the typical folk group, the so-called Mariachi.

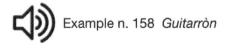 Example n. 158 *Guitarròn*

It has 6 strings and this is its tuning:

The real sound is a low octave, like the double bass.
The peculiarity that immediately stands out when you see this instrument's tuning is that the first and last strings are placed at an octave distance. From an executive point of view, this is also an essential element: the guitarròn player often octaves the bass by also using barrè.

This guitar on the right is the *Chilean Guitarròn.*
As I mentioned before, it is a very different instrument from the classic Mexican guitarròn, even in size: it is smaller.

Its peculiarity lies in the number of strings, no less than 25 arranged in a very particular way, plus four drones that are in tune with keys attached to the soundboard.

It is an instrument widely used in traditional Chilean music and has a very particular tuning:

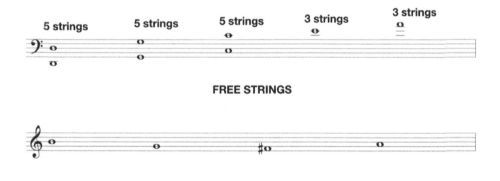

The highest strings are arranged three at a time in unison. On the other hand, the last three strings are five in number, resulting in an octave.
As you can see, the free strings are not arranged in order of height.

Example n. 159 *Chilean Guitarròn*

Let's now go to the discovery of a very particular percussion instrument: the *Washboard*.
It is a typical instrument of North America.
Originally from New Orleans, they widely used it in Dixieland and Zydeco (traditional Louisiana)

As you can see from the image, it is a friction percussion instrument that takes the features of an ancient table for washing clothes, hence the name washboard.
If necessary, especially for parades, it can also be worn and played with thimbles, usually made of metal or aluminum.

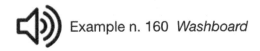 Example n. 160 *Washboard*

The last instrument I am talking about in this paragraph is the *Berimbau*.
Despite being of African origin, it is widely used in Brazil, especially to accompany Capoeira, a typical martial art.
It is composed of an arch about one and a half meters long derived from a branch of "berimba" combined with a dried pumpkin that acts as a soundboard.
It is played by striking the string with a wooden stick and is often combined with a caxixi.
A movable bridge, similar to a coin, called 'Dobrao', is used to vary the string's width, therefore, the intonation.
There are three types of Berimbau: "Viola", "Medium" and finally "Gunga", the largest and also considered a sacred instrument.

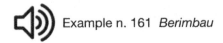 Example n. 161 *Berimbau*

ETHNIC INSTRUMENTS FROM AFRICA

The African continent is huge and highly heterogeneous for this reason.

The cultures, peoples, traditions that affect this continent are innumerable and very different.

This diversity is also clearly expressed by musical instruments.

Obviously, the musical instrument has always been linked to the culture in which it was born and developed. African music is probably the most extensive and most varied in the world.

In this context, I speak of 'traditional African music', therefore to that specific section that involves ancient and modern populations but is closely linked to the territory.

The rituality to which the music of this continent is linked should be specified here.

It is associated with solemn dances and ceremonies that define significant moments in the personal life of individuals and communities, such as birth, transition to adulthood, marriage, and funeral.

Music and dance are significant social and religious values in sub-Saharan Africa.

Each ethnic group has its musical tradition just as it has its literary tradition and its own set of rules and beliefs; each social group has a reference musical repertoire and subgenres appropriate to specific daily activities.

African music is characterized by the use of specific instruments, which have become famous worldwide. It is produced with natural materials such as pumpkins, horns, skins, and shells; many artificial materials are currently in use, mostly aluminum or metal such as cans, strings, bottle caps, and bins.

Modern African music results from the encounter between traditional African music and Western music. It has some fundamental characteristics that place it in continuity with traditional African music and at the same time distinguish it from the latter.

Africa is so large that its cultures can be divided into three large areas:

- o North Africa, which has experienced a solid Islamic influence;
- o Southern Africa, which has suffered a strong Western influence, due to numerous and vast settlements of settlers and the presence of multiple Christian churches of European origin;
- o Central or sub-Saharan Africa is the area least influenced by musical styles from outside and where traditional African music is still found, sometimes in its pure state.

Now, I will not follow the subdivisions of the geographical areas: my intent is, dear reader, to make you better know the musical instruments that affect the whole African continent.

By force of circumstances, I will not list all the instruments present in these cultures, but I will limit myself to listing the most used and most 'requested' by both the original and Western traditions.

The first instrument I am talking about is young and goes beyond the ancient African traditions: the *Vuvuzela*.

As you can easily guess, this instrument does not have an extremely musical value. It is rarely used in arrangements but has now entered the world scenario thanks to the South African World Cup in 2010.

It is made of plastic: its invention dates back to the 60s of the last century.

It produces a powerful and penetrating sound, pitched around B flat

The Vuvuzela is widely used in sporting events, although it is prohibited due to the excessive noise in many of them.

 Example n. 162 *Vuvuzela*

One percussion I haven't talked about in the book yet is the *Calabash*.
It is a percussion derived from the half of a giant dried pumpkin.
Its origin is in West Africa, in Mali, and it is played simply by placing it on the ground, hitting with the hands and fingers, and using the fists and drumsticks to obtain different sounds.
It is often used to accompany the Kora, a very popular instrument I will discuss shortly in this paragraph.

 Example n. 163 *Calabash*

KALIMBA

M'BIRA

I am now talking about two instruments very similar to each other, but with some differences: the *Kalimba* and the *Mbira*.
They are ancient percussion instruments originating in Zimbabwe.
As can be seen from the images, they are very similar.
They differ from the position of the slats, from the soundboard: in the Kalimba, it is formed by two rear holes and a large front one, even if both can be without a soundboard, so use only the vibration of the slats.
They sound very close to the orchestral Celesta and are usually played with fingers.

 Example n. 164 *Kalimba - Mbira*

Let's now explore some typically African chordophones.
Let's start with the *Timple*.

It is a plucked string instrument originally from the Canary Islands.
Of Spanish origin, its name indicates the term "acute".

It looks a lot like a ukulele with a rounded soundboard.

The rasqueado technique is used a lot.

Its tuning is also similar to the ukulele, with strings that do not proceed in pitch.

 Example n. 165 *Timple*

Another common chordophone in Africa is the *Xalam*.

The origin of this lute is uncertain, perhaps from Mali or even from ancient Egypt.
It has a variable tuning depending on where it is played but is generally tuned to play in the key of C.
Today it is widely used in West Africa, in Senegal, and has a sound very similar to the banjo; in fact, together with the Sintir, it is believed to be an ancestor of the most famous American instrument.
It is equipped with five strings and has an oval-shaped soundboard covered with animal skin.
The instrument is so rudimentary that the performers themselves often build it.

 Example n. 166 *Xalam*

Certainly, one of the most important chordophones in Africa is the *Kora*.

The Kora has very ancient origins and is a mixture of harp and lute, typical in West Africa (Senegal, Mali, Gambia).

The so-called Jali plays it, that is always male storytellers.

The construction of this instrument is very rudimentary; in fact, it is built using a half gourd emptied and then covered with animal skin, usually of cow or antelope.

It has many strings: 21 arranged in two rows of 10 and 11 strings.

They play it by placing it in front of the body, holding it by the wooden protrusions, and plucking the strings using the thumb and forefinger.

It can have four different tuning types based on: major scale, minor scale, Lydian scale, and the blues scale.

The tuning is changed using the leather rings on the neck.

The strings are tied to the handle by these leather rings;

by moving the rings, the instrument's tuning is varied, and it has a considerable extension.

Example n. 167 *Kora*

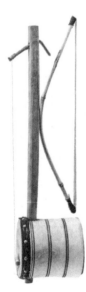

A very characteristic instrument is the *Orutu*.

It is a traditional instrument of East Africa, particularly the area of western Kenya, the north of Uganda, and the south of Sudan, or the northern part of Tanzania. The Orutu is a bowed chordophone with strings parallel to the soundboard (a cylindrical shape, similar to a tiny barrel).

It is composed of a resonance box, usually covered with leather, sometimes even well decorated, with a handle at the end of which there is a mechanism to adjust the single string; the size of the musical instrument is around 55-65 centimeters.

The sound of the Orutu is very similar to the violin, the sound technique of which is similar.

The position used to play the Orutu is standing, with the instrument held in one hand and resting on the abdomen. With the other, they modulate the sound with the bow; alternatively, it can also be played seated, but always with the instrument resting on the abdominals or the side.

Example n. 168 *Orutu*

Another very common chordophone is the *Sintir*.

They widely use it in North Africa: it is originally from Morocco.

It is sometimes referred to as "the ancestor of the banjo", (it has a sound very similar to the American instrument). It is composed of a wooden neck, with a rounded shape, a set of three strings, and a soundboard usually made of wood, trapezoidal in shape, covered with leather (usually that of bovine or camel).

The instrument's dimensions are roughly similar to a guitar's; the strings are traditionally in goat gut, or more recently, in nylon. The neck is often strengthened by metal rings, which can also have a sonic function in the instrument, modifying the sound caused by the strings' vibrations once plucked. The soundboard and the neck of the musical instrument are often finely decorated, giving rise to Sintir, which, in addition to performing their musical function, are also objects of art.

It is often used in the company of drums and castanets and songs of various genres.

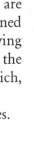

 Example n. 169 *Sintir*

Another very special chordophone is the *Valiha*.

It is an instrument originally from Madagascar. We can say that it is the national instrument, despite its ancient origin is in Indonesia.

It is a kind of zither made from a giant bamboo cane usually of large diameter, carved and used as a soundboard, and equipped with various slots that allow the vibrations to resonate correctly.

On the bamboo cane, there are holes applied on which other pieces of wood are mounted and the slots that allow it to function as a resonance box. They will act as a bridge for each of the valiha strings (and whose positioning allows you to establish the instrument's tuning).

The strings, usually from 10 to 36, which today are made of nylon or metallic threads like the strings of the guitar, were made using the threads of the bamboo bark.

Near the two ends of the bamboo cane used to build the musical instrument, there are individual rings of steel or other metals in each end to fix the strings on the instrument in a firm way.

It can measure from 60cm to one meter in length.

 Example n. 170 *Valiha*

In this paragraph, the last instrument I consider has the African sound inside: the *Balafon*.

It is a direct percussion idiophone of South Saharan origin and particularly widespread in Gambia, Mali, Guinea, and Senegal.

It is a very ancient instrument; it dates back to the 12th century. Like many instruments of this type, it is produced handmade using rosewood. The most popular model has 21 frets, but there are also simplified versions with 8 and 13 frets. As seen from the image, the resonance boxes are made from pumpkins which, once emptied, are perforated. The holes are then covered with thin membranes originally with the web of a particular spider species or with bat wings, then with cigarette papers and only recently with plastic film.

The sticks used to play this instrument are generally made of bamboo, and the upper part is made of natural rubber or covered with vegetable parts to make the sound cleaner.

The Balafon is usually tuned on the pentatonic scale, although there are also tuned diatonically.

 Example n. 171 *Balafon*

ETHNIC INSTRUMENTS FROM THE MIDDLE EAST

The Middle East has a millenary culture. Music has always been connected with the tradition that has sprung up over many centuries.

When we talk about Middle Eastern music, we mean that music united not only by the Arabic language but also by an essential element: Islam.

Religion in this context has been the fulcrum of the whole musical tradition of the Middle East, not so much in a positive but in a negative sense.

The Islamic musical tradition has never been so rich. The fact that Islam has always found music as a problematic experience has led to the development of currents close to Arab culture full of music.

Middle Eastern music is rich in improvisation and based on the ' Maqam' modality system.

A typical performance consists of alternating sections of a compound and improvised material. The compound parts are accompanied by percussion instruments that beat the many standard patterns that articulate the rhythm mode.

Popular music and dance are still alive and well-loved in the various regions of the Arab world, even if globalization is inexorably leveling all artistic manifestations on a single homogeneous level.

Considering the vastness of the Middle Eastern territory, we can distinguish five different schools:

o Middle Eastern School: Egypt, Syria, Jordan, Lebanon, Palestine.
o Maghrebi School: Morocco, Algeria, Tunisia, and Libya.
o Iraqi School
o Gulf School: Saudi Arabia, Bahrain, UAE, Kuwait, Qatar, Oman, and Yemen. In these countries, the musical tradition is closely linked to popular cultural origins: until a few years ago, few in historical terms, before the economic revolution that oil generated in the area, in these countries the population was dedicated to fishing, sheep farming, crafts, and this influenced the musical production.
o Arab-African school: Sudan, the southernmost region of Egypt, Nubia, and Mauritania. In these regions, the music is strongly influenced by African sounds.

However, Arabic music has solid and distinctive features:

In Arabic music, there are no tempered notes: the intervals between the notes are irrational and influenced by the musician's creative sensibility. We should not forget that this type of music is more monodic: all the instruments produce the same melody together, unlike what happens in a Western choir or orchestra, in which the melodies produced by the various instruments are different and governed by the laws of musical harmony. The only exception is the possibility that other instruments hold the base note of the scale, producing a continuo during an improvised solo.

In this context, as I mentioned earlier, the concept of 'Maqam' is fundamental, a real musical phenomenon within which the composition moves, which brings emotionally solid contents with it.

Although Islam has not been excessively influenced musically, one cannot fail to consider the importance of reciting the Koran to develop Middle Eastern musicality.

In this very rich context, musical instruments of all types are born and developed, belonging to all classifications made and masters of a tradition that continues to grow inexorably while retaining that ancient taste of a tradition of millennia.

The first instrument I consider is the *Oud*.

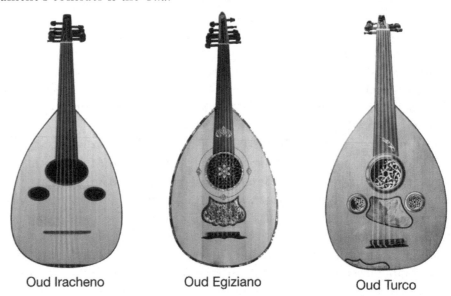

Oud Iracheno   Oud Egiziano   Oud Turco

Oud is of Middle Eastern origin and is very important and widely used in the Arabian-Persian area.
As can be seen from the image, the instrument is the direct ancestor of the European lute, and its manufacture is also similar.
Its similarities with the lute are found in the shape of the soundboard, the peg (bent from 45 ° to 90 °), and it differs from the fact that it is a fretless instrument without frets.
Compared to the lute, the Oud has a much shorter neck.
There are three popular Ouds:

- Iraqi

- Egyptian

- Turkish

Technology has also influenced the Oud.
There is electric Oud (the IOud - on the right).
The name means "strip of wood" in Arabic, referring to the strips used to give life to its typical pear shape. With a short neck compared to the body, the player can be very in tune despite the absence of frets. For this reason, the Oud is ideal for performing the Arabic 'Maqamat' (Arabic improvisation technique based on maqam, that is, specific scales of the Arabic tradition).

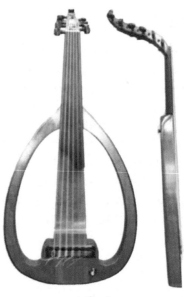

I-Oud

Since the Maqamat is a melodic tradition far from equal Western temperament, the fretless keyboard of the Oud is perfect for moving the fingers slightly to play intervals smaller than a semitone.
The Oud usually has five pairs of strings tuned in unison and a single bass string, although some have an extra pair.

Here is its tuning:

Modern strings are made of steel wrapped in nylon.
Like all chordophones of this type, the strings were first made of gut.
The Oud is played with a particular pick called 'risha', which is made of plastic, turtle shell, animal horn, or even bamboo.

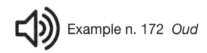
Example n. 172 *Oud*

risha

A common chordophone used in the Middle East is the *Kanun* (or Qanun).

The origins of this instrument date back to before Christ, in the civilizations of Mesopotamia and Egypt.
It is a chordophone - held on the legs - whose strings are plucked by a particular pick.
Trapezoidal in shape, its name derives from the Greek "kanon" which means 'law'.
Throughout its history, the Kanun has undergone many changes.
Still, the morphological characteristics have always been the same: a narrow wooden box, which acts as a resonator, on which the strings are stretched. The box has an acute-angled shape on one side and the other running diagonally. On the straight side, there is a stretched leather section. The feet of the long bridge on which the strings slide press on the skin. The strings are stretched between the bridge and the pegs, three for each string. The Turkish Kanun, for example, has about 24 to 26 sets of strings, for a maximum of 75-81 strings.
The ropes can be lengthened or shortened using latches placed under them. For this reason, the Kanun can also play intervals of less than a semitone. Its trapezoidal shape is functional to the length of the strings (on the small side, there are the small strings, on the large side, the longer ones).
Its range can be about three and a half octaves.

Example n. 173 *Kanun*

A bowed instrument widely used in the Arab area is the *Rebab* or Rabab.

Although the origin is Afghan, it has spread widely in the Arab area of the Middle East. We find many types of a rebab, sometimes even different from each other.

The typically Afghan one, for example, is completely different from the one you see on the left, which is the classic Arab rebab.

Unlike the Afghan, the Arab rebab has up to 4 strings, which has many more. It has become so prominent that it is used in Arabic and Persian classical music.

There are precious Rebabs with the soundboard covered with a beaten copper and decorated.

In the image on the right is the *Afghan Rebab*.

As we can see, it is completely different from the Arab rebab.

First of all, it is larger and has more strings.

The strings are 5: 3 primary and two additional, with 13 drone strings.

🔊)) Example n. 174 *Afghan Rebab*

Here is its tuning:

As is evident, the II and IV strings produce the same sound, as well as the III and V; this is because the first three are leading, and the others are additional.

Drone strings also often repeat themselves.

Seen from another point of view, the Afghan rebab looks like this (right):

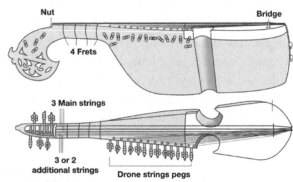

348

Another very ancient and still very popular lute is the *Qanbus*.

The Qanbus is the classic Yemeni lute, although widespread in Oman, Indonesia, Malaysia, and East Africa.
It has 6 or 7 nylon strings played by a pick similar to the Oud. Usually, the first three strings are coupled, and the last is single.
It is a fretless instrument widely used in the last century, then supplanted by the Oud.
Today it is used to accompany the traditional Yemeni dance called Zapin.

Here is its tuning:

EFFECT ONE OCTAVE BELOW

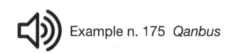 Example n. 175 *Qanbus*

Another important lute is the *Buzuk*.
It is a lute of Greek origin and is a cross between the Greek Bouzouki and the Turkish Saz. However, it is also widely used in traditional Lebanese and Syrian music. Unlike the other lutes in this area, which all have short necks, the Buzuk has a very long neck and frets, so it's not a fretless instrument.
For the execution of the Maqamat, however, they can move the frets to create intervals of less than a semitone.
The strings, up to 4 coupled, are made of metal and are played with a pick.

Here is its tuning:

EFFECT ONE OCTAVE BELOW

 Example n. 176 *Buzuk*

A lesser-known but essential instrument with a vibrant sound is a typical chordophone of the Turkish lute family: the *Saz*.

The most common is also called Baglama.

This instrument is also ancient: it was the instrument of minstrels in Turkey for centuries.

As can be seen from the photo (right), it is a typical long-necked lute and is widely used now in the Türkü, a typical Turkish musical genre.

It is part of an entire family of musical instruments, from the highest to the lowest: Cura, Baglama, Tambura, and Divan Saz.

They are all tuned one octave below the previous one starting from la Cura.

It has seven strings: the first triple and the other two coupled

Here is its tuning:

EFFECT ONE OCTAVE BELOW

Example n. 177 *Saz*

On the left, a very present instrument in many iconographic sources: the *Simsimiyya*.

It is a zither of Egyptian origins, also known as a pharaonic zither because it was born on the banks of the Nile.

They are used for Sawahli, popular music from northern Egypt, and a typical dance of the Suez Canal area, the Bambutiyya.

Example n. 178 *Simsimiyya*

Another zither, very similar to Simsimiyya, is the *Kissar*.

It comes from Egypt and the North of Sudan. Unlike the Simsimiyya, there are some different sizes, but they are all 5-stringed played with a pick.
The greatest of the Kissars is called Tanbura.

 Example n. 179 *Kissar*

One of the most commonly used wind instruments throughout Arab culture is the *Ney* or Nay.
It is a flute with a classic embouchure at the top, like a recorder or an ancient Baroque flute.
The Nay is of Persian origin and has been widely used in all Middle Eastern music for thousands of years. It is enough to look at all the iconographic elements that have come down to us to understand how ancient this instrument is.
It is usually made from bamboo cane and can have 5 or 6 holes plus a thumb hole.
There are many sizes of this instrument. Often an instrumentalist brings a lot of them with him precisely because they are cut according to the tonality.
Its range is not vast: at most 2 or 3 octaves.
Today, the most popular Nay are three: Persian, Turkish, and Arabic (left).
They are a little different, also in terms of playing and quality. For this reason, it is advisable to study them all to understand which one to use.
Nay's instrumentalists usually play them all.
For example, the Persian Nay is played by placing it in the mouth's lateral part, and not all sounds are tempered.

 Example n. 180 *Ney*

The *Duduk* is one of the ethnic instruments dear to me, which I have used a lot in my productions.

Of Armenian origin, the Duduk is practically the symbolic instrument of this population - it is always present in every party, wedding, or popular event.

It is ancient, probably over 2000 years old, and a very warm-sounding double-reed instrument.

Originally it was built in bone, now in wood with a mouthpiece carved at the end of the reed.

The reed is now separated from the body because in ancient times, when it was built in a single piece, it broke easily, thus becoming unusable.

Aged Apricot wood is used for the construction.

The reason lies in the very warm sound of this wood, pleasant and particularly close to the human voice.

There are different types of Duduk, from 28 to 40 cm, with a range that goes from one to 4 octaves.

The sound of the Duduk can express various moods depending on the content of the piece or the context of the performance.

The 40 cm long Duduk, for example, is considered the most appropriate for love songs; the smaller one accompanies the dances.

The one that is now most used is in A and is 35 cm long.

It usually has 8 holes in the front and 2 in the back and is divided into four parts: barrel, mouthpiece, regulator, and cap.

Being made of apricot wood, it is very fragile. In fact, instrumentalists often use walnut oil to give strength and shine, protecting it from atmospheric events.

The intonation can still be slightly adjusted (at most one semitone) using the regulator, i.e., the clamp in the center of the mouthpiece.

The sound of the Duduk is so penetrating that it is often used in film music.

Hans Zimmer himself used it a lot in the soundtrack of the 2001 film "Gladiator".

 Example n. 181 *Duduk*

Another wind instrument typical of the Arab area is the *Zurna*.

It is a double-reed instrument of Turkish origin, basically like an oboe, with a very bright sound.

It is widely used in Turkey and throughout Central Asia.

Depending on the size, there are different types of Zurna, and her voice is surprising despite having a very narrow sound range; in fact, it has a range of about 2 octaves.

It can be built using many species of trees: juniper, ash, willow, plum, mulberry, etc.

Its length is about 30cm, and it has a clamp attached to the upper part of its body.

This gripper is used to modify the fundamental register of the instrument.

They often play it with the Davul, a typical Turkish Bassdrum and can have up to eight holes on the front and the thumb hole on the back.

Since Turkish music is made up of often continuous melodies, most of Zurna's players are very skilled in circular breathing.

Example n. 182 *Zurna*

As I explained to you in the bagpipe chapter, Bagpipes are widespread all over the world. There are many and very different from each other.

Arab culture also has its bagpipe: the *Mizwad*, a typical bagpipe from Tunisia.

Unlike the classic Italian bagpipes, this one has two chanters instead of one, and both end with a sort of horn.

It is a simple-reed instrument that is often accompanied by the Darbuka, which I already told you about in the chapter on percussion.

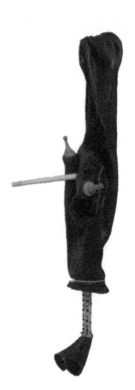

Example n. 183 *Mizwad*

Let's start talking about percussion instruments widely used in the Middle East.

On the right is the *Daf*, a large frame drum of Persian origin that is used extensively in Iranian and Pakistani folk and classical music.

It is so widespread that it has become the national instrument of Pakistan.

It has thin metal plates or rings attached to hooks in three or four rectangular holes in the circular wooden frame.

It can be very large, even reaching a width of 50 cm. According to some Muslims, it was the only musical instrument allowed during the celebrations by the Prophet Muhammad.

 Example n. 184 *Daf*

Another popular percussion instrument is the *Bendir*.

Like the Daf, it is a frame drum widely used in Southwest Asia and North Africa.

Its peculiarity is given by some gut strings that cross the drum starting from the sides of the frame.

Like the Daf, it can also reach considerable dimensions.

 Example n. 185 *Bendir*

I close the paragraph with an instrument widely seen even outside Arab culture, representing its sound and tradition: the *Finger Cymbals*.

They are nothing more than small cymbals worn on the thumb and middle finger of the hands.

They have a tiny diameter, about 5 cm.

They are used in different areas, but, as you may have guessed, they are widely used for belly dance, typically Middle Eastern.

Some finger cymbals are used in Tibet for Buddhist prayers and meditations.

They are practically like Spanish castanets: while those are in wood, these are in metal.

 Example n. 186 *Finger Cymbals*

ETHNIC INSTRUMENTS FROM THE FAR EAST

The culture of the Far East is probably the oldest of all.

Music has always accompanied the history of these peoples, from India to China, from Japan to Indonesia.

Since ancient times, the fact is that it has outlined distinctive features that make it unique all over the world.

Music has always been linked to religious worship, giving birth, and progressing to unique musical instruments with distinctive traits in India.

In the countries of the Far East (China, Japan, Korea, Mongolia, Vietnam), music is very similar to the point of being treated almost as a single core, although there are significant regional differences.

The main scale used is the pentatonic, the only one recognized by the ritual music of ancient China, while subsequent musical styles in the non-religious field have expanded the scale to seven sounds and beyond.

Oriental music is, however, fundamentally melodic: musical instruments and voices all play the same melody in unison or octave, differing only in the presence of embellishments.

The Korean orchestras, which implement polyphony imported from Indonesia, are an exception.

This is a somewhat old concept. Today the music of the Far East is more westernized while retaining its ancient roots.

In this geographical area, musical instruments are usually classified according to the material they are made of.

Indeed, the Chinese culture, the oldest of all, has influenced all the music of these areas. In this context, music also has a solid spiritual value. In a very similar way to how it happened in Ancient Greece, whoever ruled established the rules of which repertoires were to be used and which ones were to be banned.

Even in Japan, music has always had great value: for example, 'gagaku', Japanese court music of Chinese inspiration, and Japanese theater have always been the basis of the tradition of these places.

There is also a trend of popular music, which includes the songs of the peasants, the music of the shamans, and dances. To catalog them all, also considering the long-lived culture of this area of the globe, would be truly impossible. Still, giving a distinctive look at the main instruments can help construct any particular arrangements and orchestrations. This paragraph will try to follow the most important geographical areas by highlighting the instruments with a specific relevance. I want to start with the musical instruments of the Indian region. I have already talked about the most important instrument of this area in the chapter on plucked string instruments, the Sitar, since the westernization path of that instrument has been very evident.

All Indian music is based on ragas, precise musical structures that often have spiritual values. In this context, a widely used instrument is the *Sarangi*: a bowed instrument with a leather-covered resonator. The typical Sarangi is handmade, usually from a single block about 66-69 centimeters long. It has three main gut strings and many brass or steel vibrating sympathetically (up to 36). Sarangi is very common throughout the Indian area: they are several, and the shape can vary from region to region. For example, the Nepalese Sarangi is generally much smaller than its Indian counterpart, and not all Sarangi have strings that vibrate in sympathy. It is widely used in Indian folk music and Bangladesh, and Pakistan. The three gut strings are tuned like this:

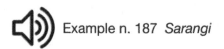

The resonance strings are divided into four parts, with two tuning pegs, one on the right and one on the top. Inside there is a row of 15 chromatically tuned strings and on the right two rows of nine diatonically tuned strings plus a few extra strings. Additional strings are tuned following certain ragas.

 Example n. 187 *Sarangi*

A characteristic instrument for its extreme 'Indian' sound is the *Tànpura* or Tàmbura.

It is an extraordinary plucked string instrument not used for melody but the harmonic accompaniment of a soloist or a voice.
The repeated plucking of the strings in cycle creates a particular harmonic canvas typical of Indian countries.
The shape of the Tanpura is similar to the sitar, but it is a fretless instrument. It has four or five (rarely six) metal strings, which are plucked one after the other in a regular pattern to create harmonic resonance on the base notes of a tonality.

There are two types of tuning: one for the Male Tanpura and one for the Female.
The tuning must be chosen in some way according to the piece because both Tanpuras are tuned on distinct octaves.

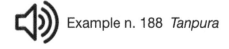 Example n. 188 *Tanpura*

The image below shows the two types of tuning used for this instrument.

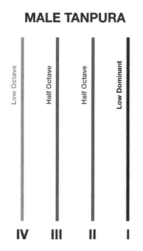

Usually, the middle strings are tuned first, and then, based on that tuning, the other two outside are tuned.

Here is a hypothetical Male Tanpura tuning:

As you can see, the two central strings express a note (in this case, a B flat, but it changes depending on the context); you must tune the lower string one octave below and, consequently, the first string on the dominant of the fourth.

A descendant instrument of the Sitar is the *Veena*.
The term Veena, however, indicates all the instruments of this type. There are many and different from each other.
The Veena is a chordophone instrument from the lute family up to 150cm long. The shape is derived from a stick zither. It is generally characterized by a long and wide neck that constitutes the axis of the instrument, with a large number of frets and the presence of resonators, usually two hollowed-out pumpkins. The neck is inserted into the hemispherical soundboard, also made of pumpkin or wood. It is a typical instrument of northern India, and the most common has seven strings, four of which are main strings for touch and three that stretch on the left / right side of the neck.
The strings can also be not plucked by a pick but by the musician's fingernails allowed to grow. There are also fretless Veena, but they are less common. The tuning of the Veena changes according to the chosen scale (raga).

 Example n. 189 *Veena*

However, if we choose, for example, to play in E, we will have this tuning:

As you can see, the high strings are towards the player, and the low ones are far from the player. This is because it is played by placing it on the ground, almost like an American steel guitar.

An instrument widely used in the Indian subcontinent and as famous as the Sitar is the *Sarod*.

The Sarod is a stringed instrument from the lute family. It has a deep sound contrasting with that of the Sitar. Like the Sitar, it has sympathetic strings, giving it a resonant quality. The important thing about this instrument is that it is fretless; in fact, glissandi are used a lot. The classic Sarod has from 17 to 25 strings: four to five main strings used to play the melody, one or two additional strings, two 'chikari' (i.e., rhythmic) strings, and nine to eleven sympathetic strings. It is an adaptation of an Afghan rabab, which I have already told you about. It is about one meter long and has a slightly wrapped wooden body with a leather belly. It is now the backbone of Hindi music and is often accompanied by the Tablas, which I already told you about in the percussion lesson.

 Example n. 190 *Sarod*

This is the tuning of the 4 main strings:

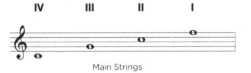

Main Strings

This of the 4 external strings:

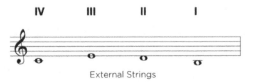

External Strings

Then the other external string is tuned an octave above.
And this instead is an example of tuning of the strings that vibrate out of sympathy:

Sympathetic Strings

Another typical stringed instrument is the *Ektara*.

With the term Ektara, the Indians denote any musical instrument consisting of a string attached to a gourd, coconut, wood, or metal resonator. There are several models of Ektara. Each specific model differs from the others for several reasons, such as the structure of the neck, which can be formed by a cane or a split bamboo cane, the construction materials, the presence or absence of frets. The word Ektara derives from combining two Sanskrit words, 'eka' and 'tara', respectively, 'one' and 'string'. There is also the Dotara, a very similar instrument but with two strings. And the word Dotara means "two strings". Ektara can be plucked and bowed (as you see in the images: left plucked, right bowed).

 Example n. 191 *Ektara*

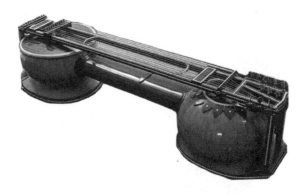

Another type of Veena, scarce in the Indian area but with an unmistakable sound, is the *Sagar Veena*.

It is a large instrument that, placed on the ground, you can play with a slide (like the bottleneck of the steel guitar, but with a larger and ball shape).

It is a fretless instrument and is of Pakistani origin. Etymologically, the word "sagar" stands for Ocean, and Veena, as I have already explained, is the term to indicate all these types of instruments. Its vibrating part consists of nine sounding strings, two additional strings, a wooden bridge with silver transmitters, and the resonance chamber. The nine strings are a combination of the three Asthans in Indian music, the Mandrasthan (bass), Madhasthan (midrange), and Tarasthan (treble).

 Example n. 192 *Sagar Veena*

Another typical stringed instrument is the *Dilruba*.

It is very similar to the sitar, but instead of being plucked, it is bowed. The bow is called Gaz.

This instrument is found in different parts of northern India and is used in religious ceremonies. It is used alone and as an accompaniment instrument in northern classical music.

It has four main metal strings, twenty sympathetic strings, and nineteen elliptical frets.

 Example n. 193 *Dilruba*

A small percussion instrument of the Indian tradition is the *Kanjira*.
It is simply a percussion from the tambourine family.
It is a small circle tambourine with only two little cymbals and lizard skin (although lately it has been banned to protect the animal species)
It is mainly used to accompany Mridangam in South Indian classical music. The Kanjira is quite difficult to play, especially for reasons which include the complexity of the percussion patterns used in Indian music. It is played generally with the palm and fingers of the right hand, while the left hand supports the drum. You can use the fingertips of the left hand to fold the skin by exerting pressure near the outer edge, thus varying the intonation.

 Example n. 194 *Kanjira*

Another important percussion, which I mentioned a little while ago, in South Indian music is *Mridangam*.
It is a double-sided drum whose body is usually made using a hollowed-out piece of jackfruit wood about one inch thick.
The two mouths or openings of the drum are covered with a goatskin and fastened to each other with leather straps along the length of the drum. These straps are put in a state of high tension to stretch the circular membranes on both sides of the hull, allowing them to resonate when hit. These two membranes are different in diameter to produce both low and high sounds from the same drum.
The smaller membrane, when struck, produces high-pitched sounds with a metallic timbre.
The wider aperture has lower pitched sounds. The goatskin covering the smaller opening is greased in the center with a black disc made of rice flour, iron oxide powder, and starch. This black paste gives the Mridangam its distinct metallic tone (like the tablas).

 Example n. 195 *Mridangam*

Let's now look at some wind instruments of Indian culture
The first one I consider is the *Shehnai*.
It is an instrument native to the Indian subcontinent, made of wood, with a double-reed at one end and a flared bell made of metal or wood at the other end.
It is used extensively at weddings, processions, and in temples, as its sound is thought to create and maintain a sense of good luck. But it is also played in concerts.

 Example n. 196 *Shehnai*

Another wind instrument typical of the Indian region is the *Bansuri*.

The Bansuri is a transverse flute originating from the Indian subcontinent, widely used in classical Hindi music.

It traditionally consists of a single hollow bamboo stem with six or seven finger holes. Some modern designs are available in ivory, fiberglass, and various metals. The range is two and a half octaves. It is typically between 30 and 75 centimeters long. One end is closed, and its vent hole is a few centimeters from the closed end. Longer Bansuri has deeper tones and lower tones. The traditional design has no keys, and the player creates the notes he wants by tapping the various holes with his fingers.

 Example n. 197 *Bansuri*

I conclude this section dedicated to the instruments of the Indian area with the *Pungi*.

Many will recognize it because, in street performances, it is used to charm snakes.

The instrument consists of a tank into which the air is blown and then conveyed into two pipes. It is played without pauses since the performer uses circular breathing.

The Pungi consists of a solid coconut cover, to which pieces of bamboo are joined, and has two components: a hollow vessel made from a gourd and two tubes, each with a single rod with eight or nine finger holes.

The musician blows air through the top of the instrument's tube. One reed makes sounds similar to those of staff, and the other produces the melody.

The tube that produces the melody has seven holes and an octave extension, while the staff tube has only one hole.

Traditionally, both sounds are played simultaneously using circular breathing to create a hypnotic effect.

The Pungi is usually played alone, as it is difficult to play with other instruments.

 Example n. 198 *Pungi*

There are many musical instruments from the Chinese-Japanese area and neighboring areas. In this paragraph, I will talk about the most important ones.

The first instrument I would like to talk about is probably one of the most indicative of this culture: the *Koto*.

The researchers believe that the Koto was originally a Chinese zither but is now a unique instrument commonly used in Japanese music.

Just looking at it, it isn't easy to distinguish it from other instruments from Mongolia, Korea, Vietnam, and China. However, it has a distinctive feature, which makes identification easier for experienced people. It has an elongated body: it is usually about 1.80m long and about 20cm wide.

It has 13 bridges and 13 strings (although there are 17 to 21 strings), and they usually make it of Paulownia wood, a tree with a light and strong wood.

Traditionally the bridges were made of ivory, but the more recent ones are made of wood or plastic; instead, the strings can be made of silk or plastic.

The Koto has remained popular in Japanese culture for hundreds of years, primarily due to its popularity among Japanese royal houses.

The Koto results from many other similar instruments that I will talk about shortly.

It is played with fingertips while wearing picks on the fingers and has become so popular that it has even swept into Western culture.

Many famous music authors have used it: David Bowie, Queen, the Rolling Stones, Genesis, and even Paul Gilbert, the guitarist of Mr. Big.

Note the tuning of the classic 13-string koto: it recalls the Japanese pentatonic culture.

Example n. 199 *Koto*

Another instrument belonging to the traditional Japanese zither is the *Guzheng*, practically the ancestor of the Koto.

He is called Zheng. The word 'Gu' stands for ancient, hence ancient Zheng.

Like the Koto, it is played by plucking the strings with the fingertips and worn picks.

Modern Guzheng has 21 to 23 strings.

The Guzheng soundboard is rectangular and made of Wutong wood.

Being fully part of Japanese culture, it accords on the pentatonic scale.

It is an instrument of great extension.
Here is its tuning:

Pressure is applied to the string beyond the bridge to play notes other than the pentatonic. They use the same technique to vibrate.

Example n. 200 *Guzheng*

The oldest of the instruments belonging to the zither family is probably the *Guqin*; it has approximately 2500 years of history.

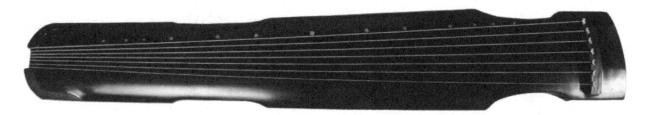

It is a 7-stringed instrument. Its structure recalls the human body: it has a head, forehead, neck, shoulders, and womb in which the embryo of sound can be born.

The body of the Guqin doubles as a keyboard. The frets are indicated by ivory buttons inlaid on the side of the soundbox.

It is played like all tabletop instruments of this type, using the fingertips of the right hand.

Example n. 201 *Guqin*

I now focus on a distinctive instrument used in Vietnam: the *Dan Bau*.

It is an ancient instrument, but they still use it in Vietnamese classical music. Believed to be as old as Vietnam's early dynastic era, the Dan Bau creates soft, serene sounds.

It is a detailed presentation of Vietnam's unique culture. A single-string musical instrument, the Dan Bau is simple but very unique.

The word's etymology also says so: 'Dàn' means a stringed instrument, and 'Bau' means 'pumpkin'; the instrument is exactly what the etymology says. In general, it consists of a few components: the soundboard, the spout, the gourd, the string, and a tuner. However, the instrument was initially composed of four parts: a bamboo tube, a wooden shaft, a half coconut shell, and a silk rope. Today's Dan Bau is built using wooden soundboards instead of bamboo. The traditional silk cord has also been replaced with an iron one. The spout of the instrument, which is a flexible rod that varies the string's tension, is made of a buffalo horn with a square frame at the root, while it is flat and gradually bent at the top. It plays a vital role in producing sounds of different pitches in addition to the fundamental harmonics of the instrument. The pumpkin used to cover the spout where the string is tied, acting as a resonator, still exists, although it was replaced by wood and is nothing more than a decorative element. Its tuner, which could be bamboo or wood, is located in the inner frame towards the bottom of the wooden soundboard. The iron string passes through a small hole at the end of the instrument's surface towards the tuning peg. A pointed stick made of bamboo or rattan is commonly used to pick this instrument. Usually, it is tuned to the note C. It is played by plucking the string touching it lightly with the side of the hand at a point that produces a harmonic. While you don't need to be highly skilled to play the Dan Bau, great precision is imperative to allow for pitch increase and decrease along with lengthening and shortening of notes with the help of the flexible rod, which allows the changing tension of the string. The technique consists of gently tapping the string with the little finger of the right hand while the other fingers pluck the string using a long pick. With the left hand, you can lower the note's pitch by pushing the flexible rod using the index finger or pulling the rod away with the thumb if a higher pitch is desired. Used to be played solo or in an ensemble in poetry recitals or accompanying plays.

 Example n. 202 *Dan Bau*

A very common lute in the Isan region of Northeast Thailand is the *Phin*.
It is a three-stringed instrument used a lot in today's electric version.
Here is its tuning:

EFFECT ONE OCTAVE BELOW

 Example n. 203 *Phin*

Another widely used lute in China and Japan is the *Shamisen* or Sangen.
It is of Japanese origin, probably from Okinawa, and is a three-stringed fretless lute.
Although it has only been used in Japan since modern times for performances of puppets and other similar theatrical music, singing accompaniment, and folk songs from many regions, the Shamisen is widely loved.
There are different types of Shamisen depending on the neck length of the instrument.
Its soundboard is square with front and back cat skin (formerly lizard skin).
They play it with a large pick; different types of picks produce distinct colors for specific types of music.
A groove cut in the neck near the upper bridge causes the lower string to touch the fretboard, creating a distinctive hum called 'sawari'.
There are several tunings for the Shamisen.

This is the most common one:

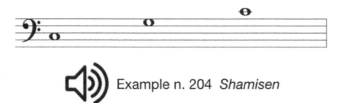

 Example n. 204 *Shamisen*

Let's go on with the Japanese lutes talking about the *Biwa*.

It is a short-necked Japanese lute featuring a graceful pear-shaped body. The Biwa has a shallow, rounded back and silk cords (usually four or five) attached to thin side pegs. The musicians play the instrument with a large wedge-shaped pick called 'bachi'. The strings are tuned by fourths, and the melody is played almost exclusively on the highest string.

Here is its most common tuning:

The Biwa can accompany various types of narrative as part of a gagaku (court music) ensemble or as a solo instrument. Performers of the instrument often pluck two notes at once, producing a variety of intervals, especially when the singer is silent.

 Example n. 205 *Biwa*

Another instrument that fully identifies Chinese culture is the *Erhu*.

As can be seen from the image, it is a bowed instrument.
It is like a violin that is played vertically by resting it on the knee in practice.
It has only two strings, generally tuned for fifths, stretched over a wooden drum-like resonator covered in a snakeskin membrane.
The Erhu has no fretboard: the strings are supported by a vertical upright that pierces the resonator, and the player stops the strings by pressing the fingertips on them.
It is used both as a solo instrument and in an ensemble and can be found in all Chinese music, from popular to pop or jazz.
Its characteristic sound is produced precisely by the vibration of the snakeskin.
Unlike the classical violin, whose bow also separates from the instrument, in the Erhu, the bow's horsehair is permanently glued to the strings (that is, it passes through the strings and not on top). The two strings are very close to each other; the musician plays it as if there was only one string.

The two strings are usually tuned this way.

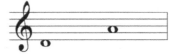

Here is its range:

A typical Erhu measures approximately 81 cm and is often made of fine woods or red sandalwood. His performance is characterized by subtle contrasts in the powerful vibrato and glissandos. A sharper version with a smaller resonance surface and the shorter pole is the gaohu or nanhu. A larger and lower version of the Erhu is called zhonghu. All three dimensions are valuable members of the orchestra.

 Example n. 206 *Erhu*

Another bowed instrument is the *Banhu*.

It is a Chinese bowed violin.

The instrument traditionally has two strings stretched on a small bamboo bridge that rests on a wooden soundboard, unlike other stringed instruments, which have the soundboard covered with a snakeskin membrane.

It is a very ancient instrument; it dates back to around the 16th century.

It is a member of the modern Chinese orchestra.

The Banhu is held upright like the Erhu during the performance, although it is considerably smaller.

The bow passes between the two strings.

Its strings are held taut by the hand of the performer; the bow is performed near the top of the semicircular resonator, which is made of wood or coconut shell. Soprano, alto, and tenor versions of the Banhu are available. The soprano model is the type of banhu regularly used in the Chinese orchestra due to its ability to produce extremely high tones compared to other stringed instruments. They typically use it in northern folk music, which plays an essential role in popular works.

The handle of the Banhu is made of solid rosewood.

Its timbre is usually piercing and metallic; its range encompasses the power and flavor of popular music.

Possessing a sharp and penetrating tone, the Banhu has a range of more than two octaves, and the frequent use of rapid glissandos characterizes the playing technique.

 Example n. 207 *Banhu*

Let's now see what are commonly referred to as 'Lunar Lutes' due to their shape. There are mainly two.

The first is the *Yueqin*.

It is a short-necked Chinese lute. Inside its circular body, there is a fixed metal tab. It is used to accompany songs and is popular in small opera ensembles.

The Yueqin, which evolved from the Ruan, is about 45 cm long, with a round case about 30 cm in diameter.

The fingers or a small pick plucks the strings. The modern Yueqin is generally larger than the traditional instrument, it extends up to about 67 cm, and its 3 or 4 strings are made of steel wrapped in nylon.

Here is its tuning:

EFFECT ONE OCTAVE BELOW

 Example n. 208 *Yueqin*

The other lunar lute is the *Ruan*, but, unlike the Yueqin, it has a long neck.

It originally had 13 frets; now, modern Ruans have 24 frets.
Usually, the keys are made of ivory, but lately, they are also made of metal.

It is a 4-stringed lute and has several cuts, from soprano to double bass.
There are also versions of bowed Ruan, especially in the low register.
It has the same tuning as the Yueqin.

 Example n. 209 *Ruan*

A very famous chordophone in China is the *Pipa*.

It is a pear-shaped lute with a wooden belly and, sometimes, two crescent-shaped sound holes.
It has been and continues to be used primarily for entertainment as a solo instrument or in an ensemble.
The modern Pipe has 29 or 31 frets, 6 on the neck, and the rest on the instrument's body. Also associated with Buddhism, the Pipe is often seen in the hands of angels in Buddhist iconography and incorporated into Buddhist narrative chant and is often decorated and seen in symbolic ways. For example, each string represents a season. The pinnacle at the top of its box of thorns can represent a symbolically significant creature. The front and back of some surviving old Pipe soundboards are lavishly decorated with inlays. The four strings were once made of silk. Today they are usually made of steel wrapped in nylon.
They played silk strings with a pick or with bare fingers, but steel strings are typically played with small picks attached to the fingers.
The instrument is held vertically on the musician's thigh during the performance.
The playing technique for the Pipe is quite sophisticated and can include glissandos, tremolos, and harmonics sounds.

According to a document from the Eastern Han dynasty (25-220 AD), the instrument's name derives from the techniques of the fingers, 'pi' for plucking with a forward movement, 'pa' for plucking with a backward movement. There are several varieties of Pipes in China, and closely related instruments are also found in Vietnam and Korea. Here is its tuning, different from the lutes I illustrated earlier:

EFFECT ONE OCTAVE BELOW

Example n. 210 *Pipa*

Let's leave the stringed instruments and move on to the wind instruments from the Far East.
The first one that I illustrate is the *Suona*.

The Suona is a Chinese double-reed instrument. Although it is widely used in China, it is native to Arabia. Indeed, I would say the most commonly used double-reed instrument.
The reed is fixed on a conical wooden body covered with a copper tube with eight finger holes (seven in front and one behind), to which a brass bell is attached.
Its range is generally around two octaves, and it comes in many sizes.
Suona is characterized by its shrill and piercing sound and frequent use of the tongue during the performance.
It is widely used in military music ensembles and religious processions and as a stage instrument in Chinese operas.

 Example n. 211 *Suona*

An instrument of great charm is the *Sheng*.
Native to Southeast Asia and used before the 12th century BC, the Sheng is a free-reed instrument.
It now accompanies folk songs and is occasionally used in Peking Opera to add harmony.
Similar to the Western harmonica, which inspired it, the Sheng is the only Chinese wind instrument capable of playing many notes simultaneously. It is played, like the harmonica, by blowing and inhaling.
It is usually made up of 17 bamboo tubes set in a small case in which a player blows through a mouthpiece.
Each pipe has a free reed, made of metal (or formerly bamboo or reed),
which vibrates to produce sound when a finger hole in the pipe is covered.
The reeds, of five different lengths, are arranged in two triangular shapes to symbolize the folded wings of a phoenix bird. In addition to the traditional 13, 14, and 17 tube sets, there are 21 and 24 tube sets and a 36 tube set based on the chromatic scale, with all 12 semitones. There are also other modern variants. The Chinese instrument plays melodies with occasional fourth or fifth harmonies. Contemporary Chinese ensembles include the larger Sheng capable of playing Western chords.

 Example n. 212 *Sheng*

Let's talk now about a flute: the *Dizi*.

The Dizi is a Chinese transverse flute.
Today it is used on many regional and national occasions of Chinese music, as a soloist, small ensemble, and orchestra.
It is a leading melodic instrument in many regional instrumental ensembles in the central China area. Dizi has been taught in music conservatories, and composers have created a significant repertoire of solo works for the instrument. As a result, many Dizi, highly skilled concert musicians in China today, perform as soloists and in the modern state-sponsored chamber and orchestral ensembles. The Dizi consists of a straight bamboo stem with any internal knots removed to produce a cylindrical hole. They are made in various lengths. Above the breather, the hole is blocked with a cork, leaving only the far end of the flute open. Six finger holes, positioned almost equidistant, are located in the lower half of the tube; there is no thumb hole on the back. A distinctive feature of the Dizi is the inclusion of a 'mirliton', a membranophonic sound modifier consisting of a hole covered by a bamboo membrane as thin as tissue paper that vibrates significantly when the flute is played. This hole is located between the breather and the first finger hole. Several loops of silk thread are wrapped tightly around the flute and covered with red lacquer to prevent the bamboo from breaking. Through the hyper-insufflation and the opening of the finger holes, it is possible to obtain a practical range of two octaves. Two distinct styles of Dizi characterize their use in northern and southern China. The Southern-style focuses on sweet and expressive sounds with delicate ornamentation, while the Northern style is energetic and shriller, with glissandi and dazzling tongue effects. Regardless of the style played, this flute's characteristic 'mirlitone' adds a characteristic nasality to its sound, especially when played at high volume and in the higher register.

 Example n. 213 *Dizi*

Another characteristic instrument is the *Hulusi*.

The Hulusi is a free-reed wind instrument originating from China. It is usually made of natural pumpkin and black bamboo; recent demands for higher volume, greater dynamic range, better tone control have led luthiers to do this with hardwoods. The instrument works on the basic principles of compressed air, forced into the gourd. Then vibrates the metal tongue or "reed" that buzzes in the tube, producing the sound.
It is held vertically and has three bamboo tubes that pass through a pumpkin crate.
The center tube has finger holes, and the outer two are typically drone tubes.
The drone tube has a finger hole, which allows the sound to stop. Advanced setups have keyed finger holes similar to a clarinet or oboe, significantly extending the Hulusi's range to several octaves.

 Example n. 214 *Hulusi*

The following wind instrument that I illustrate is the *Hichiriki*.

The Hichiriki is a tiny Japanese double-reed wind instrument, similar to the oboe. It has a robust nasal sound. The current Japanese shape is approximately 18cm long and has seven finger holes on the front of the instrument and two thumb holes on the back.

It is made of internally lacquered bamboo and wrapped with cherry or wisteria bark bands between the finger holes. The wide and thick barrel is placed in an enlarged end of the tube, thus giving the Hichiriki an external conical shape, although the tube is cylindrical.

The player uses a wide yet controlled embouchure and gentle finger movements to create his rich and fluid melodic style. Derived from earlier continental Asian models, Hichiriki was used in ancient Japanese court music.

 Example n. 215 *Hichiriki*

A beautiful and exceptional instrument is the *Horagai*.

Horagai is large shells of different genera of sea snails and marine mollusks.

In particular, shells of the Trumpet species and the Giant Newt, as more commonly known, are generally used to make Horagai.

The conch was transformed into a horn-like instrument used for various purposes throughout Japanese history. This instrument is not exclusively Japanese; it is also found in other cultures. However, the Horagai is unique because it can produce up to 3 or 5 different notes than other clamshell horns, producing only a single pitch. This is because there is a bronze or wooden mouthpiece similar to that of a flute and other woodwind instruments on the tip of the shell.

Horagai is also used in the military by samurai as a signaling device. The Horagai earned their other name, Jinkai, which translates to "shell of war". Korea also has its version called Nagak; however, it can only produce one note used in military procession music.

 Example n. 216 *Horagai*

Let's move on to some percussion instruments.

Let's start with the *Kotsuzumi*.

The Kotsuzumi is a small hourglass-shaped drum used in Japanese drama. It comprises three main parts: a central hourglass-shaped shell, two membranes placed at the ends, and a braided rope. The instrument is held over the right shoulder, and the front is hit with the fingers of the right hand. By pressing on the lacing with the left hand, the performer can tighten the membranes and thus raise the pitch. Ropes are traditionally made with colored hemp, although a synthetic rope is often used. The shell is carved from a solid block of cherry wood. The structure of each drum skin is an iron ring (or cherry bark) wrapped in bamboo around the horse skin membrane, which has a radius of a few centimeters larger than the shell itself. The membranes differ slightly in their thickness, the thinner of the two used for the sounding part and the thicker one for the rear head.

 Example n. 217 *Kotsuzumi*

Another percussion typical of these areas is the *Kagura Suzu*.

The term 'suzu' refers to Japanese instruments associated with the Shinto ritual. Kagura stands for 'music for the Gods' and is a term that includes Shinto instrumental music, songs, and dances performed in shrines and courtyards.

Kagura Suzu is a set of bells used in the Kagura dance. Coiled brass wires suspend the three orders of bells.

The shapes of these bells are thought to have come from the fruit of the Ogatama tree.

Example n. 218 *Kagura Suzu*

We are now moving to Indonesia.

A typical instrument of the place is the *Angklung*.

It is a musical instrument made up of various bamboo tubes attached to a bamboo frame. The tubes are sculpted to have a resonant tone when struck and are tuned in octaves, similar to Western bells. The base of the frame is held in one hand while the other hand shakes the instrument, causing a repeated note to sound. Each performer in an Angklung ensemble is typically responsible for only one sound, playing their individual Angklung at appropriate times to produce full melodies. Angklung is famous worldwide, but it originated in the West Java and Banten provinces of Indonesia and has been played by the Sundanese for many centuries. Angklung and its music have become an essential part of the cultural identity of Indonesian communities.

Playing Angklung in an orchestra requires cooperation and coordination and is believed to promote the values of teamwork, mutual respect, and social harmony.

Example n. 219 *Angklung*

Indonesia is famous for Gamelan music, and a fundamental instrument for this musical genre is the *Gambang*.

It is basically a xylophone used in the Gamelan Balinese and Javanese orchestras.

The instrument bars are made of wood and mounted in a deep wooden case that acts as a resonator.

The instrument typically has 17-21 bars. They are easily removed and are held in place by a hole through which a nail is placed. They use a pair of long and thin mallets called 'tabuh' to play the instrument, made of flexible water buffalo horn with a felt tip. Gambangs are generally played in parallel octaves. Unlike most other gamelan instruments, there is no need to dampen, as the wood does not sound like the metal bars of other instruments. (there are different types of percussion keyboards with metal bars and bamboo resonators).

Different gamelan ensembles use the Gambang.

 Example n. 220 *Gambang*

A widely used instrument in Indonesia and the Philippines is the *Kulintang*.

Kulintang is an actual musical genre that identifies precisely that specific geographical area.

Kulintangs are small horizontally arranged gongs that work melodically, accompanied by larger, suspended gongs and drums. As part of Southeast Asia's broader gong-sounding culture, kulintang music ensembles played for centuries in the East Malay Archipelago regions: Southern Philippines, Eastern Indonesia, East Malaysia, Brunei, and Timor.

The primary role of kulintang music in the community is non-professional social entertainment at parties, festive gatherings, gatherings, parades, weddings, and ceremonies that mark the return of pilgrimages to Mecca. Kulintang music is also played during state services and accompanying healing ceremonies, animistic rituals, and religious ceremonies. They are also played informally at home for the enjoyment of family members. They once used this music to communicate long-distance messages from one village or longhouse to another. Traditionally, kulintang artists are volunteers whose only reward is recognition and prestige. Kulintang music is composed of modes, with a prescribed rhythm for each of the ensemble's five instruments, and the compositions are passed down orally without any formal notation. Improvisation is an essential aspect of this music. The tradition of kulintang music is slowly dying as it has been replaced with modern forms of entertainment.

These gongs are usually arranged in numbers from 5 to 9; they have dimensions from 15 to 25 cm and are generally bronze. They use light knockers to play them.

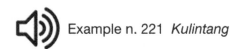 Example n. 221 *Kulintang*

The *Sasando* (right) is a traditional musical instrument of the Eastern Indonesian culture. It is a kind of circular harp.

The main part of the Sasando is a bamboo tube that serves as a frame for the instrument. Around the tube are several pieces of wood that act as wedges where the ropes are stretched from top to bottom. The function of the wedges is to hold the strings higher than the surface of the tube and produce strings of various lengths to create different musical notations. A bag-shaped fan of dried Lontar surrounds the stringed bamboo tube or Palmyra leaves that serve as the instrument case. The Sasando is played with both hands reaching the tips of the bamboo tube through the opening in the front. The musician's fingers then pluck the strings similarly to playing the harp. The Sasando can have 28 or 56 (double) strings.

 Example n. 222 *Sasando*

I conclude this long paragraph by virtually going to Australia.
One instrument that you have undoubtedly seen somewhere is the *Didgeridoo*.

The Didgeridoo is of enormous importance to indigenous Australians. Although it plays a vital role in traditional ceremonies, it is also played more casually by street musicians and around campfires.
The instrument dates back 1000 years to the northeast of Arnhem Land, but today the materials to make the Didgeridoos come from all over the Northern Territory. These fantastic instruments are also completely unique. No two didgeridoos produce the same sound.
The length, diameter, and texture of the wood all affect the tone and pitch of the instrument.
Its length can vary from 1.50m to 2.50m.

The sound of the didgeridoo presents itself with a characteristic hum and hypnotic rhythm, produced by the circular breathing in the mouthpiece of the long wooden pipe.

The traditional instrument is made from a eucalyptus branch, chosen from those whose interior is excavated by termites.

 Example n. 223 *Didgeridoo*

Glossary

ADSR Acronym (Attack, Decay, Sustain, Release) which indicates the volume envelope in a synthesizer.

AEROPHONES All those musical instruments that have air as a fundamental element for the reproduction of sound. There are wind instruments in the true sense of the word and the so-called free aerophones.

BARREL Part of the clarinet.

BASS BAR Internal part of a bowed instrument, lute or guitar characterized by one or more pieces of wood, usually in spruce, glued to the soundboard of the instrument; it has the purpose of propagating the sound on the upper part of the sound box.

BELL End part of wind instruments.

BOCAL Part of the bassoon in which the double reed is inserted.

BORDONE Term used in various situations. It can indicate in the family of bagpipes the pipes that emit a single continuous sound, or the strings (in a guitar for example), often external to the sound box, which are not felt and always reproduce the same sound (open strings).

BORE Type of tube used by a wind musical instrument; it can be conical or cylindrical.

BOTTLE NECK Cylindrical device that is worn by the guitarist to create a glissato effect on the instrument.

BOW HAIR Horse hair mounted on the bows of string instruments useful for producing sound by rubbing the string.

BOWL Part of the Timpano.

BUCKET Type of mute used by trumpets and trombones.

CHIN REST Device placed above the violin and viola useful for supporting the chin.

CORDOPHONES All those musical instruments that reproduce sound through the vibration of one or more strings.

COULISSE Fundamental part of the trombone; is a U-shaped mobile pump that is pulled by the performer to vary the length of the bore.

CUP Type of mute used by trumpets and trombones.

DAW   Acronym (Digital Audio Workstation) which indicates an electronic system for the design and recording of audio and Midi.

DRAWBAR   Command of the hammond organ with which you decide which tone-wheel should intervene.

DULCIANA   Renaissance musical instrument ancestor of the Bassoon.

E-BOW   It stands for 'Electronic bow': it is a device that magnetically vibrates the strings of an electric guitar.

ELECTROPHONES   All those instruments that require electricity to reproduce a sound.

END PIN   Device that cellos, double basses, contrabassoon and low register saxophones use to point the instrument to the ground.

FAIRLIGHT   Musical instrument dating back to 1979; it is one of the first samplers built.

FINE TUNER   Useful screw device to fine tune string instruments; is placed on the tailpiece of the instrument.

FRETLESS   Bass type without frets.

FROG   Lower part of the bow in strings instruments.

HARMON   Type of mute used by trumpets and trombones.

HARMONICS   Considered a sound, they are the multiple frequencies of a given fundamental.

HUMBUCKER   Double coil pickup type for guitar or bass.

IDIOPHONES   Musical instruments that reproduce sound through their own vibration (percussion). They are of different types (see chapter on the classification of musical instruments).

KEY   Very important mechanism in wind instruments useful for closing holes not reachable by the fingers.

LESLIE   'Rotating' Loudspeaker for Hammond Organ.

LFO   Acronym (Low Frequency Oscillator) which indicates an additional oscillator that creates motion in synthesizers.

MEMBRANOPHONES   Musical instruments that reproduce sound through the vibration of a membrane (or skin).

MIDI   Acronym (Musical Instrument Digital Interface) which indicates a standard protocol for communication between electronic instruments.

MOUTHPIECE   Device used by instruments of the brass family to reproduce sound.

NECKPart of the saxophone (alto, tenor, baritone, bass) and the harp.

OSCILLATOR   Waveform generator in the synthesizer.

PEG   Mechanism that allows the tuning of stringed instruments.

PHONOGRAPH   Useful tool for recording and reproducing sound invented by Thomas Edison in 1877.

PICKUP   Amplification device of a musical instrument invented by Rickenbacker in 1937.

PISTON   Valve present on instruments of the brass family that activate other bore pieces present on the instrument.

PLECTRUM Tool used to pluck the strings of a chordophone.

PLUNGER   Type of mute used by trumpets and trombones.

RANGE   Indicates the extention that an instrument can emit, from the lowest to the highest note.

REEDThin tongue usually of reed or plastic useful for aerophones for the reproduction of sound. It can be swing or free, simple (clarinets, saxophones...) or double (oboes, bassoons...).

REGISTER KEY   Very important key in woods (perhaps the most important).

RIBECA   Late medieval musical instrument ancestor of the violin.

SERPENT   Musical instrument of the family of cornets dating back to the sixteenth century, ancestor of the tuba.

SINGLE COIL   Single coil pickup type for guitar or bass.

SLAP   Technique used by bass players.

SOLOTONE Type of mute used by trumpets and trombones.

SOUND POST   Small wooden cylinder wedged between the right foot of the bridge of the string instruments and the harmonic back; has the purpose of transmitting the vibrations of the soundboard to the bottom and therefore to the entire soundboard.

SOUSAPHONE   Musical instrument similar to the tuba.

SPLIT COIL Type of pickup for electric bass.

STRAIGHT   Type of mute used by brass instruments.

STRING   What vibrates in the chordophones. It can be of different materials (gut, steel, nylon), covered or not with a metal wire. They can also be resonant (Sitar).

TELHARMONIUM Large electrophone instrument invented in 1897 by Thaddeus Cahill.

THEREMIN Electrophone musical instrument invented by the Russian Lev Sergeevic Termen in 1919; it is the first tool that does not require physical contact with the performer.

TIORBA   Renaissance musical instrument, similar to the Chitarrone and part of the lute family, ancestor of the guitar.

TONEWHEEL   Mechanical part of the Hammond Organ that allows sound reproduction.

TRANSPOSING   A type of musical instrument whose notes played do not match those written.

TUNING The process used to tune musical instruments according to a certain system taking as a reference point a predetermined absolute pitch. Today in the West the reference points are the A at 440Hz and the temperate scale.

VELVET   Type of mute used by trumpets and trombones.

VIELLA   Medieval musical instrument ancestor of the violin.

VOCAL FRY Entry register located in the extremely severe part.

WHISPER   Type of mute used by trumpets and trombones.

WHISTLE   Voice register located in the extremely high part.

APPENDIX I: TRASPOSITIONS OF INSTRUMENTS

INSTRUMENT	*WRITTEN*	*CLEF*
Piccolo	8va ↓	Treble
Alto Flute	P4 ↑	Treble
English Horn	P5 ↑	Treble
B♭ Clarinet	M2 ↑	Treble
A Clarinet	m3 ↑	Treble
B♭ Bass Clarinet	M9 ↑	Treble
E♭ Alto Clarinet	M6 ↑	Treble
E♭ Piccolo Clarinet	m3 ↓	Treble
Contrabassoon	8va ↑	Bass & Tenor
B♭ Soprano Sax	M2 ↑	Treble
E♭ Alto Sax	M6 ↑	Treble
B♭ Tenor Sax	M9 ↑	Treble
E♭ Baritone Sax	M13 ↑	Treble
Horn in F	P5 ↑	Treble
B♭ Trumpet, Flugelhorn, Cornet	M2 ↑	Treble
D Trumpet	M2 ↓	Treble
Tubular Bells	15ma ↓	Treble
Crotales	15ma ↓	Treble
Celesta	8va ↓	Treble & Bass
Xylophone	8va ↓	Treble
Glockenspiel	15ma ↓	Treble
Guitar	8va ↑	Treble
Bass Guitar	8va ↑	Bass & Treble
Contrabass	8va ↑	Bass, Tenor & Treble

APPENDIX II: RANGES

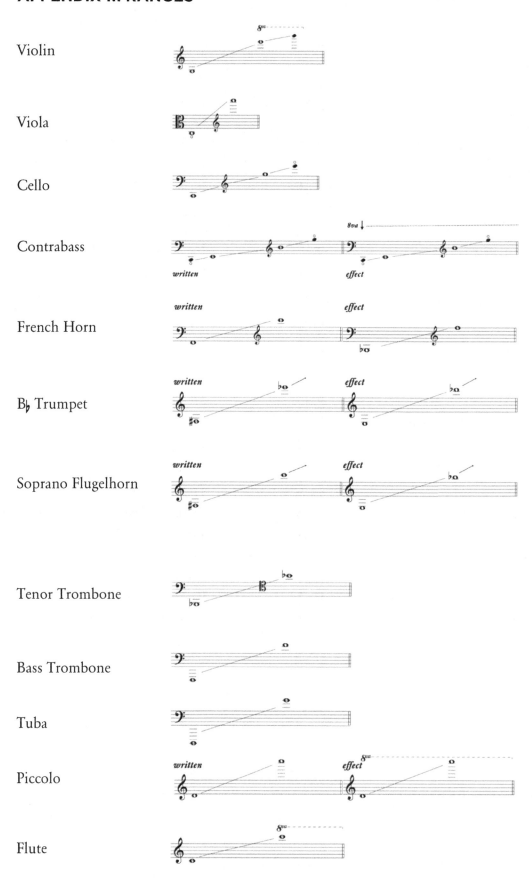

Violin

Viola

Cello

Contrabass

French Horn

B♭ Trumpet

Soprano Flugelhorn

Tenor Trombone

Bass Trombone

Tuba

Piccolo

Flute

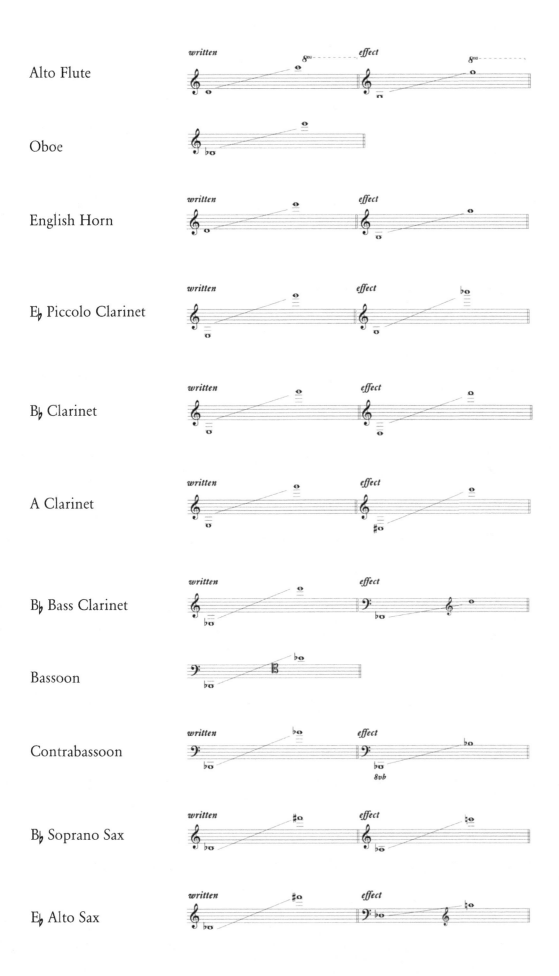

Alto Flute

Oboe

English Horn

E♭ Piccolo Clarinet

B♭ Clarinet

A Clarinet

B♭ Bass Clarinet

Bassoon

Contrabassoon

B♭ Soprano Sax

E♭ Alto Sax

Bb Tenor Sax

Eb Baritone Sax

Xylophone

Marimba

Glockenspiel

Vibraphone

Tubular Bells

Crotales

Timpani

Roto-toms

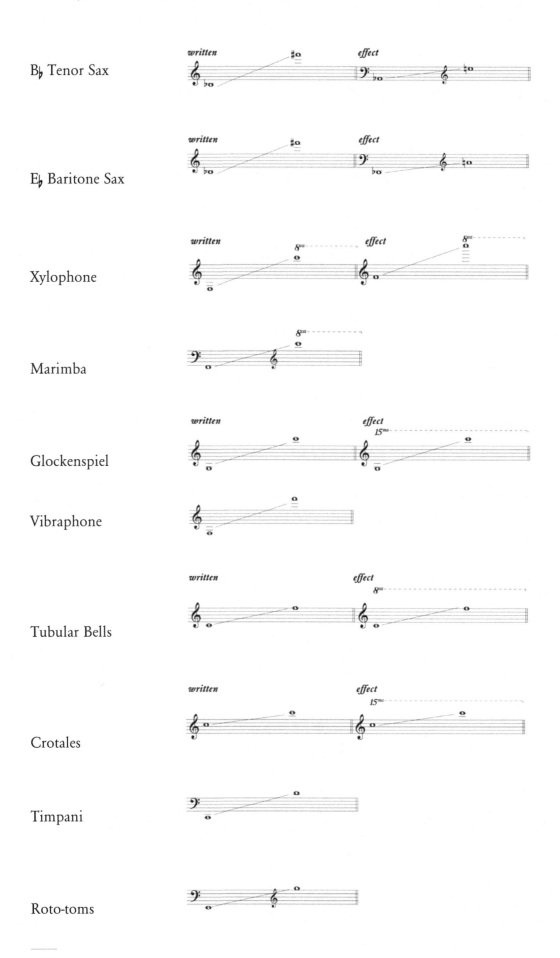

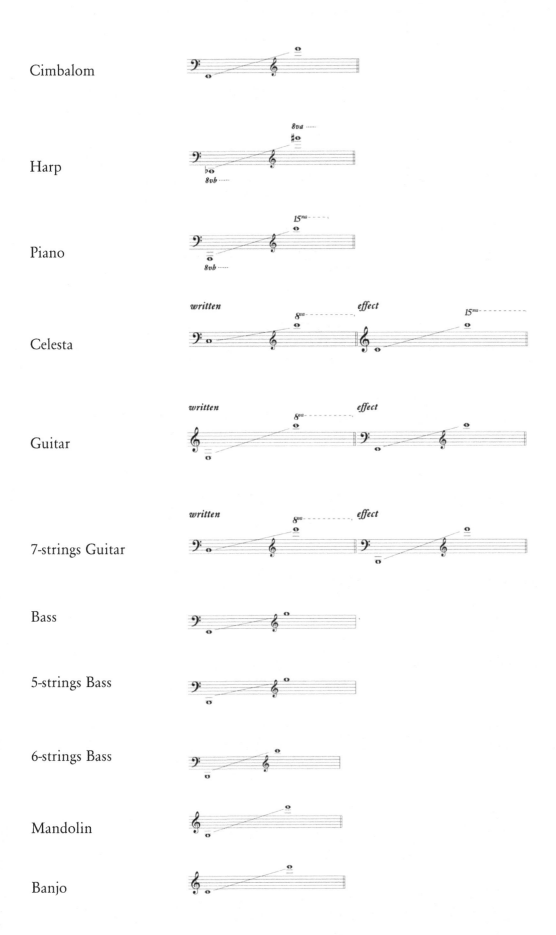

Cimbalom

Harp

Piano

Celesta

Guitar

7-strings Guitar

Bass

5-strings Bass

6-strings Bass

Mandolin

Banjo

Sitar

Ukulele

Harmonica (cromatic)

Accordion

Bandoneon

Soprano Voice

Mezzo-Soprano Voice

Alto Voice

Tenor Voice

Baritone Voice

Bass Voice

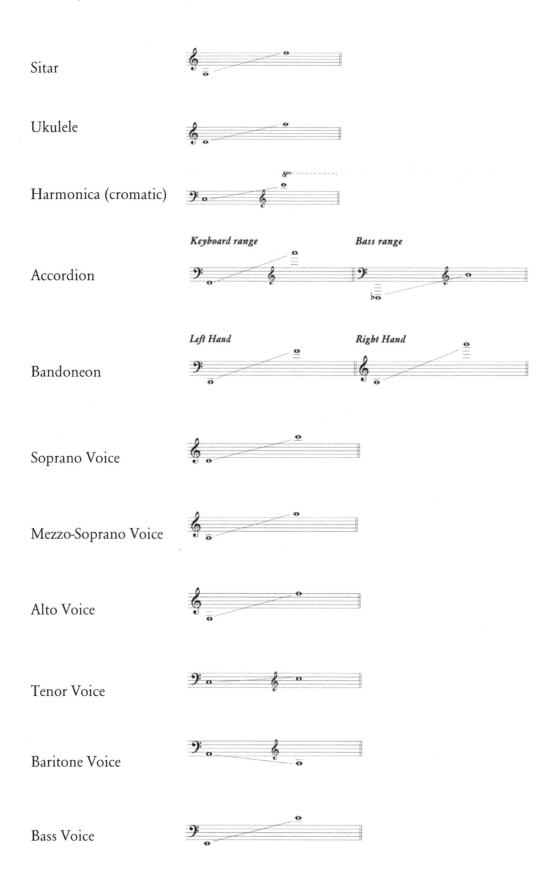

APPENDIX III: FLUTE FINGERING

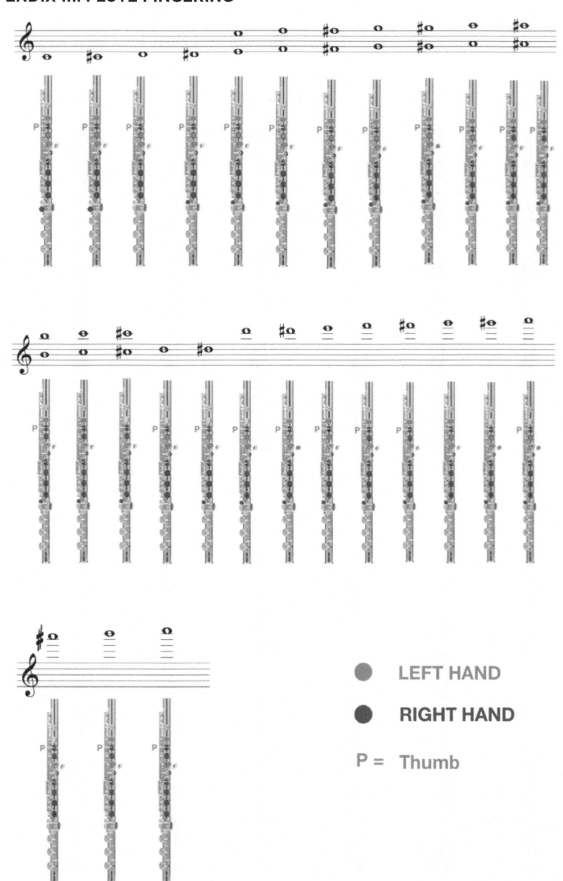

LEFT HAND

RIGHT HAND

P = Thumb

APPENDIX IV: OBOE FINGERING

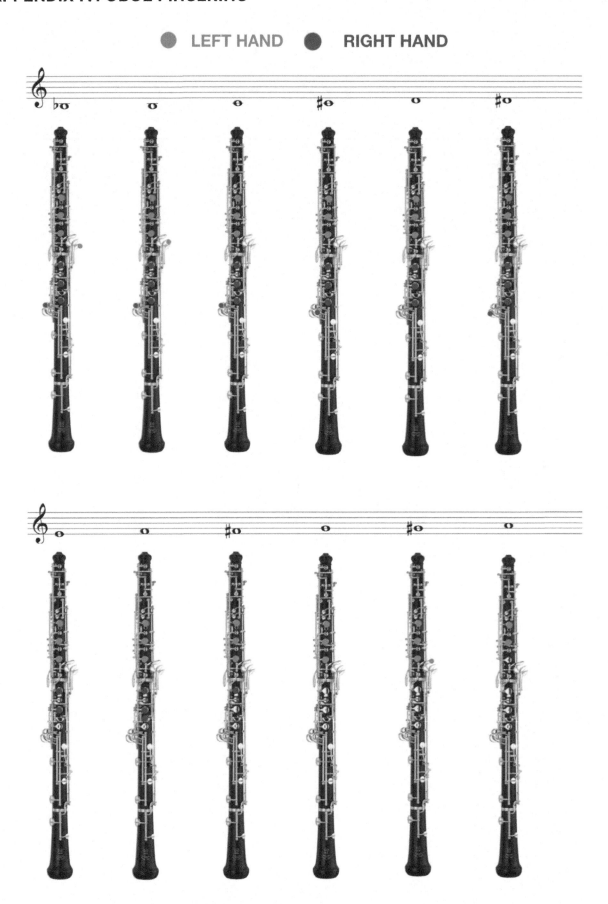

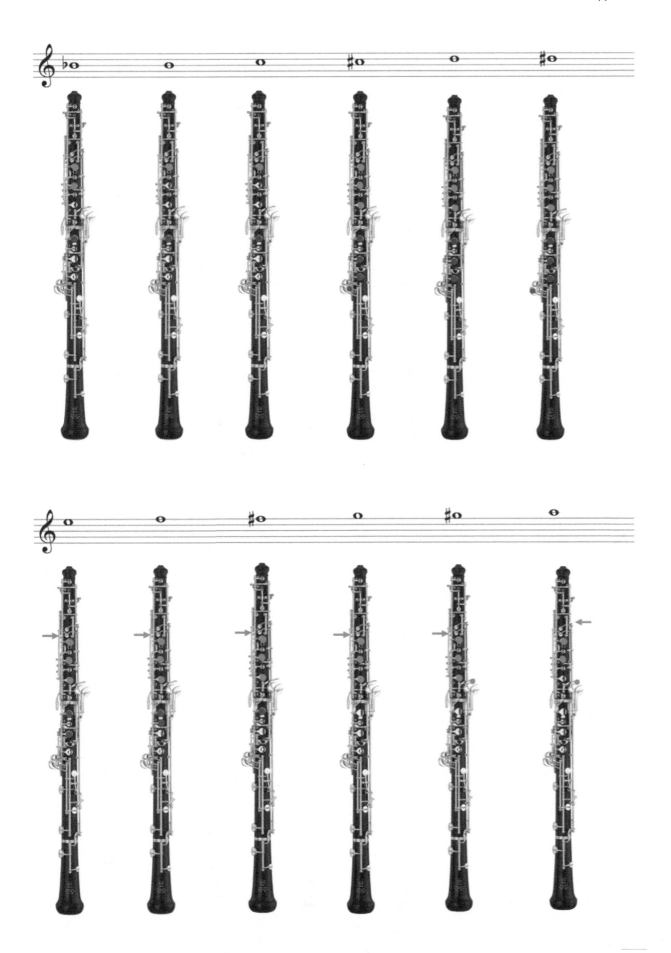

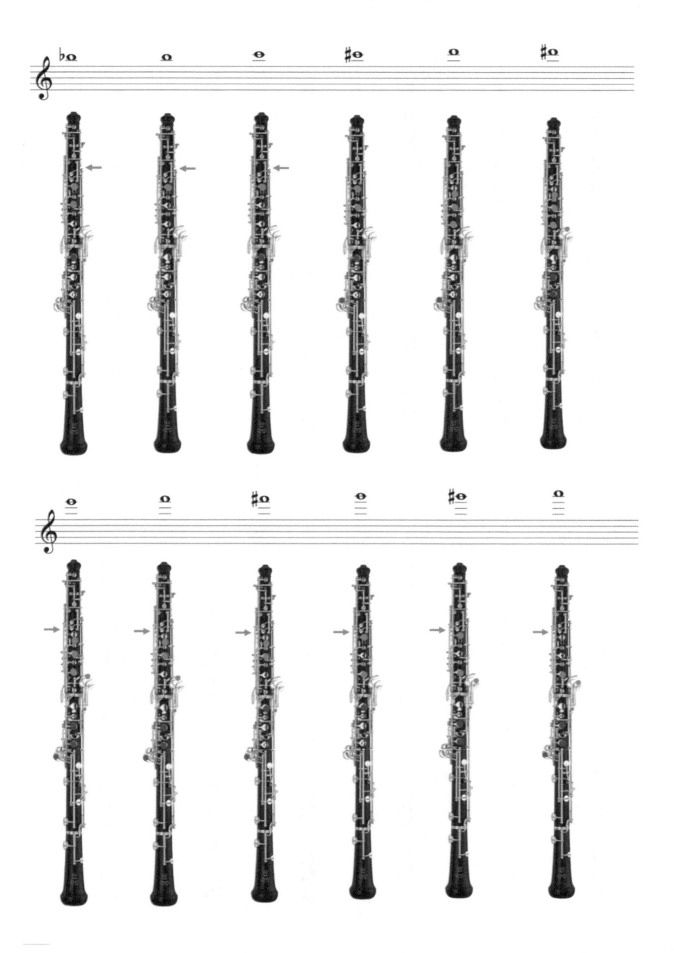

APPENDIX V: CLARINET FINGERING

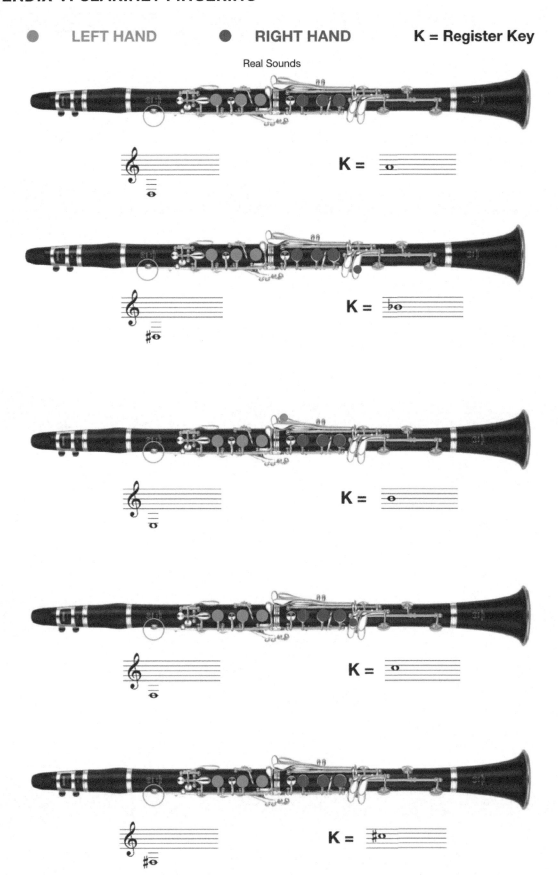

● **LEFT HAND**   ● **RIGHT HAND**   **K = Register Key**

Real Sounds

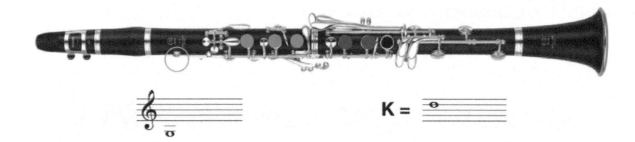

K =

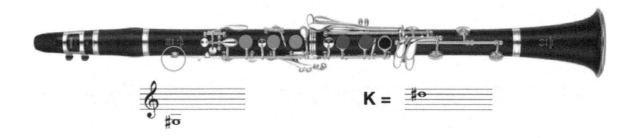

K =

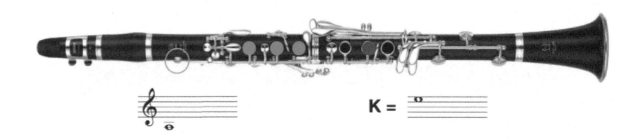

K =

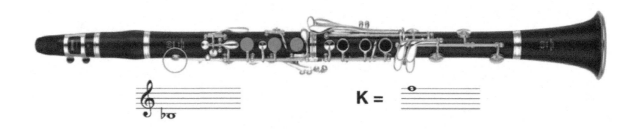

K =

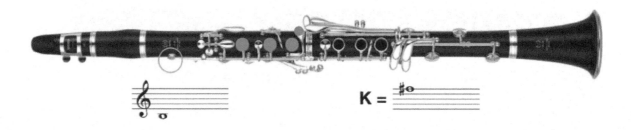

K =

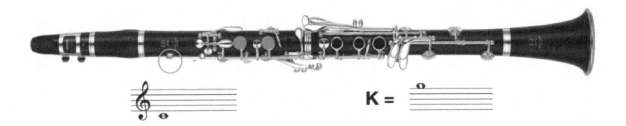

K =

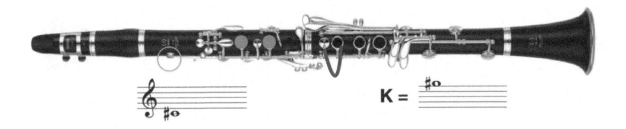

K =

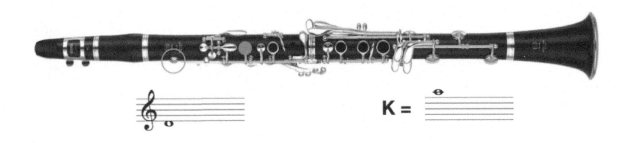

K =

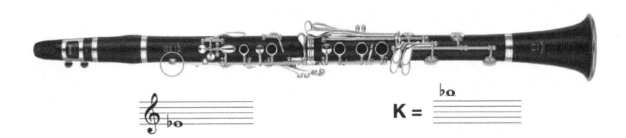

K =

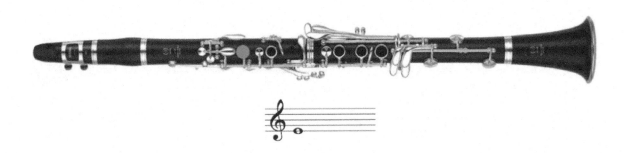

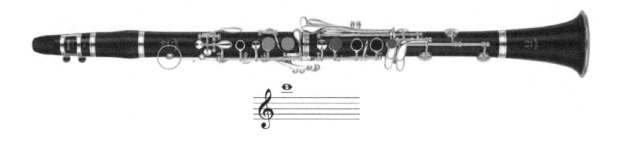

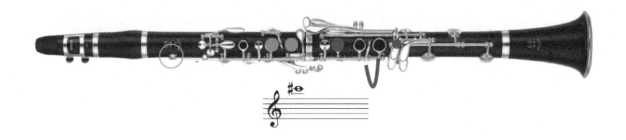

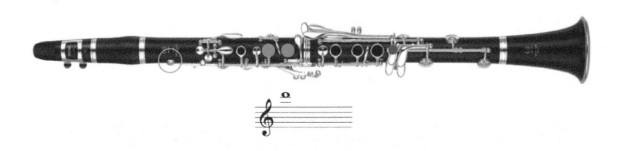

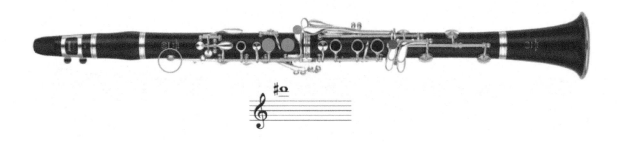

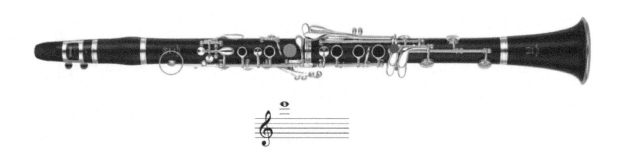

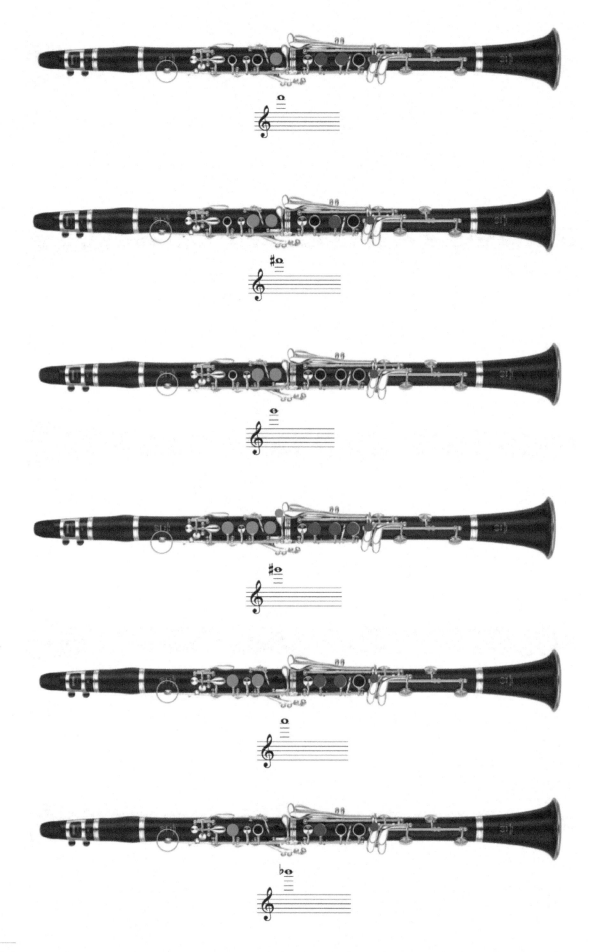

APPENDIX VI: SAX FINGERING

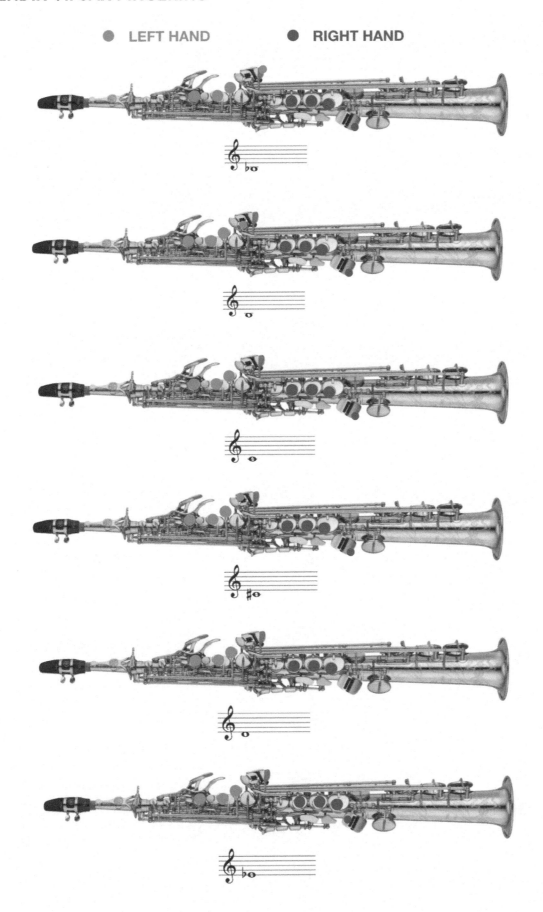

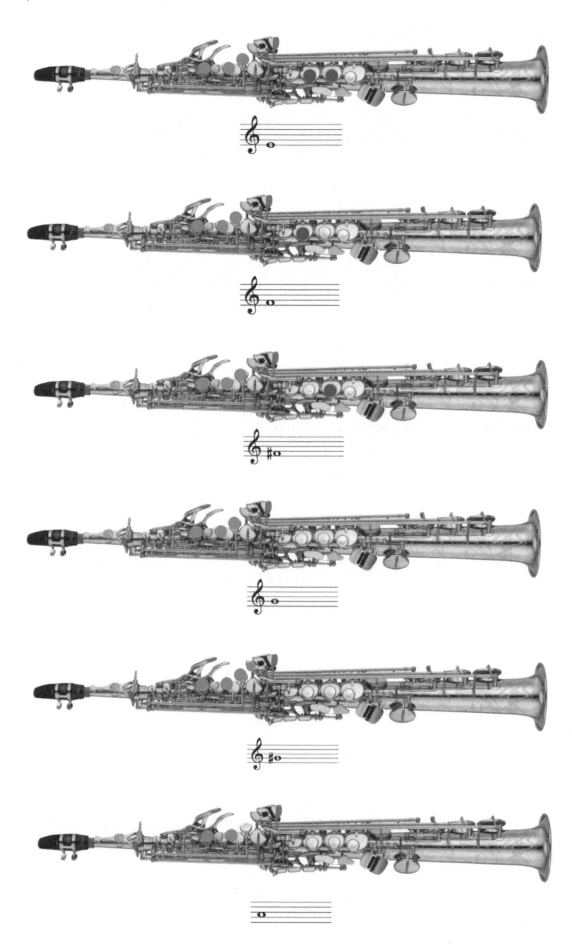

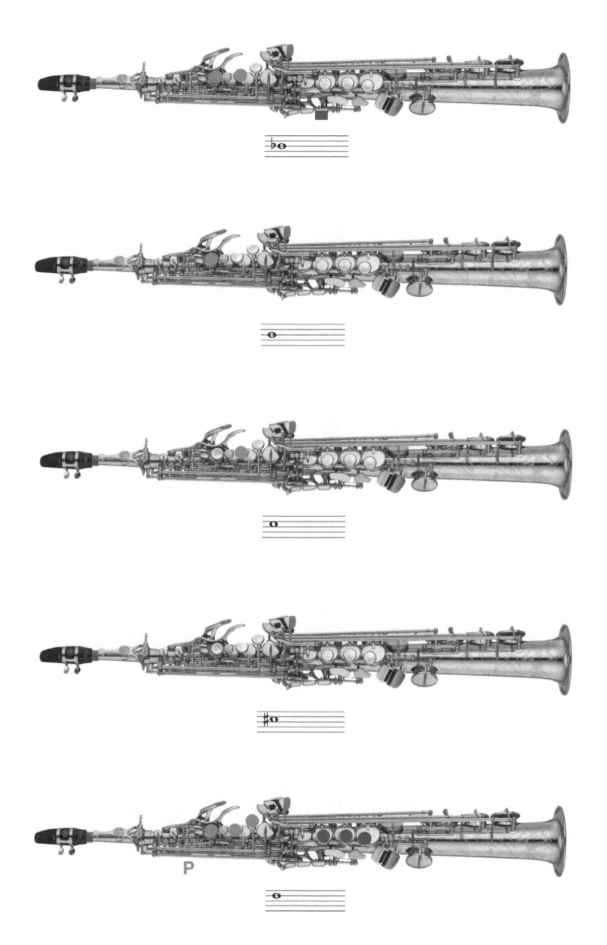

P

The Complete Modern Instrumentation

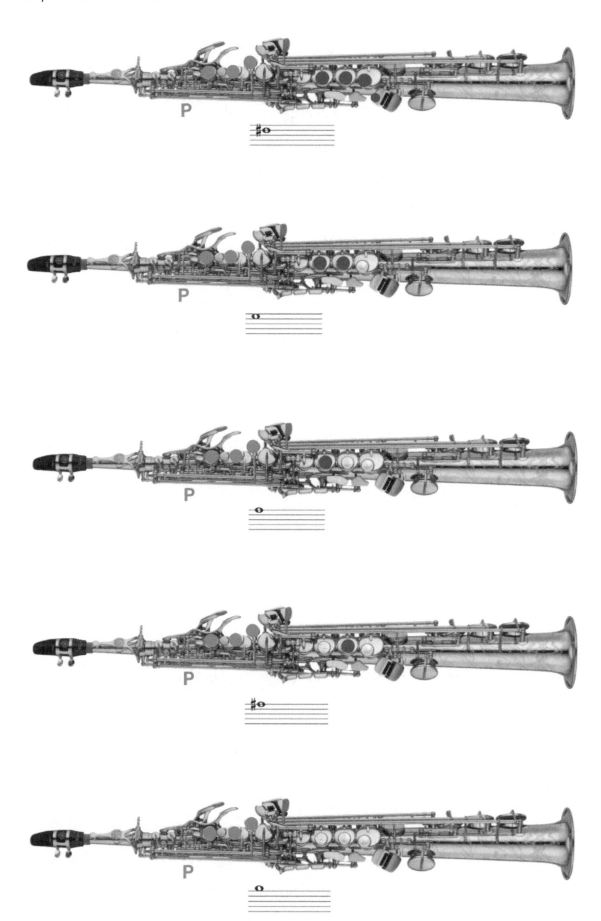

398

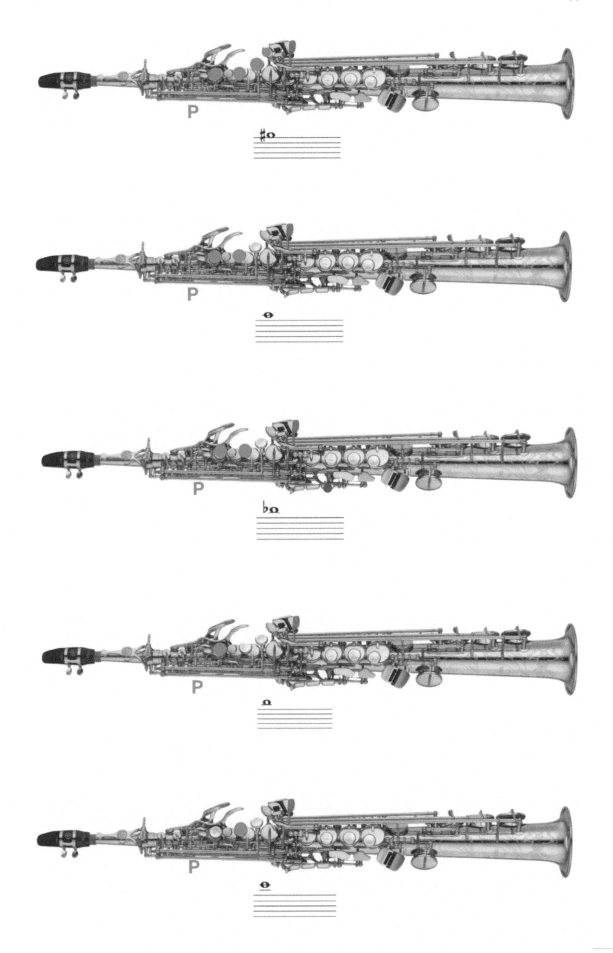

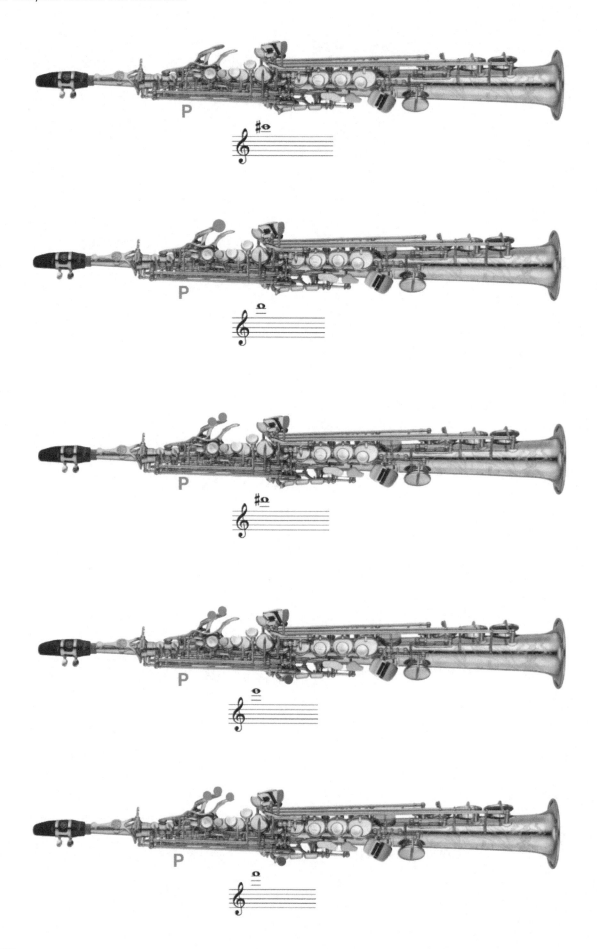

APPENDIX VII: BASSOON FINGERING

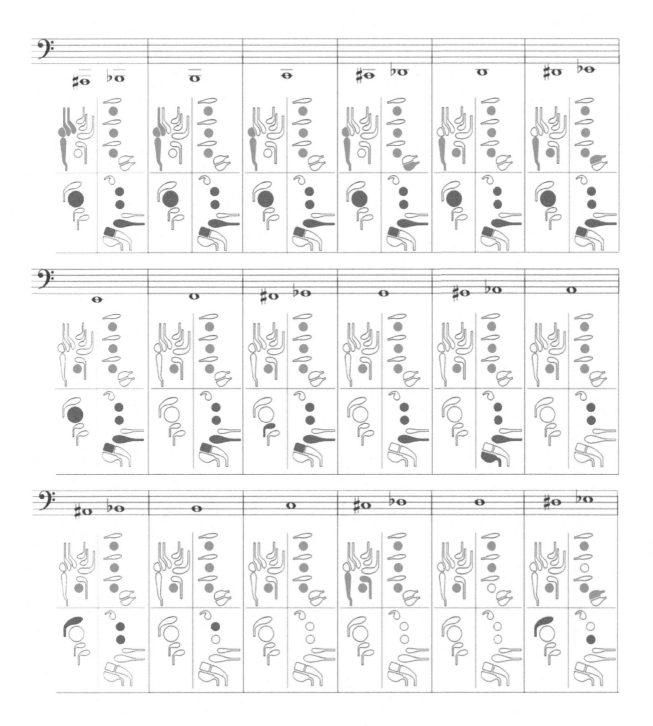

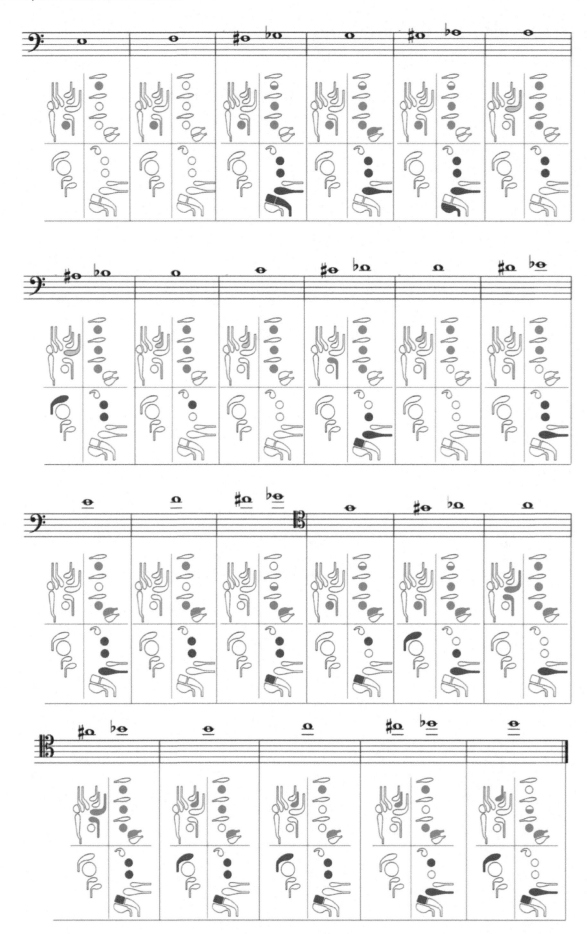

APPENDIX VIII: FRENCH HORN FINGERING

APPENDIX IX: TRUMPET FINGERING

APPENDIX X: TROMBONE SLIDE POSITIONS

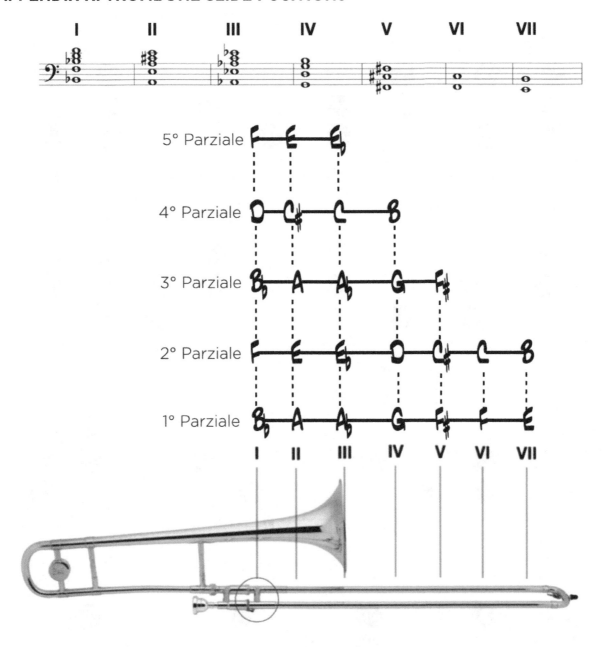

APPENDIX XI: TUBA FINGERING

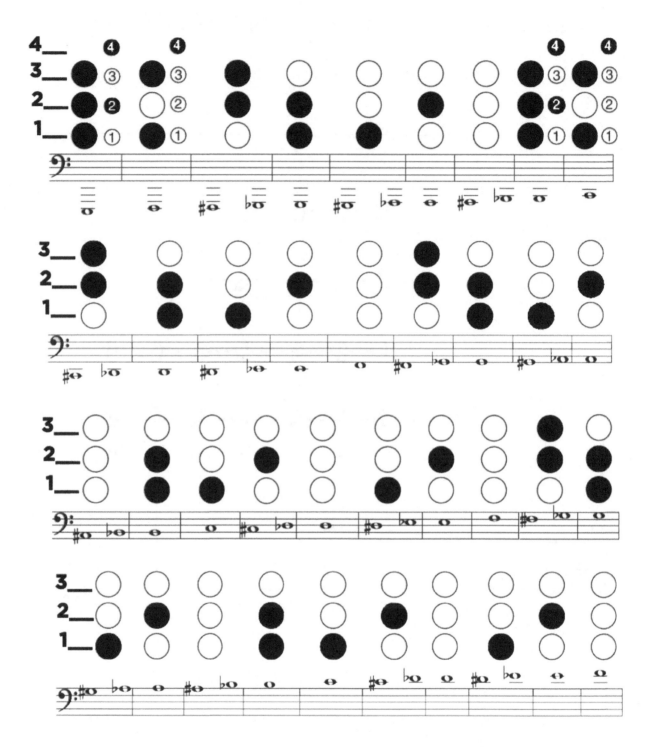

APPENDIX XII: THE HARMONIC SERIES

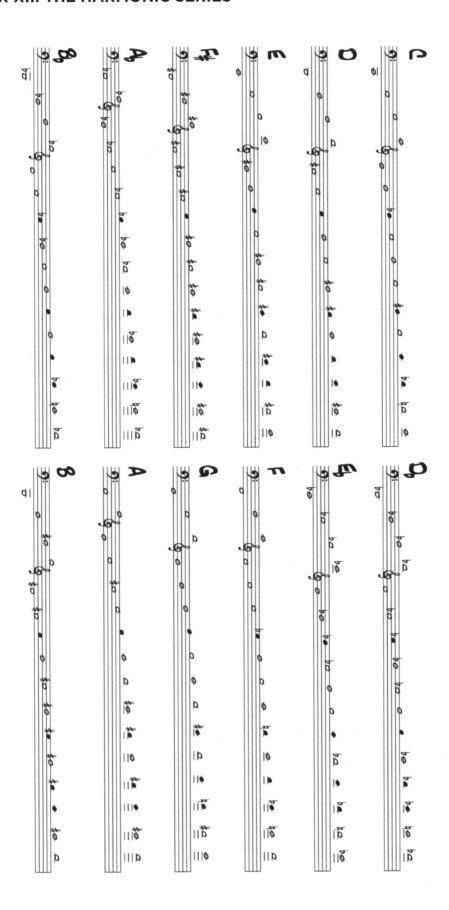

The Complete Modern Instrumentation

APPENDIX XIII: BASIC GUITAR CHORDS

BASIC CHORDS

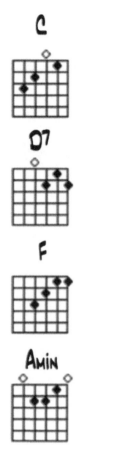

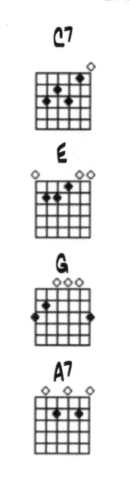

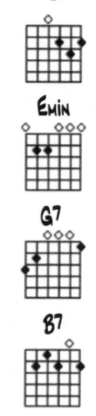

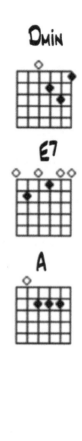

BAR CHORDS

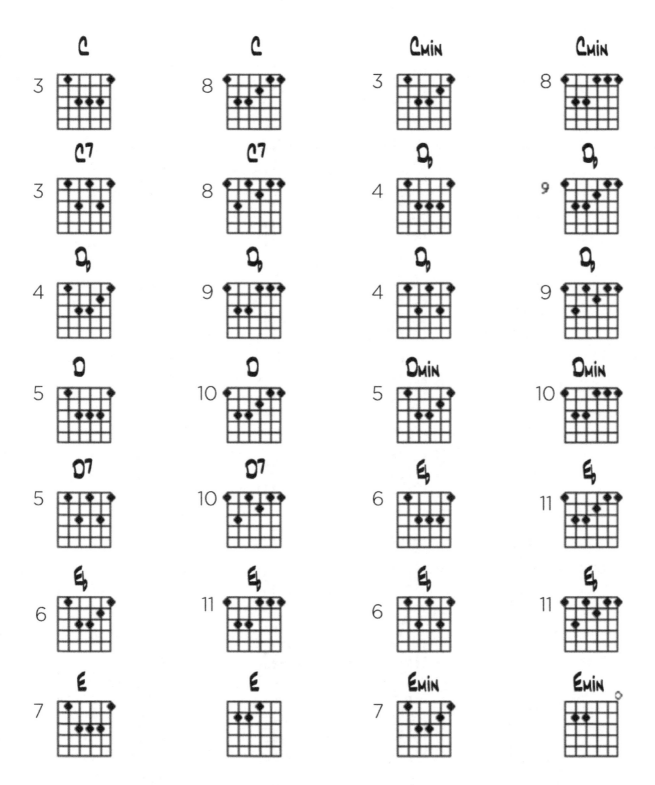

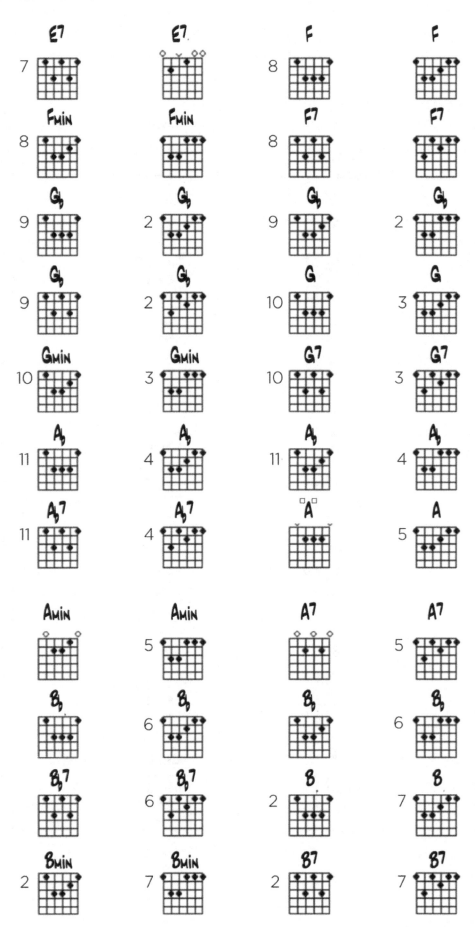

APPENDIX XIV: INSTRUMENTS RANGE

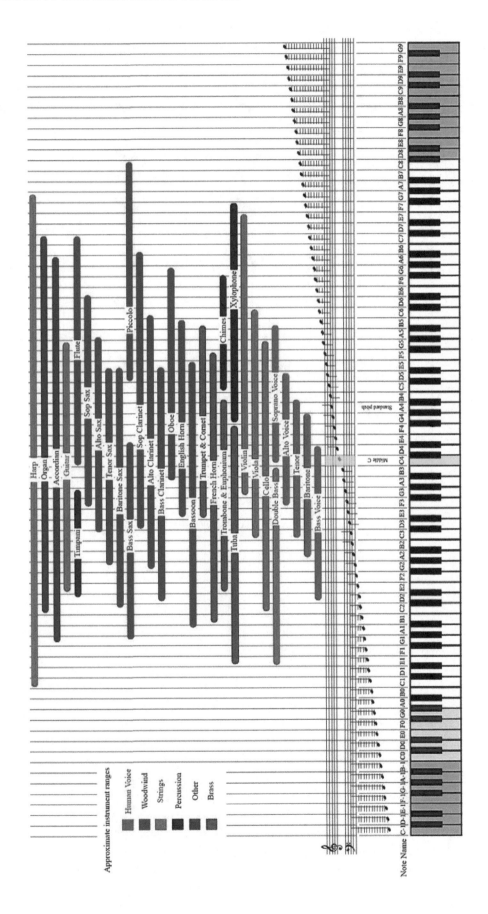

APPENDIX XV: BRASS MUTES

Mute	French Horn	Trumpet	Trombone	Tuba
Straight	✔	✔	✔	✔
Cup		✔	✔	
Harmon (wa-wa)		✔	✔	
Bucket		✔	✔	
Plunger		✔	✔	
Solotone		✔	✔	
Stop	✔			